Principles of
Grid Computing
Concepts & Applications

Principles of Grid Computing

Concepts & Applications

Dr. P. Venkata Krishna
Ph.D
Associate Professor and Division Leader
School of Computing Science and Engineering,
VIT University, Vellore

☆

Prof. M. Rajasekhara Babu
Assistant Professor (SG) and Division Leader
School of Computing Science and Engineering,
VIT University, Vellore

☆

Prof. V. Saritha
M.Tech
Assistant Professor (Senior)
School of Computing Science and Engineering,
VIT University, Vellore

Ane Books Pvt. Ltd.

New Delhi ♦ Chennai

Principles of Grid Computing: Concept & Applications

P. Venkata Krishna, M. Rajasekhara Babu and V. Saritha

Published by

Ane Books Pvt. Ltd.

4821, Parwana Bhawan, 1st Floor, 24 Ansari Road, Darya Ganj,
New Delhi - 110 002, Tel.: +91(011) 23276843-44, Fax: +91(011) 23276863
e-mail: kapoor@anebooks.com, Website: www.anebooks.com

Branch Office:

- Avantika Niwas, 1st Floor, 19 Doraiswamy Road, T. Nagar,
  Chennai - 600 017, Tel.: +91(044) 28141554, 28141209
  e-mail: anebookschennai@gmail.com, rathinam@anebooks.com

ISBN : 978-93-8061-815-9

Printed at : Sagar Colorscan, New Delhi.

Preface

Our purpose in writing "*Grid Computing—Concepts & Applications*" book is to explore the ways in which communities of design and innovation are merging and influencing each other in the world of computation to optimize computer resources and manage data and computing workloads. In order to understand the computing workloads and managing resources, students must develop both the fundamentals of grid computing and understanding key elements critical to optimize computing resources. We wrote this book to provide a framework for learning these necessary fundamentals that enable the student for advanced studies in the area of grid computing.

We had three main goals in writing this text:

Accuracy: This book is result of many years of facilitating, researching and teaching grid computing. It is important to teach our students skills that are based in research from the field of grid computing. This book places a clear emphasis on teaching basic concepts but also ensure that those skills are based on rigorous and current research.

Contemporary tools: This text describes and explains the use of contemporary tools for the development of application in the area of grid computing. In addition to examples, we have provided snapshots for the output of programs for the convenience so students can observe these results and for their practices unfold.

Approach: We have defined text in terms of five key parts that can be used to evaluate the learning effectiveness. We have organized the text in such way that the student can easily follow the basic concepts followed by advanced concepts and ends with utilization of contemporary tools for the development of applications in the area of grid computing.

Features: To enhance student learning, there are five core parts in defining structure for evaluating effectiveness of learning. The five parts are—Grid, Grid Computing Technologies, Grid Platforms, Grid Implementation and Grid Applications. At the beginning of each part, there is an overview for students about which skills they will be learning and practising in that part.

Authors

Acknowledgements

Perhaps you find it odd that a book on "Grid Computing" has been written by three authors. We can simply tell you that is not the case. Many ideas presented in this book originated in our classroom and project guidance experiences.

We applaud our M.Tech (CSE) students **Mr. Venkata Ramesh Babu G, Mr. Vinod Kumar Kavali and** M.S.(By Research) Scholar **Mr. Kalaiselvan, C-DAC** for their invaluable inputs and help. We express gratitude to our school of Computing Science and Engineering Director **Dr. Khalid M** for the support rendered by him.

We thank our honorable chancellor **Dr. G. Viswanathan**, VIT University for giving us opportunity to complete this book and we would like to thank **Sankar Viswanathan, Vice-President – Administration, G.V. Sampath, Vice-President – Operations, Dr. D.P. Kothari, Vice Chancellor, Prof. S. Narayanan, Pro-Vice-Chancellor** for their constant support and encouragement during each phase of book writing process.

Finally, we bestow our thanks to our **family members and friends** for their support, motivation and encouragement at all times.

Dr. P. Venkata Krishna
Prof. M. Rajasekhara Babu
Prof. V. Saritha

Contents

PART II

GRID COMPUTING TECHNOLOGIES

PART III

GRID PLATFORMS

PART IV

GRID IMPLEMENTATIONS

PART V

GRID APPLICATIONS

PART I

ABOUT GRID

Welcome to the world of GRID COMPUTING! In today's world there are so many problems which are completely not solved even though so many computer technologies are produced and still working in those areas. Let us take Internet. Millions of computers are connected to the internet and they are using resources bitterly even though they have different operating systems and microprocessors. Means Internet is purely heterogeneous. Shall we call grid follows the concept of internet? obviously! How? Part 1 mainly concentrates on answering this type of questions.

Here we discuss basic concepts that approach to grid computing, definitions, grid in various areas, components, concepts, virtualization in grid, grid approach etc.. Before entering into grid, let's see the fundamental concepts that are helpful for developing grid projects. These are slightly explained in *introduction* part of grid. In later sections we will go deeply about these topics. Some of those are:

- Networking
- Distributed computing
- High performance computing
- Web services and technologies

In grid computing unlimited number of machines are connected to form a grid which provides massive power to our businesses and industries every day. Presently business people wants more computational power, high speed processing machines and quality of services for solving their complex problems. Grid is the new computational approach which mainly concentrates on solving particular problem in heterogeneous environment by satisfying whatever business people wants.

The *introduction* part will provide complete information about grid. Chapter two explains Dynamic Virtual Organisation (DVO) in grid. Chapter three about distributed shared memory and chapter four about grid road map. We will also see internet concept in chapter one which gives some understanding about connection of computers.

1

INTRODUCTION

1.1 BASIC CONCEPTS

1.1.1 Networking[1]

Interconnection of any two objects/machines/computers is called a network. For forming network generally minimum two systems are required. Computers are connected by using cable or without cable (wireless). The main idea behind the network is resource sharing like memory, data, hardware etc. The world's biggest network is telecommunication and next internet. when we are knowing something about internet the first question comes to our mind is how internet works. If you are connecting all the computers in this world then that is internet. Means it is a global network of all the computers. Hardware, software and protocol are three main requirements for Internet. The computers are connected to Internet Service Provider's called clients and ISP computer is called server. One system in internet sends a request (client) to the server for some result. Suppose client has windows OS and Intel processor but server has Linux and some other processor. The instructions given by client can't understand by server because it has different processor. Then how server understands and sends reply back. One language which has platform independent so that it can run on any system on internet— that is JAVA! Almost all the available web languages are platform independent; moreover the communication between so called client and server in the internet is happening through exchanging the data packets over network..Ex(Html,Java Script-Clent side rendering,PHP,JSP-Server side scripts).

How networking related to grid! Without internetworking there is no grid concept. In grid computing heterogeneous systems must be connected then only grid solves complex and computational problems.Geographically distributed resources are connected together to solve a data and computational intensive applications With networking concept grid computing offers many solutions that are already address and resolve the problems. Grid computing environment must be constructed upon

- Coordinated resources and
- Open standard protocols and frameworks

Which are the basic things in networks. In later sections we will concentrate on mainly peer to peer grids.

1.1.2 Distributed Computing[2]

If you are connecting a collection of independent computers via a network, that are concentrate on a particular task then it is distributed system. Independent computers means they don't share memory or program execution space. Computing can be performed among network computers then it is a distributed computing. Computing in grid also achieves similar properties so distributed computing is also one of the concept for evaluating grid computing.

Grid is a loosely-coupled-means systems in grid are its own processor and memory. They didn't share the program execution space (in tightly coupled systems data can be shared using common memory space). The following diagram shows a simple distributed system.

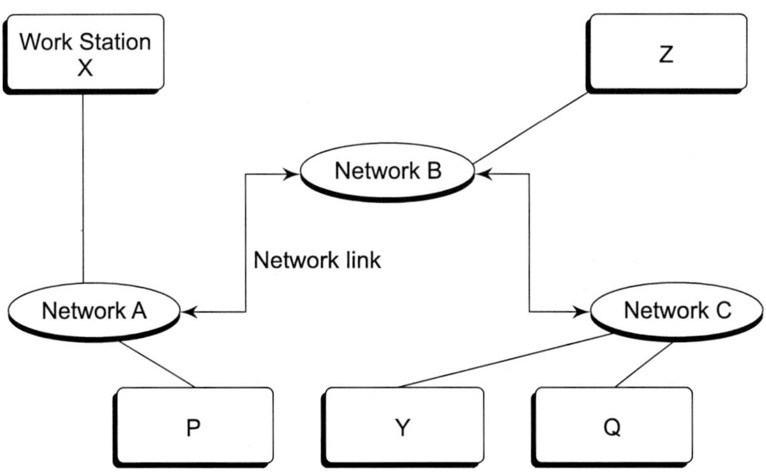

Fig. 1.1 A simple distributed system.[2,10]

1.1.3 High Performance Computing[1]

Clustering concept was comes from High Performance Computing. Computers are achieving efficient results by HPC. The basic idea behind HPC is to produce a cost-effective alternative to a supercomputer by using commercial off-the-shelf computers.

1.1.4 Web Service and Technologies

Web service is a new technology that has emerged recently. Network services are provided by web services transported by HTTP. Some of the technologies used in grid computing are WSDL (Web Service Description Language), CORBA or Java RMI, JXTA, SOAP and XML.

Following diagram shows evolution of grid from these concepts. Later sections briefly give some idea about these concepts.

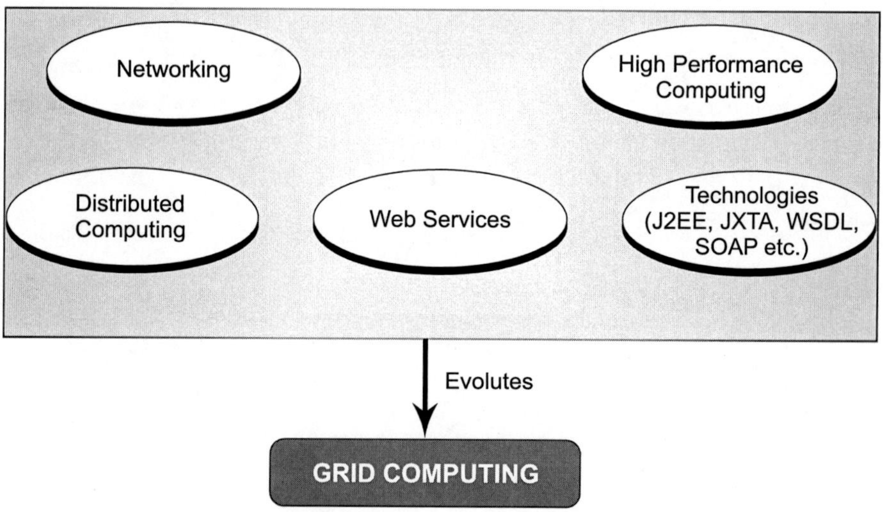

Fig. 1.2 Grid from basic concepts.[5]

1.2 ENTERING INTO GRID[5]

The word Grid computing is just the new word for Distributed computing. Grid is inspired by the 'power grids'. In the early days we started file computing and printing etc. Later we moved to program-program communication. Generally if any new technology or concept is coming into the market they solve the same problems which are facing other technologies like data format, communication protocol, security, and management. Why can't we just focus on high level task? We need to leverage existing standards and follow accepted patterns. In between heterogeneous systems the standardization of communication created the internet explosion. This emerging standardization for sharing resources, along with the availability of higher bandwidth, are driving a possibly equally large evolutionary step in grid computing. A grid is a collection of machines, sometimes referred to as "nodes," "resources," "members," "donors," "clients," "hosts," "engines," and many other such terms.

The popularity of the Internet as well as the availability of powerful computers and high-speed network technologies as low-cost commodity components is changing the way we use computers today. These technology opportunities have led to the possibility of using distributed computers as a single, unied computing resource, leading to what is popularly known as Grid computing. Grids are super Internets for ***high-performance computing***: worldwide collections of high-end resources—such as supercomputers, storage, advanced instruments, and immersive environments. These resources and their users are often separated by great distances and connected by high-speed networks. If you are developing an application that requires high-end resources which distributive in nature, for this you will want to know about grids. The computers join together to create a virtual supercomputer. Computers networked together can work on the same problems, which traditionally were reserved for supercomputers, and yet these networks of computers are more powerful than the super computers built in the seventies and eighties. Modern supercomputers are built on the principles of GC incorporating many smaller computers into a larger whole. The idea of GC originally for to handle the computation management, data movement, storage management, and other infrastructure that could handle large grids without restricting themselves to specific hardware and requirements. The technique is also exceptionally flexible.

? For what sort of "problems /applications" the grid computing is used?

The answer for this question is straight forward. Traditionally, distributed computing in general and grid computing in particular have been associated with computationally intensive scientific and numerical applications, but more recently there has been a growing interest in using grid technology for a wide range of large-scale commercial applications. The reason comes down to simple economics: you can build more powerful systems, more cheaply, by more efficient utilization of available computing resources.[14]

Those problems that are beyond the processing limits of individual computers. Right now that primarily means scientific or technical projects such as cancer and other medical research—projects that involve the analysis of inordinate amounts of data. Grid Computing applies the resources of many computers to resolve a single problem.

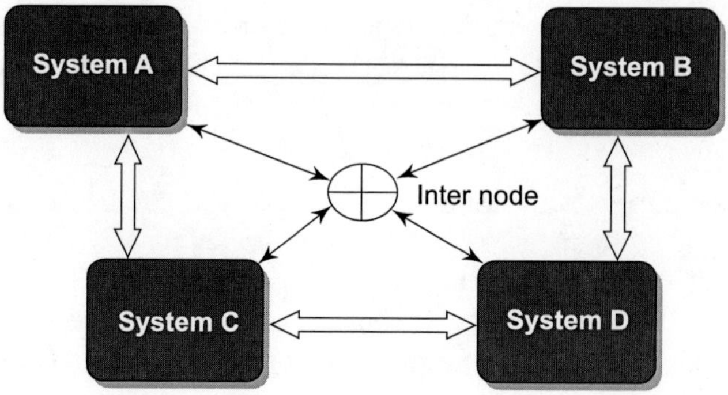

Fig. 1.3 Systems communicating in grid (simple block diagram).[2]

Now the following examples show in which areas the grid platform is used:

(*i*) Perhaps the most ambitious is Oxford University's Centre for Computational Drug Discovery's project that utilizes more than one million PCs to look for a cancer cure.

(*ii*) People around the world donate a few CPU cycles from their PCs through "screensaver time." The project eventually will analyze 3.5 billion molecules for cancer-fighting potential. More than 50,000 years of CPU power (based on a 1.5 gigahertz chip) have been put to work so far.

(*iii*) One highly publicized project is the ***SETI*** (Search for Extraterrestrial Intelligence) @Home project, in which PC users worldwide donate unused processor cycles to help the search for signs of extraterrestrial life by analyzing signals coming from outer space.

(*iv*) Nationwide electric power grid connects sources of electricity, the information Grid will connect sources and users of high-performance computing cycles, allowing these cycles to be generated in one place and used in another.

(*v*) Remote collaborators will work together on large scale projects. Scientists will be able to access extremely data-intensive instruments from across the country, in real time.

How does grid computing work in practice? Is special hardware or software needed?

In practically, grid works like Firstly, a computer tied to a network. The most far-reaching network, of course, is the Internet, which is enabling regular people with home PCs to participate in grid computing projects from anywhere in the world. Beyond that, PC owners must download simple software from the project's host site. On the other end, grid computing projects use software that can divide and distribute pieces of a program to thousands of computers for processing.

From this understanding, now definition of grid is like according to foster "Grid computing is a method of harnessing the power of many computers in a network to solve problems requiring a large number of processing cycles and involving huge amounts of data. So rather than using a network of computers simply to communicate and transfer data, grid computing taps the unused processor cycles of numerous — sometimes thousands of — computers."

Remember grid is just a concept which uses in networking for sharing high-end resources.[14]

Who wants the Grid? (Real-time scenarios)

People will use it only because they want to communicate with resources or people that care about and need to do their work. This is just an example of the local/global phenomenon mentioned in regard to previous infrastructures. We must stimulate the use of the grid by applications researchers, drawn from computational science and experimental and observational science, as well as educators and visionary corporations. Whatever the resources those are operated remotely. The following areas will use the grid technologies.[1]

Engineers and computer people wants the grid: Engineers would like to visualize their applications in real time and, for many applications. Computational people wants to transfer the results of complex simulations, as a result when they are doing this type of work an error may be detected. This is unacceptable, so that they need the ability to reach out across the grid to remote computers.

Experimental scientists: If we wish to generally influence science, we need to influence experimental and observational science. Experimental scientists enhance their remote instrumentation to supercomputers or to advanced visualization devices and, to use advanced user interfaces, such as java voice command for instrumental functions. For example computer scientists creating software which tests and working the functionality of network in the software, they need to check data is transferred to destination or not (of course this is part in internet. An internet is the good application to the distributed system. Grid is generally new word to distributed system).

For Corporations: Almost all organizations in this world are global in extent. This organizations need to share the information and data from other branches which are located in some other areas. For example take the manufacturing of product so that suppliers, manufactures, and customers spread all over the world and could imagine linking these people over the grid.

Training and Education need the grid: One of the first applications of the grid technologies will be in remote training and education. Some of the schools and institutions began the grid technologies to share the e-learning, on-line exam, virtual world games, and to share some other resources. While sharing the question arise is what new types of collaborative education will arise using a national-grid?

Real-time situations: the area of biomedical applications, the study of the cardiac electrical activity, especially under pathological conditions, requires the execution of several parametric simulations in order to analyze, for example, the influence of certain anti-arrhythmic drugs. On the other hand, the structural analysis of buildings in civil engineering design can require the simulation of a large number of different structural alternatives under diverse load conditions, in order to find that which best accomplishes with all the economic limitations, design aspects and safety requirements.

Not only these examples some others like environment grid for weather forecasting, nations and states, consumers and producers. In word almost entire world needs the grid. (Referred from Grid2 by Ian Foster.)

Grid computing technology enables the collaborative usage of computational resources across different organizations. Nowadays, the Globus Toolkit represents the industrial standard for Grid computing, and is involved in a large number of research projects. The Globus Toolkit is considered the de facto standard for Grid computing. However, its steep learning curve has discouraged its widespread adoption. In order to overcome this disadvantage, object-oriented software has been developed, which provides an intuitive interface that completely hides the direct interaction with Globus.

From the figure, a grid is a computational, integrated and collaborative environment and a high-level view of activities within the Grid organization. For solving complex type of problems users interact with the resource broker who in turn performs resource discovery, scheduling, and the processing of application jobs on the distributed Grid resources. Following are the some of the services provided by the grid.

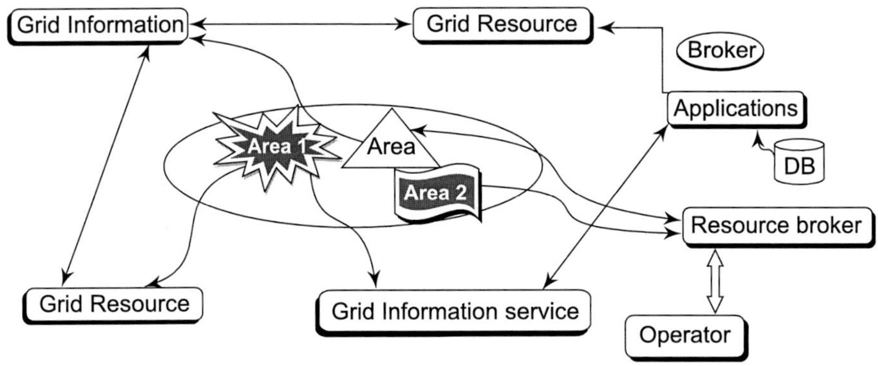

Fig. 1.4 Grid in worldwide and interaction between its entities.[2–5]

Web services in computational environment. Services are generally provided by the resource brokers. Services are web in nature especially in internet point of view. These resources are generally distributed in nature. Computational services are provided by the computational grids. In later section we will see about computational grids. Some examples of computational Grids are: NASA IPG, the World Wide Grid, and the NSF TeraGrid.

Shared and end-to-end services. The shared infrastructure is the foundation for business communication, collaboration and trade. As such, it has to meet much higher expectations than the Internet of old. Delays, interruptions and errors in these activities cost the participants money. When we are talking about end-to-end services mainly three characteristics arise, they are:

(*i*) **Support for applications:** We know grid is a concept. The original Internet made it possible to send and receive email and to share access to files, which is also uses the concept of grid. In the grid environment the task of the web infrastructure is to support commercial-grade application functionality. When grid is become popular we consider the following operating requirements when we are operating in this technology:

(*a*) **Consistency:** Each separate component must act within certain parameters, such as availability response times.

(*b*) **Authenticity:** There must be some way of assuring the identity of each of the participants in the process.

(*c*) **Timeliness:** Processes must execute in the correct order, and promptly—especially if a user is waiting on the result in order to continue with their work.

(*d*) **Integrity:** There must be mechanisms to avoid data becoming corrupted as it passes between participants

(*e*) **Persistence:** Each participant in the process must maintain a permanent record of their part in the transaction.

(*ii*) **Multiple providers:** A *grid* is a collection of computers working on a particular problem. So network also play a very important role. It will providers contribute server management, data storage, edge caching, security, VPN and wireless services. the network and software layers, is within individual enterprises. They too thus participate as providers.

(*iii*) **Essential standards:** Standardization is the effective mechanism to enable co-operation between so many different and varied participants. They are two alternative standards namely:

(*a*) Vertical-integrated infrastructure-owned by single provider of enterprise.

(*b*) Co-operated infrastructure-partnership between multiple participants.

Parallel-job services: Parallel systems are well suited to work-loads in which tasks are small and have similar requirements. These are concerned with parallel execution management and providing access to remote software and libraries transparently. Grid assigns a task from work list to a suitable resource. They build on computational and data services provided by the Grid.

Business services: A service domain represents a collection of comparable or related Web services through a common services entry point in business area. A service domain applies autonomic computing principles for aggregating Web services and grid services. The service domain technology provides a service grid and can create, filter, discover, cluster, organize, select, route, recover, and switch Web services and grid services autonomically. Using service domain objects enables you to implement business solutions easily and quickly. These service domain objects instantiate multiple service instances into a virtual service, multiple virtual services into high-level virtual services, and so on.

Quality related services: Efficiency, integration and a higher quality of service are some of the most significant ways in which technology like e-business is benefited from grid computing. For this type of services OGSA, one of the services architecture in grid available to permitting the resources in an automated fashion which as heterogeneity in nature. OGSA provides configure, optimize, heal, and protect the resources and open protocols- which are self-managing.

Distributed file systems and caching: Distributed applications, more often than not, require access to less distributed among many servers. A distributed le system is therefore a key component in a distributed system. From an applications point of view it is important that a distributed le system can provide a uniform global namespace, support a range of le I/O protocols, require little or no program medications, and provide means that enable performance optimizations to be implemented, such as the usage of caches.

Security and authorization: Any distributed system involves all four aspects of security: condentiality, integrity, authentication, and accountability. Security within a Grid environment is a complex issue requiring diverse resources autonomously administered to interact in a manner that does not impact the usability of the resources or introduces security holes/lapses in individual systems or the environments as a whole. A security infrastructure is the key to the success or failure of a Grid environment.

System status and fault tolerance: To provide a reliable and robust environment it is important that a means of monitoring resources and applications is provided. To accomplish this task, tools that monitor resources and application need to be deployed.

Computational economy and resource trading: As a Grid is constructed by coupling resources distributed across various organizations and administrative domains that may be owned by different organizations, it is essential to support mechanisms and policies that help in regulate resource supply and demand. An economic approach is one means of managing resources in a complex and decentralized manner. This approach provides incentives for resource owners, and users to be part of the Grid and develop and using strategies that help maximize their objectives.

Programming tools and paradigms: A Grid should include interfaces, APIs, utilities, and tools to provide a rich development environment. Common scientic languages such as C, C++, and FORTRAN should be available, as should application-level interfaces such as MPI and PVM. A variety of programming paradigms should be supported, such as message passing or distributed shared memory. In addition, a suite of numerical and other commonly used libraries should be available.

1.3 DEFINITIONS[1]

Today there are many definitions of *Grid Computing*: "What is the Grid? A Three Point Checklist", Foster lists these primaries attributes: Computing resources are not administered centrally, Open standards are used. Non-trivial QoS is achieved.[5,14]

- Grid is a type of parallel and distributed system that enables the sharing, selection, and aggregation of geographically distributed "autonomous" resources dynamically at runtime depending on their availability, capability, performance, cost, and users' quality-of-service requirements.[5,14]
- Plaszczak/Wellner- define grid technology as "the technology that enables resource virtualization, on-demand provisioning, and service (resource) sharing between organizations".[5,14]
- IBM defines grid computing as "the ability, using a set of open standards and protocols, to gain access to applications and data, processing power, storage capacity and a vast array of other computing resources over the Internet. A grid is a type of parallel and distributed system that enables the sharing, selection, and aggregation of resources distributed across 'multiple' administrative domains based on their (resources) availability, capacity, performance, cost and users' quality-of-service requirements" An earlier example of the notion of computing as utility was in 1965 by MIT's Fernando Corb. Fernando and the other designers of the Multiuse operating system envisioned a computer facility operating "like a power company or water company".[5,14]
- Buyya/Venugopal- define grid as "a type of parallel and distributed system that enables the sharing, selection, and aggregation of geographically distributed autonomous resources dynamically at runtime depending on their availability, capability, performance, cost, and users' quality-of-service requirements".[5,14]
- CERN, one of the largest users of grid technology, talk of **The Grid**: "a service for sharing computer power and data storage capacity over the Internet".[5,14]

Grids can be categorized with a three stage model of departmental grids, enterprise grids and global grids. These correspond to a firm initially utilizing resources within a single group i.e. an engineering department connecting desktop machines, clusters and equipment. This progresses to enterprise grids where non-technical staff's computing resources can be used for cycle-stealing and storage. A global grid is a connection of enterprise and departmental grids which can be used in a commercial or collaborative manner.[5,14]

1.4 GRID PROJECTS

Some of the national and international grid projects are:[3–14]

- D-Grid (German)
- GARUDA (Indian)

- National Grid Service (UK)
- Open Science Grid (USA)
- VECC (Calcutta, India)
- INFN Grid (Italian)
- EGEE Grid(European Grid) (Used in Larger Hadron collider Project)

We will see details about our national grid project named GARUDA in later sections.

1.5 GRID LAYERED ARCHITECTURE

The grid architecture is a layered architecture. There are mainly four layers in architecture:[5–14]

- Fabrication layer
- Grid core middleware
- Development layer
- Applications

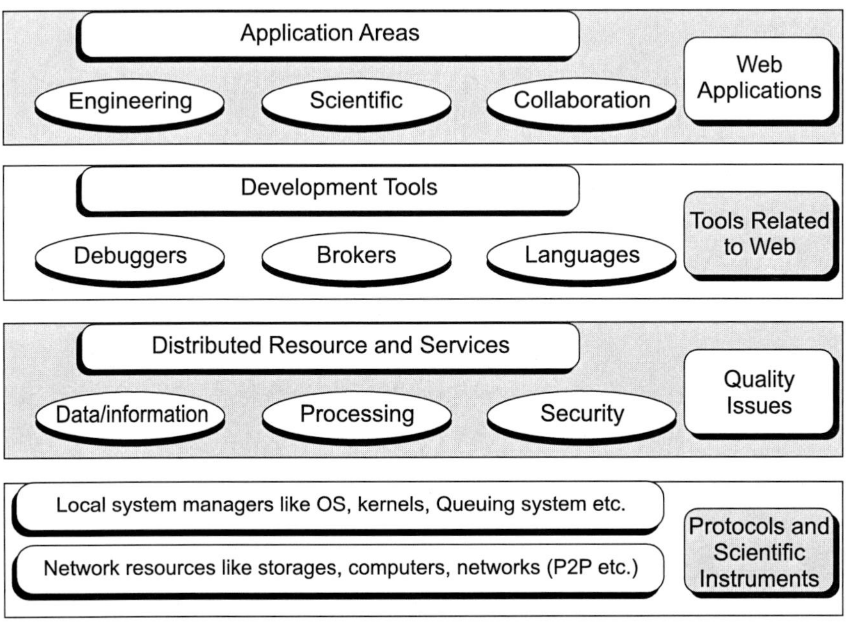

Fig. 1.5 Grid layered architecture.[7–12]

According to diagram grid contains

- Heterogeneous components
- The bottom layer has resource managers which are in local machines and also network resources like data sources, secondary storages etc. It will take care about network protocols.
- The next layer was purely related to distributed services. Security mechanisms are applied here like GSI. Quality of Service (QoS) one also considered here. Resources are shared the information efficiently in distributed environment.
- Development environment provides tools and languages for developing grid applications.
- Application layer is the top layer in layered architecture. Users are interacting and they applied problem solving skills from this layer.[5–14]

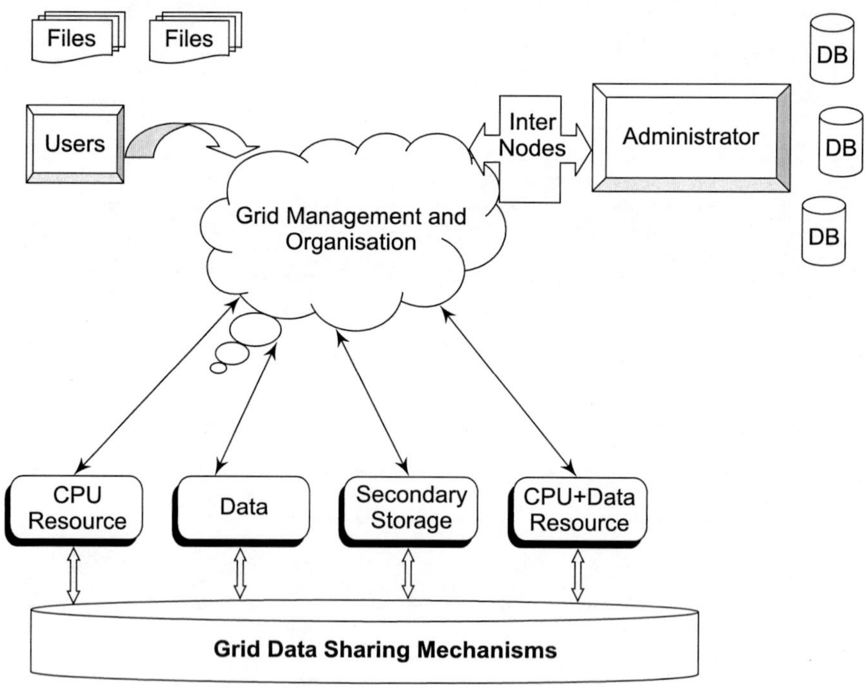

Fig. 1.6 A simple grid.[5–12]

Clusters are usually deployed to improve performance and/or availability over that provided by a single computer, while typically being much more cost-effective than single computers of comparable speed or availability. Some people would call a "cluster" implementation rather than a "grid".[5–14]

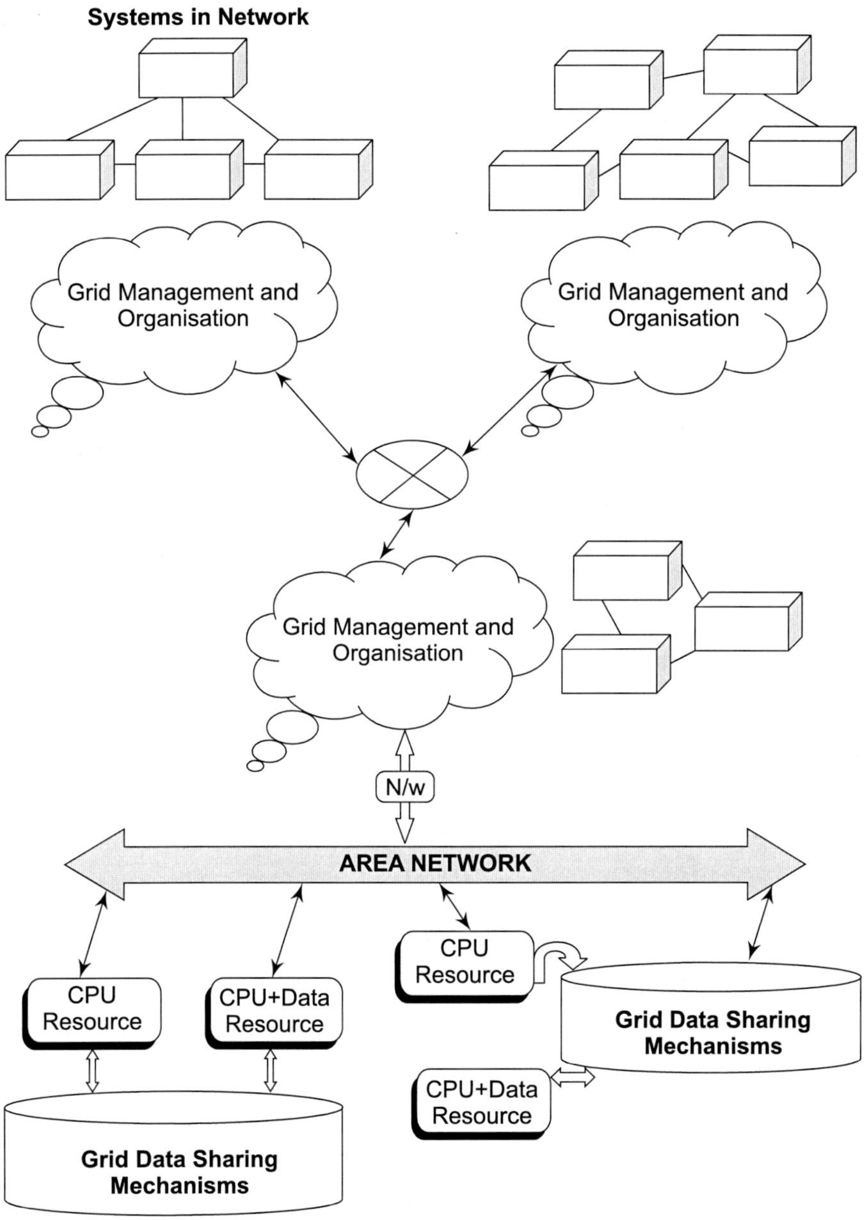

Fig. 1.7 A complex intergrid.[5–12]

1.6 DISTRIBUTED COMPUTING

Distributed computing is a process of computation, where a program is divided into modules and is processed on different computers of a network in parallel. Distributed environment is established by forming a network of computers where resources are shared mutually. For establishing a distributed environment there are some weak assumptions.[2,8,10,11]

1.6.1 Flawed Assumptions of Distributed Computing

Flawed assumptions are a set of fault assumptions made by programmers while developing distributed applications.

(*i*) **The network is reliable:** The network must ensure reliable transmission of data among the nodes.

(*ii*) **Latency is zero:** There must be no delay in the transmission.

(*iii*) **Bandwidth must be infinite:** The network must allow max bandwidth that there must be no data loss and no data flooding.

(*iv*) **The network is secure:** The network that exists among the nodes of distributed environment must be secured and should defend any kind of threats.

(*v*) **Topology doesn't change:** Once a network is designed with a particular topology, it must persist forever. There must be no intermediate changes of network topologies.

(*vi*) **There is one administrator:** An administrator should be present who controls the distributed network. An administrator may be one among the nodes of the distributed network.

(*vii*) **Transport cost is zero:** The transmission of data on the network should be exactly like the transmission of data from folder to folder in a system.

(*viii*) **The network is homogeneous:** The network established for a distributed environment must be homogenous. That is all the sub-networks existing in a distributed network must be of same kind (similar).

(*ix*) **System clocks are identical:** The clock time maintained by the systems of the network must be the same as the time of the administrator (though this is not possible, algorithms like Lamport clock synchronization algorithm, etc must be used to do it).

The above assumptions are easy to assume but not possible to implement. That is why they are called as 'false assumptions' or 'fallacies'. So a distributed environment must be established with more or less same as the above assumptions.[2,8,10,11]

1.6.2 Distributed Computing Environment

Distributed computing environment (DCE) is a software system developed by major companies like Hewlett-Packard (hp), IBM, etc in 1990's. DCE provides a framework and toolkit for developing client-server applications, which includes *remote procedure call* (RPC) mechanism known as DCE/RPC, a naming (directory) service, a time service, an authentication and a distributed file system (DFS) known as DCE/DFS.

Distributed computing environment was fairly encouraged till early 1990s. But the development of competing technologies like java, internet, web-services, etc empowered DCE from mid-to-late 1990's. As this grew well Microsoft's DCOM and ODBC systems, etc used the DCE/RPC in their network transport layer. Several years later this technology is being developed and released versions of DCE (DCE1.2.2 in 2005 by The Open Group).

1.6.2.1 *DCE architecture*

Most important unit that manages DCE is a ***cell***. Almost all the privileges had been assigned to a role called *cell-administrator*. Privileges can be assigned or removed from following categories: user_obj, group _obj, other_obj, any_obj for any specified DCE resource.

Major components of DCE within every cell are:

(*i*) **The Security Server:** Responsible for authentication.

(*ii*) **The Cell Directory Server (CDS):** Which is a repository of resources and ACL's.

(*iii*) **The Distributed Time Server:** Which provides an accurate clock for proper functioning of the entire cell.

Implementing a distributed file system using the DCE , by adding filenames to the CDS and defining the appropriate ACL's on them might not be user friendly, but support replication of a fileset on multiple DFS servers (it will have one Read/Write copy and zero or more read-only copies). In addition, DCE/DFS also supports 'backup' filesets, which are capable of storing a version of the fileset with prior to last replication.

Features of DCE/DFS:

- World's only file system that correctly implements the full POSIX file system semantics, including byte range locking.
- Sufficiently reliable.
- Stable to run the back-end file system for a website.

- Seamlessly and automatically distributed.
- Edited worldwide in different time zones.

1.6.3 Distributed Hash Table (DHT)

Distributed Hash Tables are a group of local distributed system that provide indexing services as a hash table. A hash table consists of (key, value) pairs and if any node in the network wants to use the DHT , should provide a key associated with a value. Actually, the DHT is constructed based on the orientation of nodes across the network and if any of the node change their state of being, may cause large disruption in the DHT. That's why DHT is allowed to *scale* to a high extent and must have a capability of main-taining the status(arrivals, departures, etc) of all the nodes of the network at every time.

DHT's infrastructure can be used to build complex services like *distributed file system, peer-to-peer file sharing* and *content distribution systems, cooperative web caching, multicast, anycast, domain name services* and *instant messaging.*

1.6.3.1 *Properties*

DHT's characteristically maintain the following properties:

- **Decentralization:** the nodes collectively form the system without any central coordination.
- **Scalability:** the system should function efficiently with huge (million say) no. of nodes.
- **Fault tolerance:** the system must be reliable even when nodes continuously join, leave or fail.

1.6.3.2 *Real World DHT's and their differences and improvements over basic shemes*

The following are the most frequently identified differences in 'real world' DHT implementations:

- One of the parameter of DHT is *address space*. Several real world DHT's use 128-bit or 160-bit.
- Some real world DHT's use hash functions other than SHA-1.
- Key *k* is formed mostly with the hash of file's content rather than file's name. So, the renaming of the files cannot prevent users to access the file.

- Some DHT's allow objects of different type. Take for e.g., key *k* may be node ID the define a node of the network, but in some cases it may a random number. Key representing node ID can be used for optimizing DHT operations.
- DHT's reliability can be improved using *redundancy*, i.e., replicating a key in more no. of nodes corresponding to that key.
- Some advanced DHT's like Kademlia[kademlia.scs.cs.nyu.edu] can perform iterative look ups , using which unwanted traffic can be reduced.

1.6.4 Distributed Resource Management System (DRMS)

Resource Management is nothing but managing and monitoring resources of a system. When this process is implemented in a distributed environment , then we call it as distributed resource management. Collectively we can define DRMS as a system, which is responsible of managing resources among the system of a distributed network.

In IT firm, a DRMS network need to be coordinated with the ever changing demands of business activities across different platforms. Hence the easiest way of implementing a decentralized resource management in an IT environment is through installing a software application. Main concepts of DRM include *jobs, dependencies, job streams, users.*

1.6.4.1 *Basic Features*

- Interfaces which help to define workflows and/or job dependencies.
- Automatic submission of executions.
- Interface to monitor the executions.
- Priorities and/or queues to control the execution order of unrelated jobs.

Any software that includes that includes all or some of the above features, then the software is said to have job scheduling capabilities. These kind of software include one of the following architectures:

(*a*) **Master/Agent Architecture:** It is a historic architecture for job scheduling software, where a small component of software is installed on a single machine and is awaited for the commands from Master, executes them and returns the result back to the Master.

(*b*) **Cooperative architecture:** It is a decentralized model where every system is equipped with scheduling and is capable of distributing the scheduled jobs to other cooperating system. This helps in dynamic workload balancing to maximize hardware utilization and high availability to ensure service delivery.

For a job scheduler to perform efficiently must include the following parameters:

- Job priority.
- Compute resource availability.
- Execution time allocated to user.
- Number of simultaneous jobs allowed for a user.
- Estimated execution time.
- Elapsed execution time.
- Availability of peripheral devices.

1.7 COMPUTATIONAL GRIDS

The current high speed computing has evolved very rapidly computers have became extremely powerful from five years ago. Even home-based systems available on commercial markets are powerful enough for implementing complex computations. Due to this reason the quality and quantity requirements for some business related advanced computing applications are also becoming more and more complex.[3–5, 12]

1.7.1 Definition of Computational Grids

Thus the industry needs some computational requirements in order to perform some complex computations like numerous complex scientific experiments, astronomical research and real time personal portfolio management etc.[3–5, 12]

"The grid computing environment which provides a demand driven, reliable, powerful and yet inexpensive computational power for its customers" ***—Foster and Kesselman***

These computational grids change the understanding on the utility and availability of computer power. This environment consists of one or more hardware and software enabled environments that provide dependable, consistent, pervasive and inexpensive access to high-end computational capabilities.[3–5, 12]

1.7.2 Reasons for Computational Grids

The following are the reasons for building the computational grids:[3–5, 12]

- To allow the users for independent management of computing resources.
- Provision of mechanisms that can intelligently and transparently select computing resources capable of running user jobs.

- Failure detection and failover mechanisms.
- The understanding of current and predicted loads on grid resources.
- Ensure appropriate security mechanisms for secure resource management, acess and integrity.

1.8 DATA GRIDS

The data aspects of any grid computing environments must be able to effectively manage all aspects of the data including qualities of data like location, transfer, access and critical aspects of security. These grid systems must also capable of providing data virtualization services to provide transparency for data access, integration and processing.[3–5,12]

The following are the core functional data requirements for grid computing applications:[3–5, 12]

- Integration multiple distributed, heterogeneous, and independently managed data sources.
- Provision of efficient data transfer mechanisms.
- Provision of data caching or replication mechanisms to minimize network traffic.
- Provision of necessary data discovery mechanisms.
- Capability to implement data encryption and integrity checks.
- Provision of backup/restore mechanisms and policies to prevent the data loss.

Example

The data intensive grids focus on management of data, which is being held in a variety of storage facilities in geographically dispersed locations.[3–5, 12]

Definition

"The grid computing environment which is able to effectively manage all the aspects of the data, including data location, data transfer, data access and critical aspects of security".[3–5, 12]

SUMMARY

Initial concept was suggested by Ian Foster and Carl Kesselman. According to them a grid refers to an aggregated system comprising of geographically sparsely located computing devices, storage devices, instrumentation devices and control devices built a top internetworks. From this a grid is a collection of computers working on a particular problem to achieve good performance. Frankly a grid is a just concept; we have to implement this concept for achieving efficiency, reliability, consistency, and durability in network. Here we discussed about the clusters-which are heterogeneous in nature where as computers in grid are homogeneous. From this a group of computers mainly work for particular services.

Some of the points which relates to grid computing are:

- High performance, cluster computing, networking (P2P) and internet computing areas are umbrella to grid computing.
- A grid is a hardware and software infrastructure that provides dependable, consistent, pervasive, and inexpensive access to computational resources.
- The difference between web and grid is web provides us information where as grid process it.
- Grid is flexible, transparent, secure, coordinated resource sharing among dynamic collections of individuals, institutions, and resources.
- A *resource* is an entity that is to be shared. It can be computational such as a personal digital assistant, laptop, desktop, workstation, server, cluster, and supercomputer or a storage resource such as a hard drive in a desktop.

KNOWLEDGE TESTING

1. By understanding definition of grid provided by different organizations and people, define grid in terms of your own words and explain the functionality of systems who are in part of grid?
2. How is grid different from other technologies and explain the working of grid by taking your own real life examples?
3. What are key Design Issues in Grid Computing? Who is addressing this grid?
4. What all software technologies are needed to build a Grid network? (for this question you also refer second chapter)
5. What kinds of applications are best suited to grid computing?
6. Compare and contrast grid computing, cluster computing and distributed computing.
7. How a Distribute Hash Table can be implemented in real world scenarios? Explain with some examples.

Contd...

8. How a distributed computing environment can be established? What are the pros and cons of a DCE?
9. What are the functionalities of Computational grids and Data grids? For space oriented applications, what type of Grid do you prefer? Justify your statement.

REFERENCES

1. Foster, C. Kesselman, S. Tuecke "The Anatomy of the Grid: Enabling Scalable Virtual Organisations", *International Journal of Supercomputer Applications and High Performance Computing*, 2001.
2. I. Foster, J. Geisler, W. Nickless, W. Smith, S. Tuecke "Software Infrastructure for the I-WAY High Performance Distributed Computing Experiment" in Proc. 5th IEEE Symposium on High Performance Distributed Computing. pp. 562-571, 1997.
3. *http://www.research.ibm.com/journal/sj/434/joseph.pdf.*
4. *http://www.redbooks.ibm.com/redpapers/pdfs/redp3613.pdf.*
5. Ian Foster and Carl Kesselman (eds), *The Grid: Blueprint for a New Computing Infrastructure*, Morgan Kaufmann, July 1998. ISBN 1-55860-475-8.
6. National Research Council. *National Collaboratories: Applying Information Technology for Scientific Research.* National Academy Press, 1993.
7. *www.cse.mtu.edu/cseri.html.*
8. *http://research.microsoft.com/users/lamport/pubs/distributed-system.txt.*
9. *http://www.ncbi.nlm.nih.gov/sites/entrez?db=pubmed&list_ uids=16711722 & cmd=Retrieve.*
10. *http://www.cs.technion.ac.il/~cs236370/main.html.*
11. *http://www.youtube.com/watch?v=8iSRLIK-x6A.*
12. *http://www.ngp.org.sg/seminars/Slides/DavidAnderson-Seminar@NLB.pdf.*
13. *http://www.ebizq.net/topics/web_services/features/1565.html.*
14. *www.gridcomputingplanet.com.*

❑❑❑

2

Dynamic Virtual Organisation

2.1 INTRODUCTION

In a grid environment, there will be many kinds of resources, like software resources, hardware resources, specialized resources, etc. A client can access only one resource related to his problem domain. But a client can have many kinds of resources in the repository for solving his problem. If he wants to access another resource, he has to free the previously accessed resource and gain another resource. This may result in delay on any conflicts during the processing. In order to solve this problem we adopt a mechanism called resource sharing. Here a client makes an agreement with service provider and other clients to mutually share the available resources. This scenario is collectively referred as *coordinated resource sharing*. By using this, a client can access any resource on demand.[2]

2.2 FUNCTIONALITY

The functionality of the coordinated resource sharing can be explained in detail as following. First of all, service providers will come forward with the services they can provide. Then a client or a user will choose the service providers depending on the services they provide that can solve the problem. Then the client forms a virtual organization with the hardware and software service providers. After forming a virtual organization, the client submits his problem and the resources he require to solve his problem. Then service providers will provide access to those requested resources for the client and thereby he can solve his problem. During this process, if any other clients find the formed virtual organization is suitable for their problem domain, then they also can do an agreement between the service providers to access the resources they provide.[4]

After a client finishes his job, he may resign from the virtual organization. Thereafter, the organization may persist or may collapse to form another VO with other clients. This decision depends on the client's requirement of the resources.[4]

2.3 IMPLEMENTATION

The implementation of the dynamic virtual organization can be explained further with the following example.[2,4]

- A virtual organization for Disease Diagnosis: Consider a user (say doctor) wants to make a survey on a newly found disease. First the user forms a VO with the software service provider who can offer a *Disease Diagnostic System* as a software resource. Using this resource the user will perform the diagnosis on the required disease. The user may also be permitted to use some hardware resources like system, network, etc and some specialized resources like database.
- A virtual organization of stock exchange: Consider a user wants to make a report on statistics of stock market. First the user forms a VO with the software service provider who can offer him a web service to obtain the information of latest stock exchange right from the National and International stock markets. Using this information and some specialized resources like report generation etc, the user can make a consolidated report on the latest stock exchange.

A resource provider in a virtual organization must provide a resource with the following criteria:[2,4]

- A provision for dynamic discovery of any other resources.
- Allocation and provisioning of resources immediately based on the user requirements.
- Efficient management of all the offering resources.
- The resources must be equipped with a feature that they are auto-monitored based on the command given by the user.
- The resources must guarantee secure accesses and bindings with the local servers or nodes.

A virtual organization must be able to provide the following features:

- Should establish project teams and group leaders to share the work given by the user.
- Should dynamically link the resources the user wishes to point to.

- Must identify the problem and its solution dynamically and required resources.
- Should form secured group and corresponding management for all the resources of the virtual organization.
- The secured commission must identify the mappings to the local resources.
- Must manage the resources as well as utilization, allocation within the economic criteria.

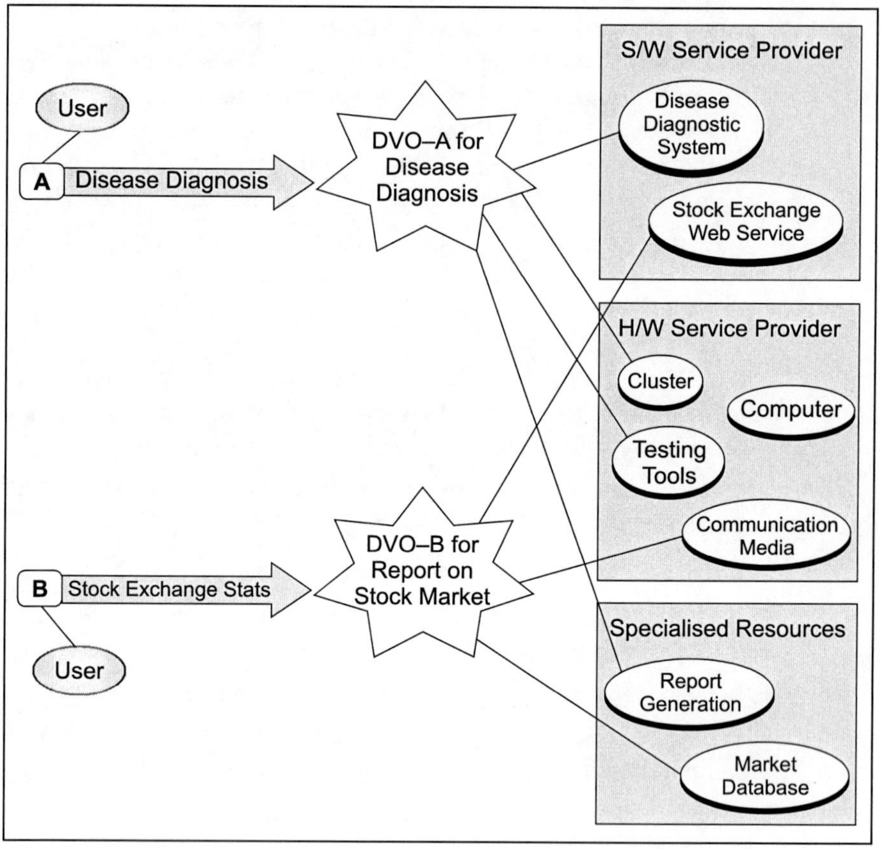

Fig. 2.1 Coordinated resource sharing using a DVO.[2]

2.4 SINGLE SIGN-ON AUTHORIZATION IN VIRTUAL ORGANIZATION

Though many organizations and communities evolve Grid faces a potential problem, which is *security*. Many solutions and technologies are been introduced to enhance grid security, such as CAS [Certification Authority service], GSI [Globus Security Infrastructure], PERMIS [Privileged Management Infrastructure], VOMS [Virtual Organization Management Service]. At certain time the security issue is cleared by PKI [Public Key Infrastructure]. PKI provided security by using public key authentication based security models.[2,4]

Grid security still relies primarily on PKI authentication mechanism because it validates the identity of the requesting user. PKI is more advantageous and widely accepted because it supports *single sign-on*. Where there will be a Certificate Authority [CA] responsible for issuing certificates to authenticate users. With this certificate authorization, user gets access to the resources available in a virtual organization. Certificate path analysis in this model is easier since there will be only on step between a certificate and its corresponding CA. Hence this model is called *Single sign-on*.[2,4]

In general, some resources will be obtained with multiple site accesses. In these situations grid will face scalability issues for large scale grid infrastructures. It will become a bottleneck for the server to serve all the requests and even more complex when more number of users joins. With a single SOA (service oriented architecture) the grid infrastructure may not be succeeded. So, it should lookout for a delegation security mechanism. As it is not realistic to implement, single sign-on mechanism is helpful. Single sign-on mechanism provides web services for issuing certificates for the authorization purpose.[2,4]

SUMMARY

Whenever user needs to use the resources present in remote servers, he forms a virtual organization via coordinated resource sharing mechanism with various resource providers. After forming a virtual organization a user can avail the services provided by all the resource providers on demand by the user. In this way a user establishes a coordinated resource sharing environment. For the security purpose in a virtual organization, the user uses some security mechanisms such as PKI, CAS, Single sign-on, etc.

Some examples of a virtual organization are:

- Boeing's Blended Wing Body design team located in numerous Boeing offices around the world.
- Worldcom's Global VPN Product Management team with members in 28 countries working on defining product specifications.
- An accounting department of a company.
- An emergency response team created to tackle an oil spill in the Gulf of Mexico.

KNOWLEDGE TESTING

1. What do you mean by coordinated resource sharing? How it is implemented in a virtual organization?
2. Take any real time application and how a DVO is formed to solve the problems in that application. Mention the limitations.
3. "Security is still a Big-fish in Grid infrastructure". Comment on the statement with a solution to the problem. What are the pros and cons of your solution?

REFERENCES

1. R.O. Sinnott, O. Ajayi, A.J. Stell, J. Watt, J. Jiang (National e-science centre, University of Glasgow, Glasgow, Scotland), J. Koetsier (National e-science centre, University of Edinburgh, Edinburgh, Scotland), "Single Sign-on and Authorization for Dynamic Virtual Organizations".
2. Joshy Joseph, M. Ernest, C. Fellenstein, *Grid Computing*. Pearson Education, 2005.
3. *www.wikipedia.org.*
4. Ahmar Abbas, *Grid Computing—A Practical Guide to Technology and Applications*. Charles River Media Inc. 2004.

❑❑❑

3

Distributed Shared Memory in Grid Environment

3.1 INTRODUCTION

Distributed shared memory is a mechanism where single memory is shared among different nodes simultaneously. For implementing shared memory mechanism, there are various algorithms and schemes. Among them, *Central Server Algorithm* is one. In the central server algorithm, there will be one central server with a shared memory and some clients who will share the memory offered by the server. Here a client sends a request for every read or write operation to the central server. The server responds with data in case of a read operation and with an acknowledgement in the case of a write operation.[1–2]

The central server uses a simple request-response protocol for communication with the clients. The requests are retransmitted if the response time is out, otherwise a failure condition may arise. This retransmission of the messages shows the reliability of the distributed network. For implementing the entire scenario, two messages are used in the algorithm, one message for client to request for a resource and another one for server to response to the client. This algorithm has a limitation that the server may be a bottleneck. That is, the server may fail or crash due to some problem and may not be available further after. But if the server is available every time, the algorithm shows maximum performance than remaining algorithms. After all the clients request for the shared memory data, the central server pushes all the client requests into a queue. Then it allows the clients to access the shared memory in a round robin fashion based on a time quantum. After the time stamp is over, the server allows another client to access the shared memory. Like this the process continues till all the clients finish their jobs with the shared memory.[1,2]

3.2 PROBLEM DESCRIPTION

Distributed shared memory, is a mechanism where a single memory is shared among different client nodes. All the clients cannot access the shared memory at a time. So the server needs to manage the clients to access the shared memory. So, the server uses Central server algorithm that enables all the clients to communicate with the data sever with requests and responses. In this algorithm, a client who wishes to access shared memory data sends a request to the central server. Then the sever grants the permission to access the shared memory in a response to the client.[1–2]

3.3 ANALYSIS USING CENTRAL SERVER ALGORITHM

The Central server algorithm is implemented using a simple request-response protocol. If there is no response after certain period of the request, then the request is re-transmitted. This shows the reliability using this protocol. Along with this, the server needs two messages to communicate with the client. One message from client to request server for the shared memory and one from server in a response to the client. This scenario can be represented in the form of an algorithm as shown.[1–2]

Algo_Central_Server()

```
{
    If(client wishes to access shared memory)
       Send_req_to_Server();
       Server_receive_req();

       //Perform Shared data access.//

       Send_response_to_client();
       Client_receive_response();
}
```

3.4 IMPLEMENTATION

The code for the above algorithm was implemented using JAVA platform. There are two module of the code, one is Server module and another one is client module.[1–2]

First the Server module is executed, which starts a server. Now the server is ready to accept the client requests and allow them to access the shared memory.[1–2]

3.4.1 Server Module

```
import java.io.*;
import java.net.*;
public class Server
{
BufferedReader in= null;
PrintStream outer= null;
Socket incoming= null;
ServerSocket serversocket= null;
public static void main(String args[])
{
new Server().establishConnection();
}
void establishConnection()
{
        try
        {
                serversocket = new ServerSocket(9987);
                System.out.println("\nServer\n");
                while (incoming == null)
                incoming = serversocket.accept();
                in = new BufferedReader(new InputStreamReader(incoming.getInputStream()));
                outer = new PrintStream(incoming.getOutputStream());
                while (true)
                {
```

```
                    String msg = in.readLine();
                    System.out.println("Received..." + msg);
                    if (msg.equalsIgnoreCase("end-client1"))
                    {
                    outer.println("Byee client1...*** End of Session ****");
                    }
               else if (msg.equalsIgnoreCase("end-client2"))
                    {
                    outer.println("Byee client2...*** End of Session ****");
                    }
               else if (msg.equalsIgnoreCase("end-client3"))
                    {
                    outer.println("Byee client3...*** End of Session ****");
                    }
               else if (msg.equalsIgnoreCase("end"))
                    {
                        outer.println("Byee ...*** End of Session ****");
                    System.out.println("Byee ...*** End of Session ****");
                        incoming.close();
                    }
               else {
                    //String msgst = new String("\nauthorized user :"+
msg+"\n>>>  Access shared memory data  <<<");
                    outer.println("hello client");
                    System.out.println("\nacessing....");
                    System.out.println("\nauthorized user :"+ msg +"\n>>>
Access shared memory data  <<<");}
               }
          }
          catch (Exception e)
          { }
}
}
```

Second Module is Client Module. When Client module is executed, it automatically connects to the server and an informing message is displayed. There by multiple clients can be connected to the server who wishes to access the shared memory.[1–2]

3.4.2 Client Module

```
import java.io.*;
import java.net.*;
public class Client
{
BufferedReader in=null;
PrintStream out=null;
Socket socket=null;
public static void main(String args[])
{
new Client().connect();
}
void connect()
{
try{
        DataInputStream input =new DataInputStream(System.in);
        socket=new Socket("127.0.0.1",9987);
        System.out.println("\nClient side\n\n");
        if(socket!=null)
        {
        System.out.println("\nConnected to server:"+socket.getInetAddress());
        }
        else
        System.out.println("\nConnection failed");
        in= new BufferedReader(new
InputStreamReader(socket.getInputStream()));
        out= new PrintStream(socket.getOutputStream());
        Client obj=new Client();
```

```
        while(socket.isConnected())
        {
        System.out.print("\nEnter any string(end to quit):");
        String msg=input.readLine();
        if(msg.equalsIgnoreCase("end"))
        {
          out.println(msg);
          System.out.println(in.readLine());
          socket.close();
          break;
        }
        else if(msg.equalsIgnoreCase("end-client1"))
        {
          out.println(msg);
          System.out.println(" message received:"+in.readLine());
        }
        else if(msg.equalsIgnoreCase("end-client2"))
        {
          out.println(msg);
          System.out.println(" message received:"+in.readLine());
        }
        else if(msg.equalsIgnoreCase("end-client3"))
        {
          out.println(msg);
          System.out.println(" message received:"+in.readLine());
          //break;
        }
        else {out.println(msg);
        System.out.println(" message received:"+in.readLine());}
        }
      }
      catch(Exception e)   {}
  }
}
```

The combined execution of the modules at a time resembles a distributed shared memory environment.

3.5 FUTURE WORK

Central server algorithm has one potential problem that it may become bottleneck as it has to process all the client requests. For this problem the server will replicate the backend data at multiple servers. In this situation all the clients must be able to locate the newly updated servers where the required data is stored. For this purpose the central server algorithm must be equipped with more number of features or any alternative must be looked out.[1–2]

Alternatives of the central server algorithm are *migration algorithm*, *read-replication algorithm* and *full replication algorithm*.[1–2]

SUMMARY

Distributed shared memory is a mechanism that enables multiple client nodes to share a single memory. Here the shared memory mechanism is implemented using central-server algorithm. Central server algorithm involves a central server responsible for processing all the client requests. This server functionality is implemented using a server module. Multiple clients are also involved who will send requests to the server for accessing the shared memory data. This client environment is implemented using the Client module. This on executing connects to a server and allows the clients to send requests to the server for accessing shared memory data.

KNOWLEDGE TESTING

1. What do you mean by distributed shared memory? How it varies in a Grid environment compared to normal environment?
2. What are various algorithms available to implement DSM in Grid environment?
3. What are the problems arise in implementing DSM in Grid environment? How those problems are exploited? Suggest a solution for this problem.

REFERENCES

1. Michael Stumm and Songnian Zhou, *Algorithms Implementing Distributed Shared Memory*, Computer, Volume 23, Issue 5, pp. 54–64, May 1990.
2. Joshy Joseph, M. Ernest, C. Fellenstein, *Grid Computing*. Pearson Education 2005.
3. *http://www.wikipedia.org*.

❑❑❑

4

Conceptual Evolution and Pathway to Grid Computing

4.1 INTRODUCTION AND EVOLUTION

Grid started in the early 1990s as a model of Meta computing in which supercomputers share resources. Grids could help bridge the gap between grid technologies and users. After completing this chapter you would be able to understand the concepts of:[1,4,6]

- How the grid concept comes into this world
- Networking concepts in grid
- Grid road map
- Business related issues in grid

The grid has evolved in numerous distinct phases. Grid computing can be evolved by using mainly four technical concepts. Those are:[1,4,6]

- Distributed computing
- High Performance computing
- Clusters
- Finally web services

Let's see the each one of them.

4.1.1 Distributed Computing

In grid distributed computing deals both the hardware and software which containing more than one processing element in the loosely-coupled and heterogeneous environment. By using this concept the program is split up into parts that run simultaneously on multiple computers communicating over a network. Distributed uses the property of openness (each subsystem is continually open to interaction with other systems). However some drawback is there because of using DC in grid- sometimes it decreases the overall reliability of computations the unavailability of a node can cause disruption of the other nodes. There are mainly three models comes into the Distributed computing of the grid.[1,4,6]

- Internet computing,
- Peer- to-peer
- Grid enabled architecture

4.1.2 High Performance Computing

In grid HPC related to the parameters speed, performance and throughput of computing. Grid computers (Super Computers) are belongs to High Performance. High performance mainly relies on parallel processing and speedup. We improve the performance in following domains like processor, Memory, I/O devices. In the form of improving these one we can achieve the High Performance.[1,4,6]

4.1.3 Clusters

A cluster is generally built on homogeneous operating system and it relates to chip architecture. Clusters are located in one location and it has tightly coupled interconnections. A grid can be formed by collection of clusters.[1,4,6]

Are cluster and grid computing both are synonymous?

No. Cluster and grid computing both are not same. These two are different implementations to meet the application demands.

Table 4.1: Difference between Cluster Computing and Grid Computing

Cluster Computing	*Grid Computing*
Build on homogeneous operating system.	It consists of heterogeneous in nature,
It has tightly coupled interconnection.	Loosely–coupled one.
Placed in single location and rely on very low network latency.	Grid resources are distributed across LAN, MAN and WAN.
Clusters complete a grid. It has one resource on the grid (like participating computer/network resource/storage)	Collection of clusters. However it may locate in some distance. It has one or more resources.
Single operating system and chip architecture plays a important role for building cluster.	Different operating system, chips, networks and storages.

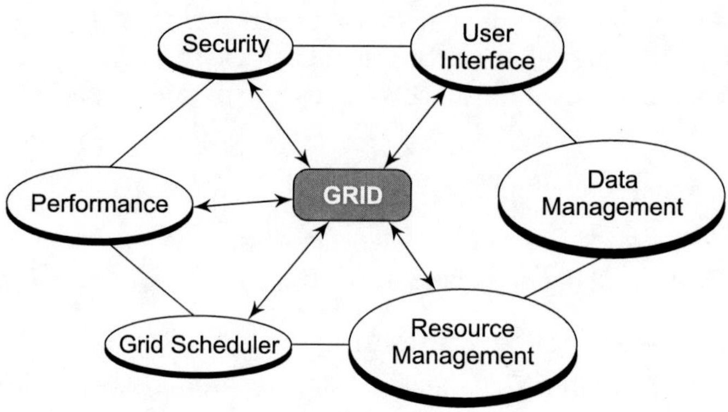

Fig. 4.1 Components tied with grid.[1,9]

4.1.4 Web Services

A service is a module of logic that maintains/contains meaningful business functions. Web services are the fundamental building blocks in the move to distributed computing on the Internet. It composed of processes, services, and components. They essentially are software components in the network. We will see more discussion on web services in second unit.[1,4,6]

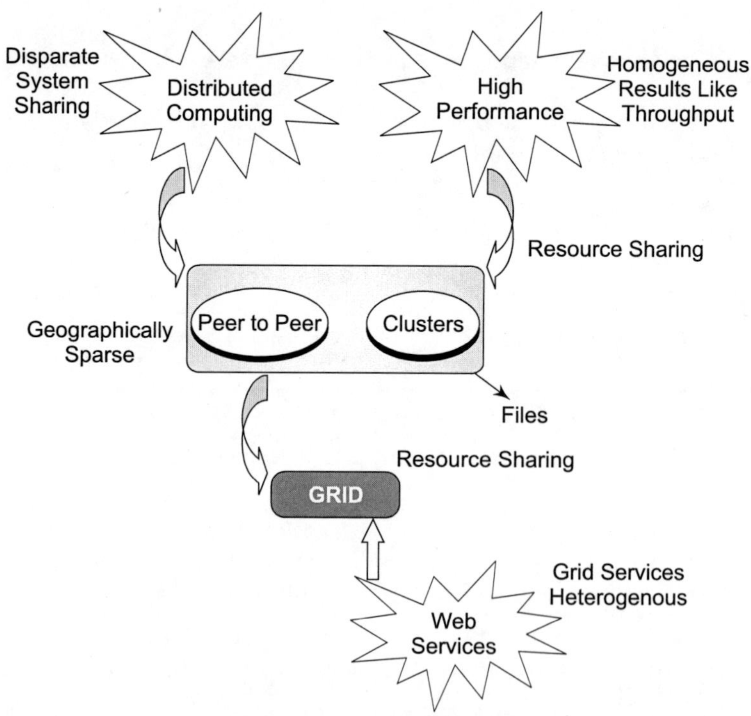

Fig. 4.2 The evolution of grid.[1]

From this a grid uses the resources of many separate computers, loosely connected by a network (usually the Internet), to solve large-scale computation problems. The necessary outcome of the grid is virtualization of resources.

4.2 CONCEPT OF NETWORKING IN GRID

Two fundamental types of relationships exist: peer-to-peer and client-server relationship.[1, 4–6]

4.2.1 Peer-to-peer Network

A peer-to-peer network defines one in which computers on the network communicate with each other as equals. Each computer is responsible for making its own resources available to other computers on the network. Peer-to-peer grid looks like.[1,4–6]

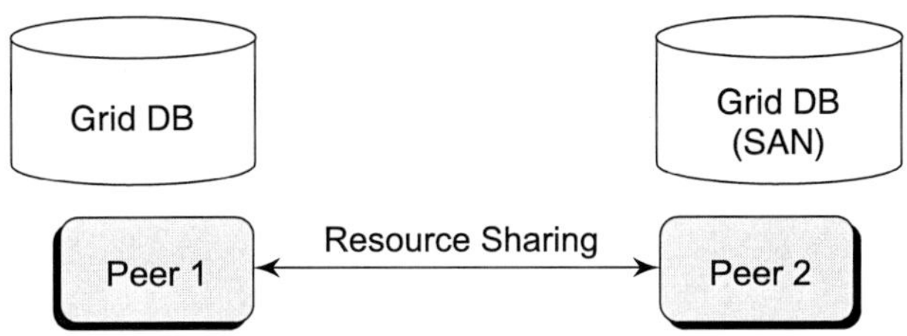

Fig. 4.3 Peer-to-peer grid.[1,4,9]

These resources might be files, directories, application programs, or devices such as printers, modems etc. The resource in peer-to-peer networks is the storage capacity of each (mostly desktops) node. Each computer is responsible for setting up and maintaining its own security for those resources. Finally each computer is responsible for accessing the network resources it needs from other peer-to-peer computers and for knowing where those resources are and what security is required to access them. Generally grid uses P2P model.[1,4–6]

4.2.2 Client/Server Network

A Client/Server is one which a distinction exists between the computers that make available network resources (the servers) and computers that use the resources (the clients, workstations). In grid, Client/server model should be a pure one for satisfying all job requests at the server side. A pure client/server network is one which all available network resources- such as files, directories, applications and shared devices- are the centrally managed and hosted and, then are accessed by the client computers. Job requests are submitted by client via grid middleware (by using resource broker) to the server. No client computers share their resources with other client computers or with the servers. Instead, the client computers are pure consumers of these resources.[1,4–6]

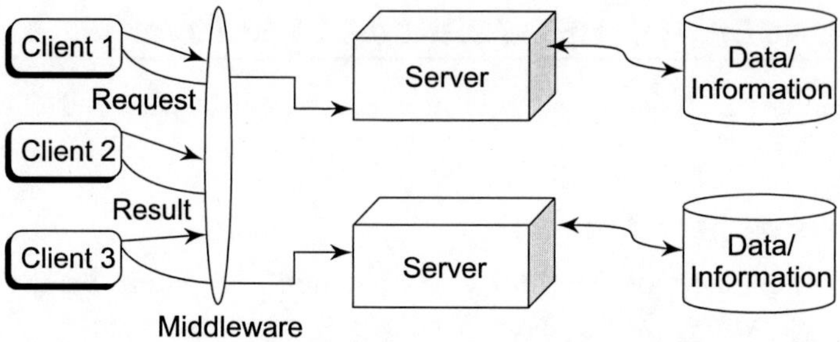

Fig. 4.4 Grid computing client/Server model.[1,4,9]

4.3 GRID PATHWAY

From generation to generation grid uses different types of information technologies and business concepts. Presently grid has in third generation and it has web services, OGSA, OGSI, Autonomic, business on demand and semantic grids.[4–6]

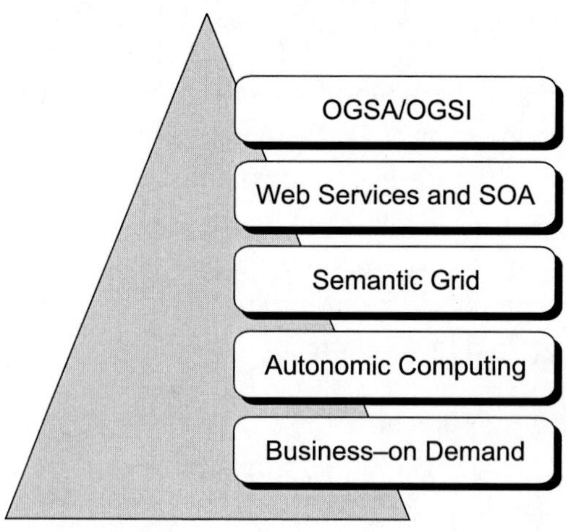

Fig. 4.5 Third generation.[1,4,9]

We discussed OGSA/OGSI, Web services and SOA in separate unit. Now we will go for remaining.

4.3.1 Autonomic Computing

"Autonomic" is the term which adjust many situations automatically without any external help either in human body or in practical systems. For managing the shared resources, solutions/outcomes, complexities we require a significant amount of autonomic functions. These functions will automatically manage the objects in the grid.[4–6]

There are mainly four basic autonomic principles which are necessary in grid computing.

- Self- configuring
- Self- optimizing
- Self- healing
- Self- protecting

In configuring, the system has able to adapt to the changes.[4–6]

In protecting, the heterogeneous systems has able to anticipate and cure intrusions.[4–6]

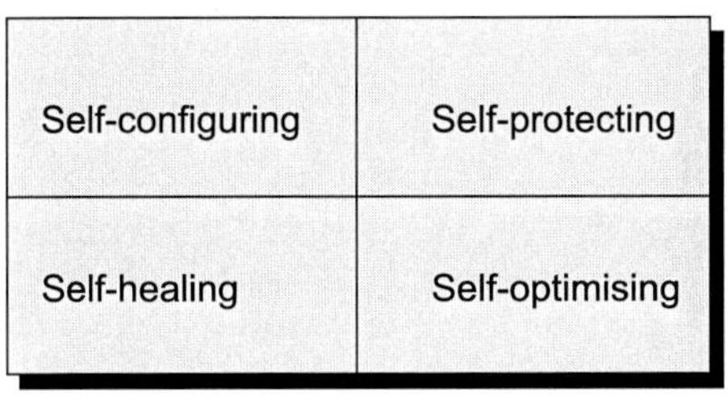

Fig. 4.6 Autonomic concept in grid.[1,4,9]

In healing, if the participating systems have fallen into any problems those should be recovered from mistakes automatically.[4–6]

In optimizing, the system shall improve his performance by better chip architectures, processors and network throughput.[4–6]

Presently, IBM implements fuse number of projects worldwide by using the concept of autonomic computing. Grid computing and autonomic computing two different topics and these two are work together for achieving reliable, efficient and self- managing grids.[4–6]

4.3.2 Business on Demand

Demand business fills the gap between IT promises and product delivers. Demand business (e-business) connects its core business systems constituencies using intranets, extranets, and the Web. Getting to e-business on demand is a natural progression that typically goes through these stages:[4–6]

- **Access:** Enable transactions against core business systems using simple Web publishing and point solutions.
- **Enterprise integration:** Use the Web to integrate business processes across enterprises. Link internal and external systems, both across enterprises and beyond enterprise boundaries.
- **E-business on demand:** Use the Web to adapt dynamically to customer and market requirements. Change business models. Combine people, technologies, and processes in new ways.

If the organizations can use the e-business in grid, they should:[4–6]

- Create new products and services faster
- Reach new customers and economically add new relationships
- Dynamically change existing relationships
- Simultaneously engage in multiple e-business models
- Improve access to information by constituents involved in these relationships

An on-demand business has these characteristics:[4–6]

- **Responsive:** Adapt to changes in the environment and to respond dynamically to emerging customer, partner, supplier and employee needs
- **Variable:** Able to adapt cost matters and business processes flexibly, to reduce risk, and to drive business performance at higher levels of productivity, cost control, capital efficiency.
- **Focused:** Focused on differentiating tasks and assets; able to use tightly integrated strategic partners to manage tasks ranging from manufacturing, logistics, and fulfillment to human resources and financial operations.
- **Resilient:** Prepared for changes and threats like computer viruses, earthquakes, or sudden spikes in demand

A business on demand must also satisfy the following capabilities.

Technology integration: Integrate the systems horizontally to link data, legacy systems, and custom applications. Technology should satisfy the transaction processing also. Use the Web services, new development tools, and open standards for building new applications.[4–6]

Openness: Because of openness capability connects the enterprises with other enterprises, other business processes, other applications, and billions of pervasive computing devices. For doing this openness is realistic way.[4–6]

Virtualized: Data centers are virtualized with an emerging technology called grid computing. Grid computing allows distributed computing resources to be shared and managed as if they were one, large, virtual computer.[4–6]

Automation: Which we discussed earlier was a frame work for on-demand operating system.[4–6]

4.3.3 Semantic Grids

Semantic grid is the natural evolution in grid computing. The evolution was towards knowledge–centric and metadata–driven computing paradigm. The Semantic Grid is clearly useful in providing support for investigations using social simulations. The 'Semantic' part provides an ontologically supported context for all of the information associated with a piece of work, from hypotheses through experiments.[4–6]

Semantic grid is the combination of semantic web services and grid services. However semantic web service combine semantic web and web service technology.[4–6]

Semantic grid = Semantic web service + grid services

Semantic web service = Semantic web + web service technology.

Semantic web is the extension of current web in which information is provided in well defined manner. There are mainly two technologies for building semantic webs:[4–6]

- XML and
- Resource description Framework (RDF).

XML provides the meaning of the structure by markup tags. Meaning is expressed and encoded by the RDF in which sentences are treated as triples (subject, object and predicate) and expressed using XML. The subject and object are identified by a Universal Resource Identifier (URI).[4–6]

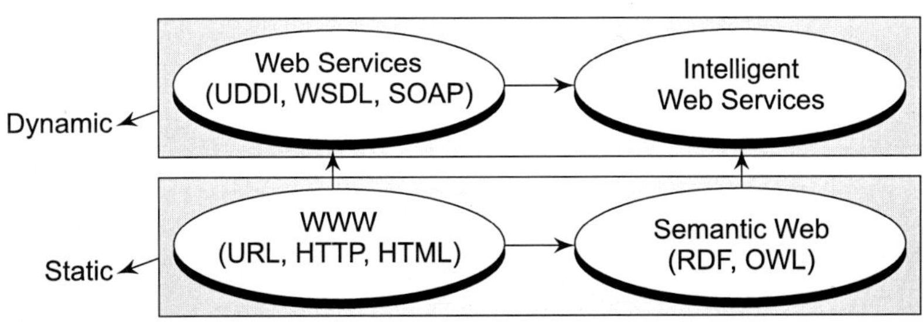

Fig. 4.7 Semantic grid and web world.[1,5,6]

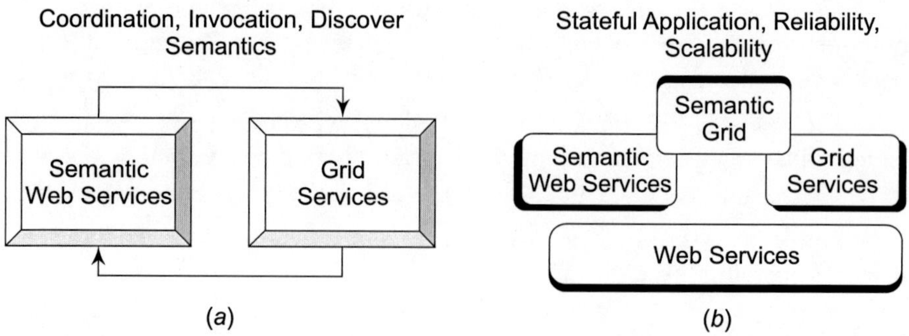

Fig. 4.8 (*a*) Semantic web services vs. grid services, (*b*) Semantic grid.[1,5,6]

4.4 GRID BUSINESS VALUES

Today companies and organizations are spending so much of amount nearly trillion dollars per year to optimize their operations in all aspects like financial, sales, marketing, engineering and product development. Grid is the one which address all these business issues. Grid successfully entered into product development from research communities like GGF (Global Grid Forum). Grid offers low cost and high throughput solution that allows companies to optimize and leverage existing IT infrastructure and investments. The following diagram shows components in grid which is related to business values.[2]

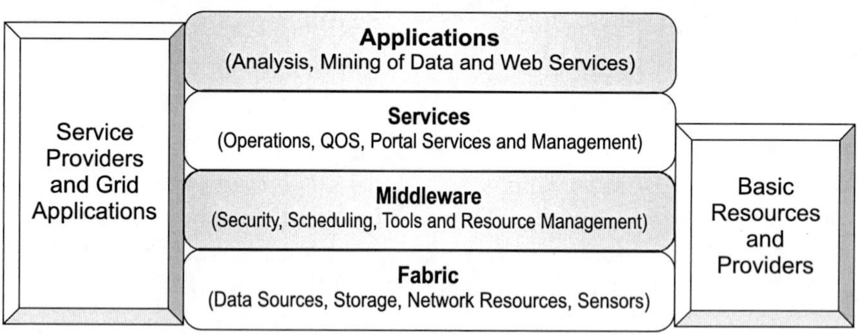

Fig. 4.9 Grid business layers.[1,2]

Fabric layer refer to hardware products that refer to grid infrastructure. These include personal computers, high performance computers, clusters, and storage devices, as well as networking devices such as routers, switches, load balancers, caching systems, etc. Software vendors, tools, scheduling are in middleware. Execution tasks are also done by middleware. Services are helped to integrate the existing systems. Services are generally end- to end services.[2]

Operations (operational support systems) are treated as services which are generally in service ware. Software vendors and applications utilize the grid computing infrastructure through application layer.[2]

SUMMARY

- A Grid Service could be viewed as a standard Web Service adapted to the requirements typically found in a Grid environment.
- The road map leads to distributed environment and meets the open standards.
- A cluster is generally built on homogeneous operating system and it relates to chip architecture. Clusters are located in one location and it has tightly coupled interconnections.
- Cluster and grid computing are not same.
- A service is a module of logic that maintains/contains meaningful business functions.
- Grid computing has in third generation and it has web services, OGSA, OGSI, Autonomic, business on demand and semantic grids.
- *Semantic grid* = Semantic web service + grid services

  Semantic web service = Semantic web + web service technology

KNOWLEDGE TESTING

1. Evaluate the grid computing technically. Explain each concept clearly.
2. Explain the:
   (i) Peer to peer
   (ii) Client-Server models in Grid computing.
3. Cluster and grid computing both are synonymous/not? justify your answer?
4. What are the technical concepts involved in grid computing? Explain each one of them.
5. Differentiating the following:
   (i) Semantic grid
   (ii) Semantic web.

REFERENCES

1. Joshy Joseph, M. Ernest, C. Fellenstein, *Gird Computing*, Pearson Education, 2005.
2. Pankaj Misra, *Sharpen Your Business Edge with Grid Computing*, *www.infosys.com/linux/white-papers/.../sharpen-edge-grid-computing.pdf.*
3. Gene Amdahl, *Validity of the Single Processor Approach to Achieving Large-scale Computing Capabilities*, AFIPS Conference Proceedings, (30), pp. 483–485, 1967.
4. *http://www.03.ibm.com/grid/pdf/it_exec_brief.pdf.*
5. *http://www.semanticgrid.org/document/semgrid-journal/semgrid-journal.pdf.*
6. *http://www.semanticgrid.org/documents/evolution/evolution.pdf.*
7. *www.deri.org.*
8. *http://jasss.soc.surrey.ac.uk/10/2/2.html.*
9. Ahmar Abbas, *Grid Computing—A Practical Guide to Technology and Applications*, Charles River Media Inc., 2004.

❑❑❑

PART II

GRID COMPUTING TECHNOLOGIES

Grid is an on-demand business related one and it supports autonomic computing. The fundamental purpose of grid is to make the distribution environment broadly across power kind of networks using open standards. For doing this service-level environment is necessary. So, in this chapter I am going to discuss briefly about some of the service level concepts and open standards.

After completing of this chapter you will be able to understand the concepts like:

- Service-oriented architecture, its role in grid computing and its applications.
- Web services and its role in grid.
- XML mechanisms.
- Web service description language and understanding XML code.

The widespread emergence of the internet is to distribute information to any corner of the world. Means what services and internet designs do this? Let us understand I am developed one service which I want to distribute among the internet.

1. What parts of the service will play a very important role?

2. What are the design/developed instructions?
3. Which action plans I need between the needs and the capabilities?
4. Which type of architecture I have to follow and what type of protocols that supports the architecture?
5. Which language describes all these whether it achieves interoperability or not?
6. How can I provide and use share data in a reliable fashion and secure way?

For answering to this type of questions we shall go to the following topics one by one. Let us initially we will see the Service- Oriented Architecture (SOA) which is a paradigm for organizing and utilizing distributed capabilities that supports different domains and technology stacks.

5

SOA, Service Oriented Architecture

5.1 SERVICE ORIENTED ARCHITECTURE (SOA)

People or organizations create domain related applications to a good solution for the problems they face in the course of their business. In the world of distributed systems, one computer agent's resources being met by a computer agent belonging to a different divisions (especially in business). There is no one- to- one relationship exists between needs and capabilities; so SOA provides a powerful framework for matching to address those needs and capabilities.[7–10]

Before providing correct definition to the SOA, let's see what a service is. A *service* is a specific function, typically a business function, such as analyzing an individual's credit history or processing a purchase order. A service can provide a single discrete function, such as converting one type of currency into another. It can also handle various operations that are belongs to multiple areas. Service may be *multiple* or *aggregated*, or *composite*. For coordinating of resources multiple services appropriated one and for complex business requirement remaining two are nice once. From this A service is a function that is well-defined, self-contained, and does not depend on the context or state of other services.[7–10]

Service-oriented architectures are not a new thing. SOA in the late 1990's to describe jini, which is an environment for dynamic discovery and use of services over a network. The first service-oriented architecture for many people in the past was with the use DCOM or Object Request Brokers (ORBs) based on the CORBA specification. A service-oriented architecture is essentially a collection of services. These services communicate with each other. The communication can involve either simple data passing or it could involve two or more services coordinating some activity. Some means of connecting services to each other is needed. A web service is the technology generally used for Service-oriented items.[7–10]

The following figure illustrates a basic service-oriented architecture (it shows very simple diagram). It shows a service consumer at the right sending a service request message to a service provider at the left. The service provider returns a response message to the service consumer. The request and subsequent response connections are defined in some way that is understandable to both the service consumer and service provider. A service provider can also be a service consumer.[7–10]

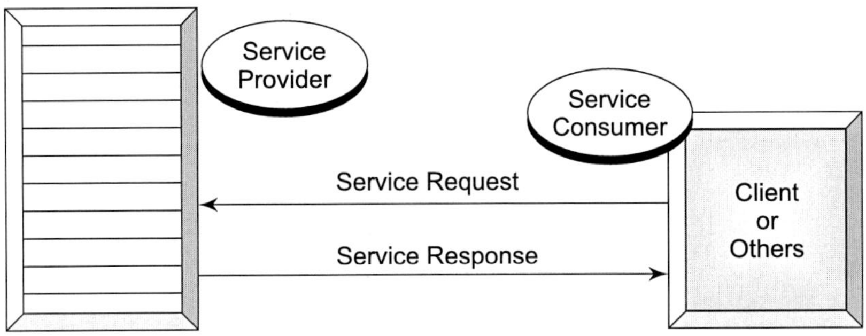

Fig. 5.1 A simple SOA architecture.[6–11]

For synchronous and asynchronous applications, it is an evolution of distributed computing based on the request/reply design paradigm. Business logic for application's or individual functions is modularized and presented as services for consumer/client applications. SOA is a loosely-coupled nature i.e the interfaces related to the services is independent of the implementations. Application developers or system integrators can build applications by composing one or more services without knowing the services' underlying implementations. For example, a service can be implemented either in .Net or J2EE, and the application consuming the service can be on a different platform or language.

Why we need SOA?

- For quickly respond to business changes
- For supporting the interoperability, heterogeneous across operating systems, applications, system software.
- Services identification and categorization, provisioning and delivery, and monitoring and tracking
- SOA bridges the gap between IT and business. Business processes can be done using the concept of SOA.
- Provides a new way of interacting with customers, partners, and suppliers
- Providing right infrastructure, business process visibility, managing enterprise applications and critical applications.
- Service Encapsulation, service loose coupling and service maintenance.

There are many reasons for an enterprise to take an SOA approach, and more specifically, a web services based SOA approach. Some of the primary reasons are:[7–10]

(*i*) **Interoperability:** Interoperability is the one which clients and services to communicate and understand each other no matter what platform they run on. It doesn't matter what the platform, systems and languages. Web services comprise a maturing set of protocols and technologies that are widely accepted and used, and that are platform, system, and language independent. Web Services Interoperability Organization (WS-I) theme is to identifies a core set of web services technologies that when implemented in different platforms and systems, helps ensure that services on these different platforms and systems, and written in different languages, can communicate with each other.

(*ii*) **Reusability:** Reusing the functionality that already exists outside or inside of an enterprise instead of developing code that reproduce those functions. So integrity applications and systems can be much simpler. Means developers can take the code developed for existing business applications, use in web services, and then reuse it to meet new business solutions. Using SOA, integrating applications and systems can be much simpler.

(*iii*) **Scalability:** SOA is loosely-coupled one. We can add other service systems easily to the existing network. Services are asynchronous in nature. An asynchronous service performs its processing without forcing the client to wait for the processing to finish but whereas synchronous service forces the browser/client to wait.

(*iv*) **Flexibility:** In loosely coupled system applications, resources and services are normally bound to each other. Because of document-based, asynchronous nature of services SOA allows applications to be flexible and easy to evolve with changing requirements.

Generally enterprises need service architecture for implementing SOA. The following diagram shows how service consumers can invoke services by sending messages. Service bus is used for transforming and routing the messages. It is lie on the service interface and implementation scenarios. This service architecture can provide a business rules engine that allows business rules to be incorporated in a service or across services. The service architecture also provides a service management infrastructure that manages services and activities like auditing, billing, and logging. In addition it offers flexible business process.[7–10]

Since SOA fill up the gap between IT and business, the benefits of SOA can be characterized into:[7–10]

- **Business aligning:** If an enterprise's architecture is SOA- based, it supports business agility. When the enterprise wants to launch a new business process, it is possible to do in business agility.
- **Technology flexibility:** Both SOA and web services uses the XML, SOAP, HTTP and UDDI. By using these technologies programmers can able to solve the problems of incompatibility.
- **Latest business opportunities:** SOA provides new business opportunities for existing enterprises. For example, SaaS is one such business model based on SOA. Presently, SOA opens windows of opportunity for new businesses.

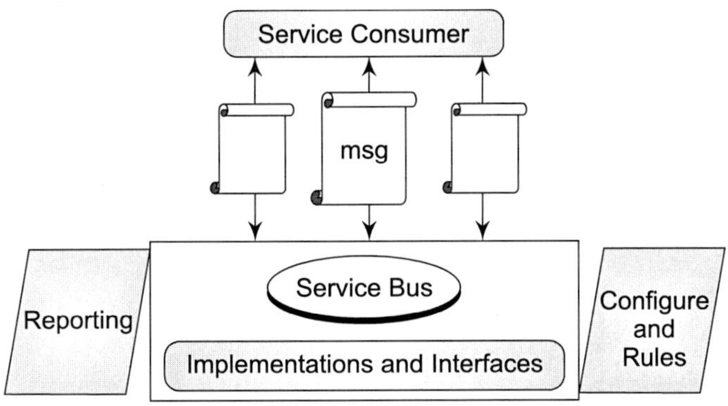

Fig. 5.2 Simple service architecture.[6–11]

SOA model has mainly includes execution phase, visibility, service description (using WSDL), policies, interactions and effect of real-world things. Here just I am giving the OASIS (Organization for Advancement of Structured Information Services).[7–10]

Service Descriptions provide declarations of aspects such as functions and technical requirements.[7–10]

Visibility is the capacity for those with needs and those with capabilities typically implemented by protocols, standards.[7–10]

The concept of *policy* also must be applicable to data represented as documents and policies must persist to protect this data far beyond enterprises.[7–10]

Execution phase deals how process are executed and what type of model it is following.[7–10]

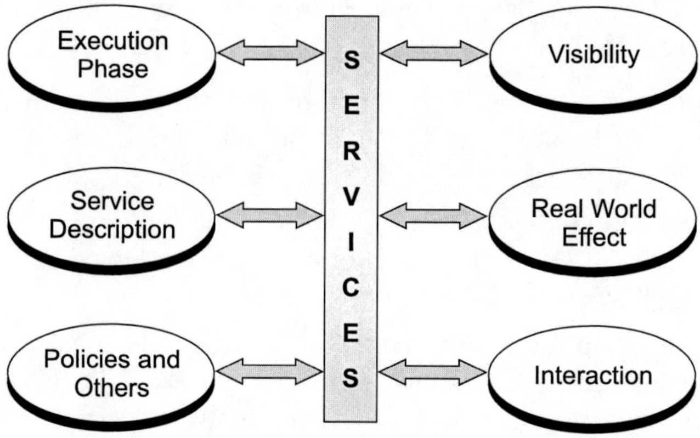

Fig. 5.3 Simple OASIS SOA's architecture.[6–11]

We remember one point here is SOA is not a web service. It creates a general confusion between SOA and web services. Gartner report, Yefim V. Natis makes the distinction as follows: "Web services are about technology specifications, whereas SOA is a software design principle. Notably, Web services' WSDL is an SOA-suitable interface definition standard: this is where Web services and SOA fundamentally connect." Fundamentally, SOA is an architectural pattern, while Web services are services implemented using a set of standards; Web services is one of the ways you can implement SOA. Implementations of SOA with Web services produce benefits that you achieve a platform-neutrality. Even in today's world vendors wants services using web. We have already seen why SOA and its importance. In one word I am telling that "*for achieving machine independence, performance over network and flexibly building business applications and also business processing SOA is necessary*".[7–10]

Let's we see roughly about SOA Infrastructure for running and managing applications.

Quality of Service (QoS)	Distributed Transaction Security Mechanisms Web Service Policies Reliable Messaging
Platform Supported	.NET Framework Java-J2EE PhP, Web Sphere etc..
Core Elements	SOAP UDDI, WSDL WS-I Basic Profile

Fig. 5.4 SOA Infrastructure.[6–11]

With an SOA, add new functions and modify existing processes by simply assembling the services required to meet the enhanced business process model. SOA Infrastructure is main part in the SOA platform. A typical SOA infrastructure contains core elements; language supporting and quality matters like distributed management, policies, security and transactions.[7–10]

Some simple points that related to the SOA's Infrastructure are:[7–10]

(*a*) WSDL, UDDI, and SOAP are the fundamental elements/pieces of the SOA infrastructure. We know already WSDL for describing the service; UDDI, directory mechanism for locating services; and SOAP, which is in XML format, as a transport layer protocol to send messages between service consumer and service provider. It is a way of packaging a message. Since XML is a universal language and human friendly, client interacts to the service easily.

(*b*) WS-I basic profile- it is used by the service providers for sponsoring the services and resources. It deals the issues related to the interoperability across different platforms and technologies.

(*c*) .NET and J2EE- Developers are mainly working on this area. They are trying to develop the applications that meet the SOA's issues and design goals. Newer specifications such as:

- Java API for XML-based Remote Procedure Call (XML-RPC)- used for invoking remote services in J2EE 1.4 facilitate the development and deployment of Web services that are portable across standard J2EE containers, while simultaneously interoperating with services across other platforms such as .Net.
- Java API for XML Binding (JAXB)- used for mapping XML documents to Java classes.
- Java API for XML Registry (JAXR)- used for interacting with the UDDI registries in a standard manner.

(*d*) In Quality of Service:[7–10]

- Deals the document type delivery. Means once only (at-most), duplicate message elimination, guaranteed message delivery, and acknowledgment.
- For addressing the issues of reliable messaging *WS- Reliability* and *WS- ReliableMessaging* standards are used and these are part of OASIS.
- Service policy describes the syntax for communicating tom the respective policies of a web service. It is important to understand that the policy framework doesn't provide a negotiation framework

for web services. For communicating providers to consumers policies are necessary. The main components of policies are discussed in OGSA.

- Security is dealing with point- to point security solutions which includes Security Socket level (SSL)/IPSec as examples. Security may be end-to-end also means security context between requester and end point web service.
- It manages the monitoring resources and business processes in distributed environment.

5.2 SOA REFERENCE ARCHITECTURE

SOA is a reference architecture model for open source. SOA takes the abstraction of functional logic to a higher level called 'service'. A service can have more than one component and number of components that a service can contain is depend upon the size and complexity of the logic behind the service.[7]

The simple architecture of SOA is looking like.

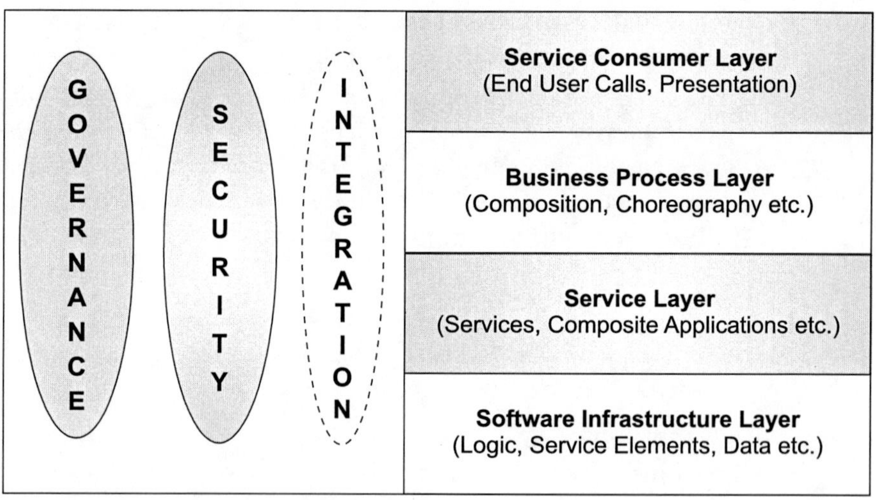

Fig. 5.5 A simple SOA reference architecture related to 'product type'.[6–11]

Functional layers in SOA are:[7]

(*i*) Software Infrastructure Layer.

(*ii*) Service Layer.

(*iii*) Business Process Layer.

(*iv*) Service Consumer Layer.

All packaged applications and traditional applications which are used by software engineers are belongs in Software Infrastructure layer. Services are exposed by Service Layer for example web services. Business process layer processes composition, choreography etc. Service consumer layer is the boundary layer to the service hosting network. It addresses the requirements of presentation and all other information services.[7]

Non-functional requirements are:[7]

(*i*) Integration.

(*ii*) Security.

(*iii*) Governance.

Security, integration and governance are the non-functional requirements. All security issues in SOA like security service, software infrastructure service are deals by Security component. Connectivity and integration of service are addressed by integration. Governance layer deals the monitoring issues and compliance. It encompasses all remaining layers.[7]

5.3 DESIGN AND DEVELOPMENT

SOA hide the details of the message issues and processing, while message is interchanged between the service providers who produce the service to a message consumer. In SOA, the service system is decomposed into a collection of network-connected components. Applications and resources should be built as loosely-coupled monolithic model. For developing this type of models Service-oriented Analysis and Design (SOAD) is used. It is a design methodology for developing high-performance systems in a consumer/producer model that abstracts implementation from process, such that a service-provider can be modified or changed without affecting the consumer.[1–6]

For developing service the following elements/components are consider into an account:[1–6]

Service contract:

Header-which includes name of service, version and owner to service.[1–6]

Functional:[1–6]

- Functional requirements.
- Service operations (methods and actions).
- URL and interfaces (ex. SOAP, REST, event triggers).

Non-functional requirements:

- Quality factors.
- Policies.
- Security constraints.
- Grammar (like semantics).
- Service level agreements and finally.
- Processes and transaction.

Architecture is not tied to one technology. It may be implemented using a wide range of technologies, including REST, RPC, and DCOM, COBRA or Web services. SOA can be implemented using one of these protocols (especially SOAP plays good role here).[1–6]

Up to here we discussed about the architecture, need of SOA, SOA model and infrastructure. What you understand from these topics. Any differences exist between traditional architecture and SOA. After I understand SOA, I observed few differences between them and I am placing these differences. I hope the reader can understood these ones, which are helpful for further proceeding to next topics:[1–6]

(*i*) Service- oriented architecture is message oriented one. It transform between service provider and consumer, which is a XML message. Whereas traditional architecture is a object-oriented one.

(*ii*) Interfaces are needed by services for separating the implementations. Traditional one doesn't need interfaces.

(*iii*) One main difference is SOA is loosely-coupled architecture whereas traditional architecture was tightly architecture. However it may support loosely also.

(*iv*) In development phase also both maintain a consistent difference. SOA belongs to iterative whereas traditional one is long developed life cycles.

(*v*) SOA is designed for approaching to the changes in business process areas but traditional didn't do this.

(*vi*) SOA is purely process-oriented. It doesn't bother about the functionality changes—this work is taken by traditional architecture.

The following graph shows the importance of SOA which address the concept of virtualization (discussed previously) related to the enterprise applications.[1–6]

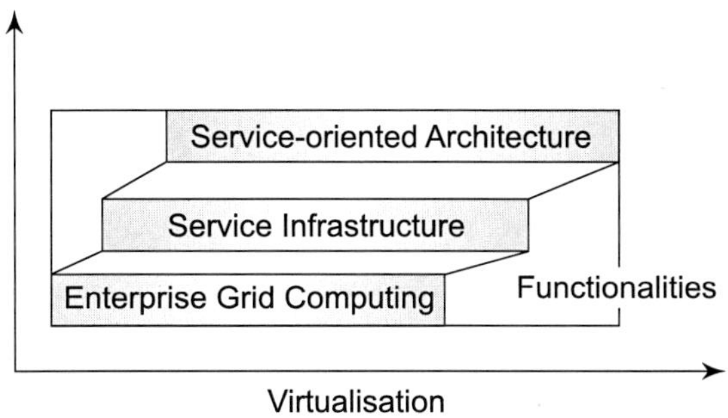

Fig. 5.6 Graph showing virtualisation concept in SOA.[6–11]

5.4 EXECUTION PARADIGM

Service-oriented architecture supports sharing functions (typically business functions) in a widespread and flexible way. The most commonly understood SOA architectures are web and web services. The web architecture has evolved even before we started talking about the SOA.The interaction pattern between the consumer and the service is a combination of message, message packaging, and transport protocols. This architecture needs to further extend by adding QoS requirements, security, and management aspects.[1–6]

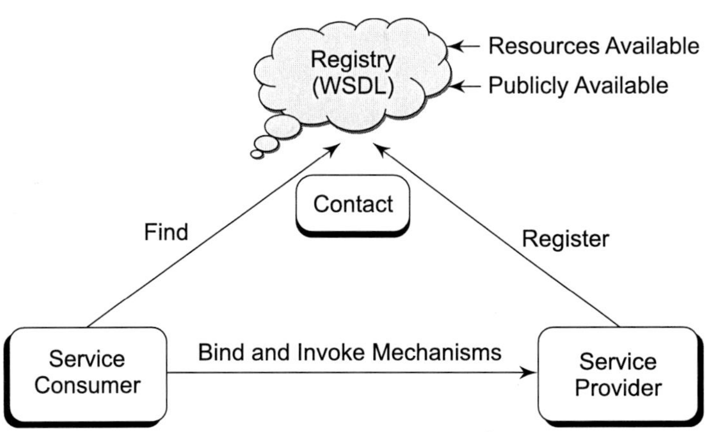

Fig. 5.7 SOA's execute paradigm.[6–11]

SOA uses the *find-bind-execute* paradigm as shown in Fig. 5.7 form the diagram service consumer, registry, service providers are main actors. In this paradigm, service providers register their service in a public registry. This registry is used by consumers to find services that match certain criteria. If the registry has such a service, it provides the consumer with a contract and an endpoint address for that service.[1–6]

5.4.1 Registry Role in Grid

The registry stores the indexes/metadata of resources. It manages the resource dependency, activity monitoring and life cycle management. Categories in resources in registry are:[1–6]

5.4.1.1 *All resources*

- Resource address.
- Service type.
- Service name.
- Service provider.
- Valid date.
- Service location.
- Service node.
- Service status.
- Service parameters.
- Service description.
- Resource shared rule.

5.4.1.2 *Algorithms resources*

- Computing status.
- Algorithm type.
- Server address.
- Parameters list.
- Algorithm description.

5.4.1.3 *Data resources*

- Data access method.
- Metadata.
- Data type.
- Data description.

SOA-based applications are distributed multi-tier applications that have presentation, business logic, and persistence layers. Services are the building blocks of SOA applications. While any functionality can be made into a service, the challenge is to define a service interface that is at the right level of abstraction.[1–6]

SOA allows for the reuse of existing assets where new services can be created from an existing IT infrastructure of systems. Let's see a simple example which illustrates the functionality of SOA.[1–6]

A good example is Credit card validation/online banking. When you log on to your account on your bank's Web site, you actually perform several processes. One verifies your username and password (and possibly shows you a security image or code to comply with multifactor authentication). Once you are logged on, another process accesses your bank records to show your current balance and past transactions. If you want to conduct an online transaction, such as transferring money to another account or paying bills online, your computer accesses another process.[1–6]

A service-oriented architecture plan is designed to tie all these processes together and present them to the user in a way that appears seamless and simple. A chief driver of SOA is that the underlying technical complexity of a linked system should not be apparent to or have to be understood to work through a process; the user should be able to easily and seamlessly initiate a process and receive results.[1–6]

SUMMARY

- Service may be multiple or aggregated or composite.
- SOA is collection of Services.
- SOA is a distributed architecture and is widely used for web services.
- The primary reasons to adapt SOA are:
  1. Interoperability
  2. Reusability
  3. Scalability
  4. Flexibility
- Service consumer, Service Provider and registry are key components of SOA's executive paradigms.

KNOWLEDGE TESTING

1. Assume you want to develop one application in web services using soa. What factors you may choose for going to the SOA? (web service is a technology used in SOA)
2. How can you present the real- world effects into the SOA? Suggest any model related to this category.
3. Discuss briefly the infrastructure and architecture of SOA. Draw a diagram that supporting these two
4. Why SOA is loosely- coupled. Are there any advantages of using loosely-coupled one.
5. Discuss briefly the pros and cons of SOA. Explain SOA by using any one example.
6. What's the role of registry in SOA? Explain the functionality of registry and also describe the working procedure of SOA?

REFERENCES

1. Sriram Krishnan and Karan Bhatia, *SOAs for Scientific Applications: Experiences and Challenges*, Future Generation Computer Systems Volume 25, Issue 4, April 2009, pp. 466–473.
2. Hongbing Wang and Joshua Zhexue Huang, *Web services: problems and future directions*, *www.elsevier.com/authored_subject_sections/P05/misc/wang.pdf.*
3. R. Akkiraju, J. Farrell, J.Miller, M. Nagarajan, M. Schmidt, AmitSheth, and Kunal Verma. Web service semantics - wsdl-s, *http://lsdis.cs.uga.edu/projects/meteor-s/wsdl-s/.* Technical Report, 2005.
4. Liliana Cabral, John Domingue, Stefania Galizia, Alessio Gugliotta, Barry Norton, Vlad Tanasescu, and Carlos Pedrinaci, *IRS-III: A Broker for Semantic Web Services based Applications*, In Proceedings of the 5th International Semantic Web Conference (ISWC 2006), Athens, GA, USA, 2006.
5. J. Euzenat, *Towards a Principled Approach to Semantic Interoperability*, In Proceedings of IJCAI workshop on Ontologies and information sharing, Seattle (WA), US, 2001.
6. Armin Haller, Emilia Cimpian, Adrian Mocan, Eyal Oren, and Christoph Bussler, *WSMX – A Semantic Service-Oriented Architecture*. In Proc. of the 3rd Int. Conf. on Web Services, pp. 321 – 328. IEEE Computer Society, 2005.

7. Martin Bosworth, *Service–Oriented Architecture*, *http://www.govexec.com/basics/ServiceOrientedArchitecture.htm.*
8. *Qusay H. Mahmoud, Service–oriented architecture*, http://java.sun.com/developer/technicalArticles/WebServices/soa/.
9. *SOA and* Specialized Messaging Patterns, *http://192.150.8.55/government/pdfs/SOA-technical-whitepaper.pdf.*
10. Hao He, *What Is Service-Oriented Architecture*, *http://www.xml.com/pub/a/ws/2003/09/30/soa.html.*
11. Joshy Joseph, M. Ernest, C. Fellenstein, *Grid Computing*, Pearson Education, 2005.

❑❑❑

6

WEB SERVICES IN GRID

6.1 WEB SERVICES TECHNOLOGIES

Internet is more than just a physical network. Web services are the fundamental building blocks in the move to distributed computing on the Internet. It is an application programming service that can be accessed remotely via standard Internet protocols using XML as the data format. It composed of processes, services, and components. They essentially are software components in the network. Like prior protocols for distributed computing—such as DCOM, DCE, CORBA and Java RMI—web services provide a framework for remotely invoking an object and exchanging data. In internet environment web service looks like:[2–4]

- Services are self-contained (perform predetermined tasks) and loosely coupled (for independence).
- Services encapsulate a business process and it provides a facility that service provider's register themselves.
- Find, Bind, and Execute are the main words involve in any services.
- Composite services can be built from aggregates of other services.

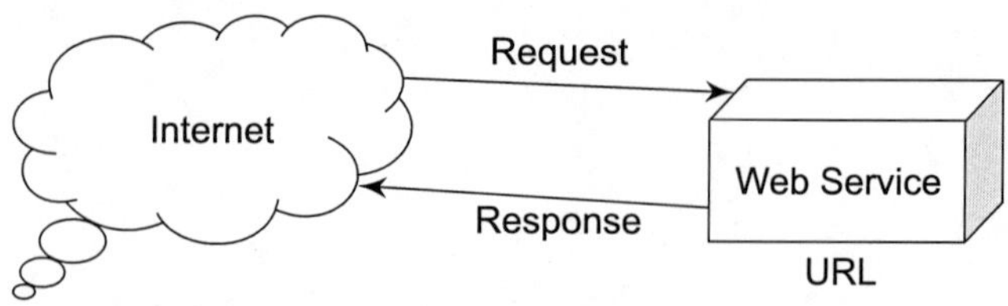

Fig. 6.1 Internet web service.[6–11]

Web services allow programs written in different languages on different platforms to communicate with each other in a standards-based way. The other significant advantage that XML Web services have over previous efforts is that they work with standard Web protocols—XML, HTTP and TCP/IP.[2–4]

What is a service? Why we need services?

A service is a module of logic that maintains/contains meaningful business functions. For example 'Credit card validation can be considered as a service. The most popular services are web services. We can discover the services dynamically. Simply we say a "service" is the atomic unit of an SOA. Service is nothing but implementation of well-defined business functionality, and such services can then be consumed by clients in different applications or business processes. Means Services are software components with well-defined interfaces that are implementation-independent. An important aspect of SOA is the separation of the service interface (the what) from its implementation (the how). Such services are consumed by clients that are not concerned with how these services will execute their requests.

6.1.1 Architecture

Architecture of web services is mainly based upon four layers. The general architecture is:[2–4]

Data layer: data layer contains data that can be accessed by the web service. It includes database or data storage that can be accessed by a web service to manage information.

Data access layer: It's intermediate one between the data layer and the business layer.

- Responsible for to retrieve the data from data layer and make available to the web service.
- Updates the data storage after a business transaction.
- Maintains the integrity of data by validating the changes that meets the business logic applications

Business layer: It implements the business logic of application and provides accessibility to the web service. Business layer is divided into two layers.

- **Business logic layer:** Applications implementations.
- **Business façade layer:** It is an interface that provides access to the services provided by business logic layer.

Listener layer: It is upper most layers in the web service general architecture. It listen the client requests that are made by web service and converts the request to form that can be processed by web service.

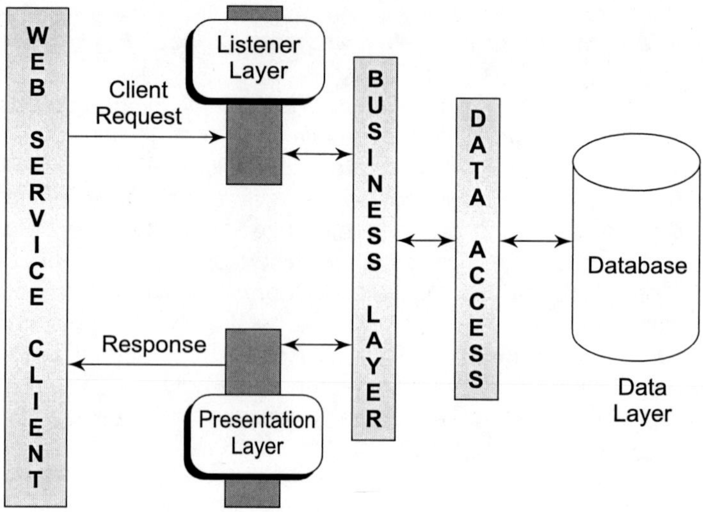

Fig. 6.2 The general architecture has four layers.[6–11]

Web service agents are exchange information in the form of messages. Web service standards are implemented by using platforms and service products from all major vendors.[2–4]

Grid will share the data, computations using web services. When people working web services they may doubt what the difference between web server and web service is.[2–4]

Table 6.1: Difference between web server and web service

Web Server	*Web Service*
It is the combination of URL plus some parameter values.	It is a XML Document (SOAP message) and returns XML document. It lokks like RPC.
It returns dynamic web pages.	Provides distributed objects for the web. It includes naming, discovery, security etc..

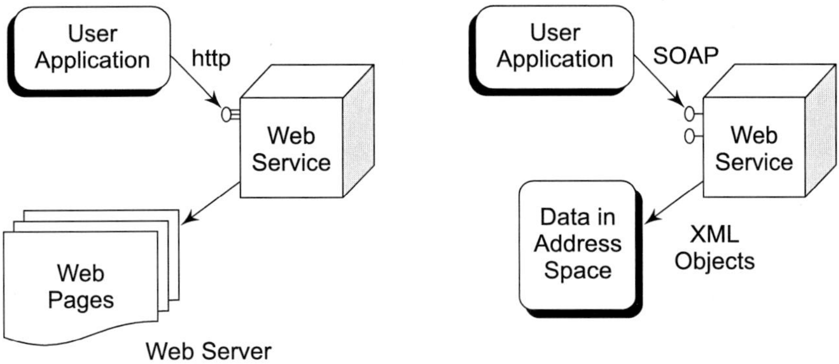

Fig. 6.3 Web server vs Web service.[6–11]

6.1.2 Architecture Related to Grid

The web service architecture is build using XML Technologies. The base layer is transport layer which contains all the transport mechanisms like HTTP, SMTP, JSON- RPC, and BEEP. Numbers of technologies are lie on this layer like.[2–4]

Description mechanisms, message format (SOAP), business processes and other XML technologies. It includes SOAP headers, security policies, and transactions.[2–4]

The familiar architecture provides same functionalities shown in next page.[2–4]

6.2 TECHNOLOGIES FOR WEB SERVICES

Web services are platform neutrality and Standards such as XML, SOAP, UDDI, and WSDL address the basics of interoperable services. These are helpful for client to find a needed service and make a request that both the client and service understand, her we need not consider where client and service reside or what language the client or service is coded in. web service is the main technology in SOA we would consider the other technologies and the standard organizations like World Wide Web Consortium (W3C) and OASIS. These are the organizations which provide standards to the web services (even these related to the grid also).[2–4]

There are two standards that are popular in the web services:

(*i*) **WS–Security:** The first question comes to our mind is how the web services provide security mechanisms in the internet environment. It is a standard released by OASIS. There are mainly three levels of security namely Secure Socket Level (SSL), Message Level Security

(MLS) and Transport level security (TLS) (for more information read web services security). Not only is these Kerberos for windows domain and Public-key infrastructure also one part in security.

It describes security-related enhancements to SOAP messaging that provide for message integrity and confidentiality. Integrity means that a SOAP message is not tampered with as it travels from a client to its final destination. Confidentiality means that a SOAP message is only seen by intended recipients. WS-Security uses security tokens to enable SOAP message security and integrity. A security token is a collection of claims made by the sender of a SOAP message (such as the sender's identity). A sender is authenticated by combining a security token with a digital signature – the signature is used as proof that the sender is indeed associated with the security token.[2–4]

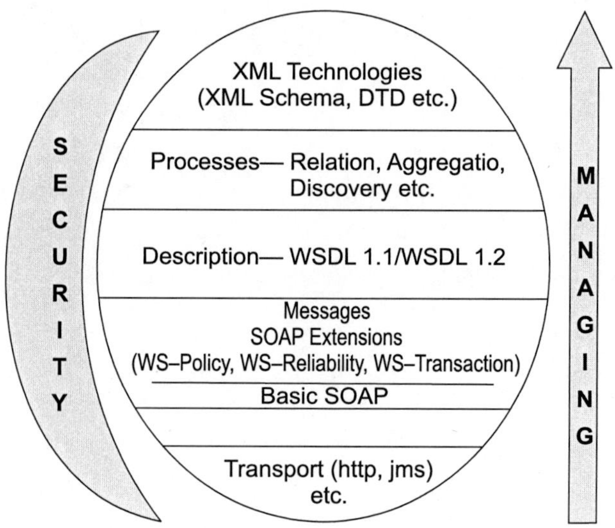

Fig. 6.4 Web services architecture.[6–11]

(*ii*) **WS–BPEL:** BPEL stands for Business Process Execution Language. It is an XML based language that is coordinates web services across a single business process. It supports the ESDL binding, means it uses WSDL to describe the web services that participate in a process and how the services interact. For example, the following WSDL entry describes one of the services in the purchase order process: portType concept is discussed later.[2–4]

```
<portType name="name of port type like purchaseOrdering">
<operation name="........ ">
        <input message="....... message "/>
        <output message="........ invoking "/>
        <fault name="anyProblem " message="pos:orderFaultType"/>
</operation>
</portType>
```

SUMMARY

In general web services are the services which are acquired from Internet (or Web). Hence the name web services. Here the service provider will be in remote location and the requester will be in another location, but they commonly engage in a medium called web service. The main concept behind the Web Service is SOA (Service Oriented Architecture, Chapter 5), where the service plays a main role in the whole architecture. Internally, a web service was built up by four main layers as seen in Section 6.1.1 which along with some important protocols like SOAP, etc., combine to provide one service called *Web Service.*

Many organizations like W3c and some technologies like WSDL, UDDI, etc were involved in providing web services. Two main standards WS-Security and WS-BPEL were available with a web service. In perspective of Grid, some of the grid services are developed using these web services and that is why this Chapter 6 is proposed.

KNOWLEDGE TESTING

1. Explain the role of services in grid computing. What is the reason clients are interested for towards services?
2. Draw a need diagram of web services and explain its functionalities.
3. Write any four differences between web server and web service.
4. Write any two standards for web services and explain the role of the standards in grid computing.

REFERENCES

1. Sriram Krishnan and Karan Bhatia *SOAs for Scientific Applications: Experiences and Challenges. Future Generation Computer Systems*, Vol. 25, Issue 4, April 2009, pp. 466–473.
2. Hongbing Wang and Joshua Zhexue Huang, *Web Services: Problems and Future Directions*, *www.elsevier.com/authored_subject_sections/P05/misc/wang.pdf.*
3. R. Akkiraju, J. Farrell, J.Miller, M. Nagarajan, M. Schmidt, Amit Sheth, and Kunal Verma. Web service semantics - wsdl-s, http://lsdis.cs.uga.edu/projects/meteor-s/wsdl-s/. Technical Report, 2005.
4. Liliana Cabral, John Domingue, Stefania Galizia, Alessio Gugliotta, Barry Norton, Vlad Tanasescu, and Carlos Pedrinaci, *IRS-III: A Broker for Semantic Web Services based Applications*, In Proceedings of the 5th International Semantic Web Conference (ISWC 2006), Athens, GA, USA, 2006.
5. J. Euzenat, *Towards a Principled Approach to Semantic Interoperability*, In Proceedings of IJCAI workshop on Ontologies and information sharing, Seattle (WA), US, 2001.
6. Armin Haller, Emilia Cimpian, Adrian Mocan, Eyal Oren, and Christoph Bussler, *WSMX – A Semantic Service-Oriented Architecture*. In Proc. of the 3rd Int. Conf. on Web Services, pp. 321–328. IEEE Computer Society, 2005.
7. Martin Bosworth, *Service-Oriented Architecture*, *http://www.govexec.com/basics/ServiceOrientedArchitecture.htm.*
8. Qusay H. Mahmoud, *Service-Oriented architecture*, *http://java.sun.com/developer/technicalArticles/WebServices/soa/.*
9. *SOA and* Specialized Messaging Patterns. *http://192.150.8.55/government/pdfs/SOA-technical-whitepaper.pdf.*
10. Hao He, *What Is Service-Oriented Architecture*, *http://www.xml.com/pub/a/ws/2003/09/30/soa.html.*
11. Joshy Joseph, M. Ernest, C. Fellenstein, *Grid Computing*, Pearson Education, 2005.

❑❑❑

7

XML, Related Technologies and their Role in Grid

7.1 ABOUT XML

XML comes from the general markup language. It is a popular data markup format. Similar to HTML, XML is tag based. Although XML doesn't replace HTML, it is a complementary format. The rules for the XML are simple and shown in below:[1–4]

- All tags must be closed. For example <portType> opening tag, then you must at some point afterward have a </pottType>. Remember XML is case sensitive.
- Tags can't overlap. For example <X><Y></X></Y> is not allowed.
- Nesting is possible in XML. It is possible we can define our own tags and we can provide attributes to that tag.

I think this matter is enough for knowing about XML (for more information refers any XML book). Here I am giving just a simple example how XML schema document looks like,[1–4]

```
<schema xmlns=http://www.w3c.org/2009/XMLSchema
            targetNamespace=http://gridworld.org/>
    <element name="verify">
            <complexType>
            <sequence>
                <element minoccurs="1" maxoccurs="2" name="a" />
            </sequence>
            </complexType>
    </element>
            <complexType name="X">
            <sequence>
                    <element ……../>
            </sequence>
            </complxType>
</schema>
```

XML has become the de facto standard for describing data to be exchanged on the Web.[1–4]

7.2 SOAP (SIMPLE OBJECT–ACCESS PROTOCOL)

SOAP, important component in web services, which is used to define a standard way of packaging a message for interoperability. Why we choose the SOAP. Reason is simple- it's a protocol that is both a simple and light mechanisms for transferring data message. To transfer message by using SOAP, the message in any form is packaged as a SOAP package, which is a well- formed XML document. The SOAP package is then transferred over protocols, such as FTP or HTTP. Remember SOAP is not a network or a transfer protocol. In addition syntax for creating the XML document defined in the specification. We will consider SOAP is a request- response format.[2–3,9]

- All big vendors, including Sun Microsystems and Microsoft, support the web services model that uses SOAP. In addition, SOAP is a widely accepted protocol for transferring data between distributed applications that are created using all recent programming languages.
- Web services model is based on the web infrastructure; therefore, you do not need to re- create the infrastructure.
- SOAP supports XML, which makes interacting application interoperable because XML transfers data in text format. The data is self- describing; therefore, the receiving applications can interpret it easily.
- It use HTTP to exchange information it can handle heavy complicated data easily by encoding the data. SOAP is secure while transferring data.

> **Note:** SOAP doesn't allow you to check for errors at the time of compiling the document. You can only test for errors at run time.

SOAP has mainly three components:[2–3,9]

(*i*) **SOAP Message:** It is a one-way communication from a sending application to a receiver's application. When the request is proceed, the result of the request is returned as another SOAP message. Because of this several SOAP messages are combined to allow communication between applications that are present on remote computer.

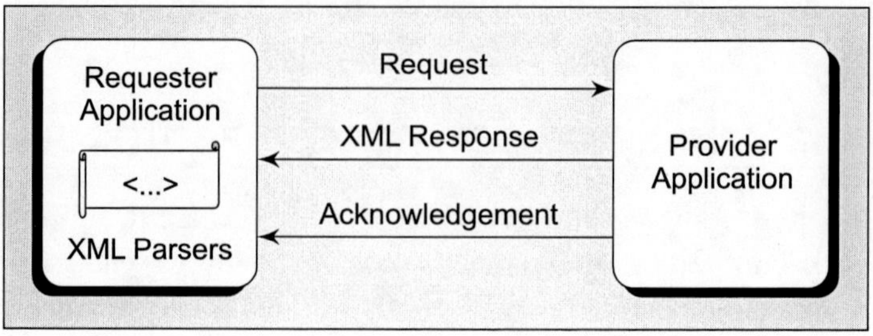

Fig. 7.1 Process of transferring data using SOAP.[1,7–9]

The components of SOAP are mainly

Envelope

Header and Body

The code with these components in the form of

<SOAP envelope: Env xmlns:SOAP

envelope=http://schemas.xmlsoap.org/soap/envelop/>

< SOAP envelope: Header>

....

</ SOAP envelope: Header>

< SOAP envelope: Body>

....

</ SOAP envelope: Body>

</ SOAP envelope: Env>

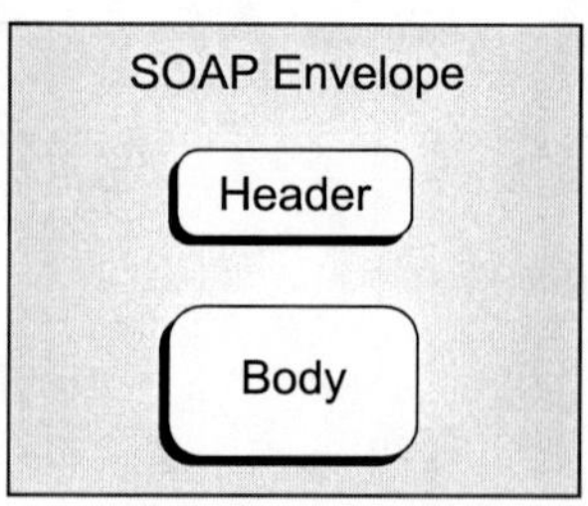

Fig. 7.2 SOAP message structure.[1,7–9]

Envelope–it defines a framework for describing message structure.

Header–it carry information such as security, transactional information and so on.

It has role attribute defines the–who is the actor and relay attribute that is set to either true or false; "role" attribute is used for targeting intermediate ones.

(*ii*) **SOAP RPC:** The process of calling a procedure from a remote computer is called RPC. The request for the procedure can be made using SOAP in the form of SOAP message. This message can includes request or response of the request. The RPC conventions can define a set of rules that can use to serialize the procedure call in the form of a SOAP message.

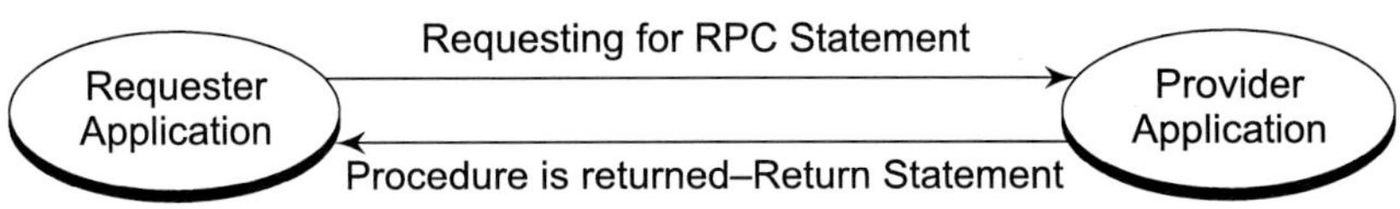

Fig. 7.3 RPC procedure in SOAP.[1,7–9]

(*iii*) **SOAP Encoding Rules:** It mainly deals the data types such as simple and compound data types, rules for serializing.

> **How the SOAP message is processed not only in grid any type of environment?**
>
> SOAP is a format for transfer data across applications on network. These applications are called SOAP nodes (grid service applications). From above point we observed one point is response is also a SOAP message. The SOAP message exchange models define the mechanism in which the messages are transferred using SOAP.

7.2.1 SOAP Processing

When a sender node sends a SOAP request, the request might need to pass through one or more intermediate applications called intermediate nodes. The path that SOAP message follows to reach the final node is called message path. When a SOAP message reaches a node that is following the message path, the receiver application process the SOAP request:

(*a*) The receiver first identifies the components SOAP message like envelope, header and body.

(*b*) Next step is receiver verifies all the components finally process the request.

(*c*) If the receiving application is an intermediate one, the optional components are removed and the final SOAP message is forwarded to the next application, as defined in the message path.

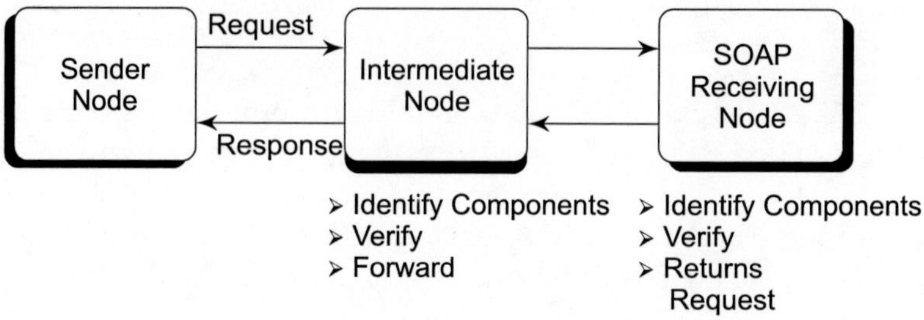

Fig. 7.4 SOAP processing.[1,7–9]

7.2.2 Supporting MEP

Message Exchange Pattern (MEP) is the main future that provided by SOAP. A SOAP MEP acts as a template, when message is exchanged between them. All request/response, one- way communication and peer- to- peer conservation are represented here only. SOAP header blocks and SOAP binding protocols are two important understandable mechanisms for implementing almost all futures in SOAP. By using these two MEP in SOAP is implemented. The above diagram is best example for illustrating MEP. One point we have to remember is MEP supports one or more underlying protocol binding either directly or indirectly.[2–3,9]

7.2.3 SOAP Modules

A SOAP module is a combination of syntax and semantics which are there in SOAP header. It also deals the issues related to the securing features means a SOAP module realizes one or more SOAP features. SOAP message can be transported through different transport bindings, such as HTTP, TCP and BEEP. The famous one is SOAP over HTTP using the GET and POST operations.[2–3,9]

SOAP (Simple Object Access Protocol) is a way for a program running in one kind of operating system (such as Windows 2000) to communicate with a program in the same or another kind of an operating system (such as Linux) by using the World Wide Web's Hypertext Transfer Protocol (HTTP) and its Extensible Markup Language (XML) as the mechanisms for information exchange. Since Web protocols are installed and available for use by all major operating system platforms, HTTP and XML provide an already at-hand solution to the problem of how programs running under different operating systems in a network can communicate with each other. SOAP specifies exactly how to encode an HTTP header and an XML file so that a program in one computer can call a program in another computer and pass it information. It also specifies how the called program can return a response.[2–3,9]

An advantage of SOAP is that program calls are much more likely to get through firewall servers that screen out requests other than those for known applications (through the designated port mechanism). Since HTTP requests are usually allowed through firewalls, programs using SOAP to communicate can be sure that they can communicate with programs anywhere.[2–3,9]

7.3 WSDL (WEB SERVICE DESCRIPTION LANGUAGE)

Web Services Description Language (WSDL) is a format for describing a Web Services interface. It is a way to describe services and how they should be bound to specific network addresses. WSDL has three parts:[1,8–9]

- Operations.
- Definitions.
- Service bindings.

Definitions are generally expressed in XML and include both data type definitions and message definitions that use the data type definitions. *Operations* describe actions for the messages supported by a Web service. There are four types of operations.[1,8–9]

One-way: Messages sent without a reply required.

Request/Response: The sender sends a message and the received sends a reply.

Solicit response: A request for a response. (The specific definition for this action is pending.).

Notification: Messages sent to multiple receivers. (The specific definition for this action is pending.)

Service bindings connect port types to a port. A port is defined by associating a network address with a port type. A collection of ports defines a service.[1,8–9]

7.3.1 WSDL Document Elements

Table 7.1: Elements in WSDL document

Element	*Description*
Definitions	It includes the definition for XML version that is used in a WSDL document.
Types	It includes schemas or references to schemas that are used in a WSDL document.
Message	Defines the structure of the message in a WSDL document.
Operation	This element associates a message with the corresponding operation.
Port Type	It declares the port type.
Binding	Binds a portType with a protocol
Port	Specifies the corresponding address of a binding.
Service	Defines the corresponding service.

The main structure of a WSDL document looks like[1,8–9]

```
<definitions>
        <types>
                definition of types........
        </types>
        <message>
                definition of a message....
        </message>
        <portType>
                definition of a port.......
        </portType>
        <binding>
                definition of a binding....
        </binding>
</definitions>
```

Example

```
<message name=”getuserRequest”>
        <part name=”” type=”xs:string”/>
</message>
<message name=”getTermResponse”>
        <part name=”value” type=”xs:string”/>
</message>
<portType name=”My work”>
<operation name=”getWant”>
        <input message=”userRequest”/>
        <output message=”userResponse”/>
  </operation>
</portType>
```

Port types are declared by using <portType> element. It combines the operations in WSDL document to from a set of operations. In this example the **<portType>** element defines “My work” as the name of a **port**, and “getWant” as the name of an **operation**. The “getWant” operation has an **input message** called “userRequest” and an **output message** called “userResponse”. The **<message>** elements define the **parts** of each message and the associated data types.[1,8–9]

How does a client know what format to use in making a request to a service?

The answers to these questions are provided by information in an XML document, called a WSDL document, which contains a description of the web service's interface. WSDL defines an XML schema for describing a web service. To uncover the description for a Web service, a client needs to find the service's WSDL document. One way, perhaps the most typical way, to do this is for the client to find a pointer to the WSDL document in the web service's registration, which can be in a UDDI registry or an ebXML registry/repository. A typical scenario is that a business registers its service.

Service description

A service description maintains some documents that combine describe the interface to a service. It may also include the service road map and functionalities.[1,8–9]

A service should be attractive nature for describing the services using syntax and semantics. It has a grammatical processing rather than human interaction processing. WSDL refers the semantic description while service doing his job. The following diagram shows the service description with semantic information.[1,8–9]

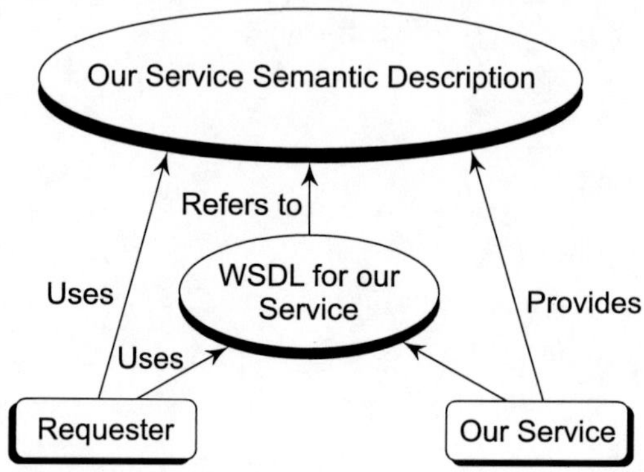

Fig. 7.5 Service descriptions with semantic information.[1,7–9]

7.3.2 WSDL 1.1

Initially WSDL (1.0) has been developed by IBM, Microsoft and Ariba to describe Web Services for their SOAP toolkit. WSDL 1.1 is the formalization of WSDL 1.0. No major changes were introduced between 1.0 and 1.1. It not only describes the document- oriented but also RPC-oriented messages. The document structure can contains mainly two sub parts—abstract and agreed upon definitions. In abstract section soap messages are placed. These messages are platform independent ones. Abstract helps for developing the services and maintains consistency relation to the agreed upon definition. It contains messages, types of operation, data types, port type and bindings. Service port and binding are the components in concrete definition (agreed upon). WSDL binding specifies grammar input, output and fault messages for the concrete one. Binding extensions defined by WSDL for SOAP and HTTP.[1,8–9]

The WSDL defines services as collections of network endpoints, or ports. The WSDL specification provides an XML format. SOAP encoding and literal encoding are the two message encoding paradigms in WSDL 1.1. Messages are constructed according to the XML schema named as *literal.* SOAP encoding rules such as *encoded* helpful for building SOAP encoding. In WSDL message transferred format can be done using two functional parameters named as document and remote procedure call (RPC): document contains the body of the message, while remoting has just parameters with specific signatures.[1,8–9]

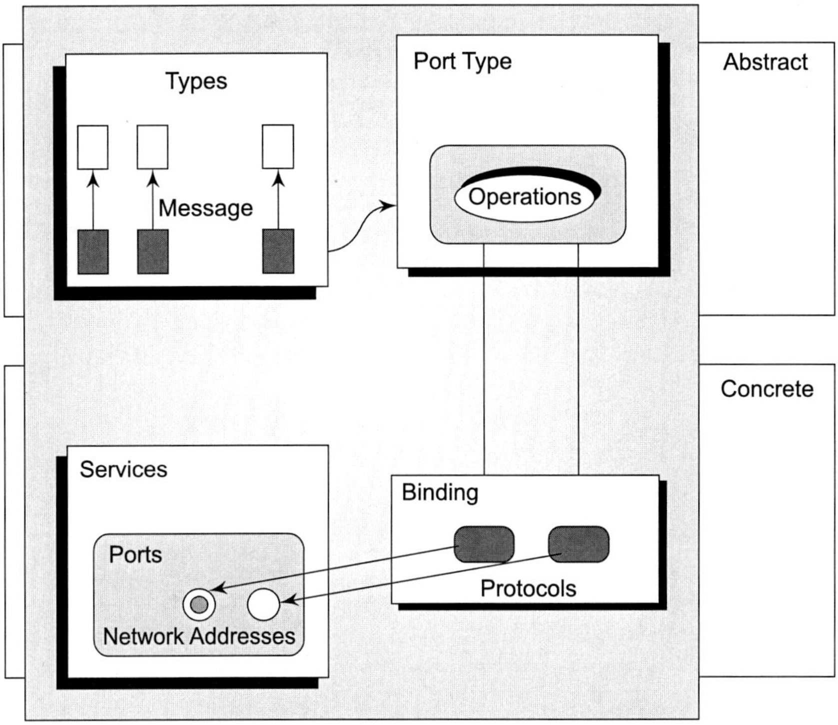

Fig. 7.6 WSDL 1.1 definition part.[1,7–9]

7.3.2.1 WSDL Document structure[1,8–9]

A WSDL document is simply a **set of definitions**. There is a **definitions** element at the root, and definitions inside. The grammar is as follows:

```
<wsdl:definitions name="Token"? targetNamespace="URI"?>
<wsdl:documentation .... />
  <wsdl:types> ?
    <wsdl:documentation .... />
    <xsd:schema .... />
    <— extensibility element —>
  </wsdl:types>
  <wsdl:message name="Token">
    <wsdl:documentation .... />
     <part name="Token1" element="……"? type="……"?/>
```

```
</wsdl:message>
<wsdl:portType name=”Token”>
   <wsdl:operation name=”inputToken”>
      <wsdl:input name=”nmtoken”? message=”gridPblm”>
         ....................
      </wsdl:input>
      <wsdl:output name=”outputToken”? message=”gridSln”>
         ............
      </wsdl:output>
      <wsdl:fault name=”faultToken” message=”.........”>
         ..............
      </wsdl:fault>
   </wsdl:operation>
</wsdl:portType>
<wsdl:binding name=”......” type=”.........”>
   <wsdl:operation name=”opToken”>
      <wsdl:input> ?
         .................
      </wsdl:input>
      <wsdl:output> ?
         .................
      </wsdl:output>
      <wsdl:fault name=”nmtoken”>
         ....................
      </wsdl:fault>
   </wsdl:operation>
</wsdl:binding>
<wsdl:service name=”services”>
   <wsdl:port name=”.........” binding=”.........”>
         ...........
   </wsdl:port>
   <— extensibility element —>
</wsdl:service>
</wsdl:definitions>
```

There are some limitations such as extension rules, service semantics with WSDL 1.1. These limitations are solved by using WSDL 1.2.[1,8–9]

7.3.3 WSDL 1.2

The view of the WSDL 1.2 is different from WSDL 1.1. This version mainly describes the features of web architecture and web service architecture in SOA. The concept of resource and service were well defined inWSDL 1.2. We know a resource is addressable by URI. These resources might be hardware or software depending upon the service interfaces defined like operational or manageable. Instead of the portType abstract definition maintains the interface. End points and bindings are defined in concrete (end points replaces the port).[1,8–9]

Port's abstract definitions and messages are separated from their concrete use or instance, allowing the reuse of these definitions (see WSDL definition diagram). A port is defined by associating a network address with a reusable binding, and a collection of ports define a service. Messages are abstract descriptions of the data being exchanged, and port types are abstract collections of supported operations. The concrete protocol and data format specifications for a particular port type constitutes a reusable binding, where the operations and messages are then bound to a concrete network protocol and message format.[1,8–9]

The WSDL 1.1 and WSDL 1.2 Bindings look identical but they have a small difference. They indicate to the client what WSDL (SOAP) version to use. If you generate a client specifying the endpoint it will generate it so that the message generated by the client would match the requirements specified in the corresponding binding. You could differentiate between WSDL 1.1 and 1.2 using the namespace. Service element and interface hierarchy in WSDL 1.2 is like:[1,8–9]

```
<definitions>
   ………
   ………
   <service name="…." Interface="xml:……" targetResourc="Web URI"?>
            <end-point />
   </service>
   …………..
   …………
   <interface name="Do">
            <operation name="multiply"
            </operation>
   </interface>
   <interface name="Doing" extends="Do">
            <operation name="PercentCal"
            </operation>
   </interface>
   …….
   …….
</definition>
```

Fig. 7.7 Service element definition in WSDL 1.2.[1,7–9]

Service is representing a single interface; of course the interface is the combination of multiple interfaces through derivation. The *target Resource* is an attribute in service which has any URI value (this URI related to the resource URI). Instead of portType WSDL 1.2 has resource part which is a logical part in abstract.[1,8–9]

WSDL 1.1 supports the operation overloading. Frankly this feature is removed from the WSDL. However interfaces have *inheritance* property. "extends" attribute in interface element defines inheritance shown in above sample code.[1,8–9]

Some points about WSDL Document structure:

- *portType* in WSDL 1.1 is replaced by *interface* in WSDL 1.2.
- *ports* are changed into *end points* in WSDL 1.2
- *Message Exchange Patterns (MEP)* are defined for complex message exchange environment.

The following simple example just shows how to define all these elements including soap tag:[1,8–9]

```
<xml version="1.0" encoding="SimpleEx">
<definition name="Illustration" targetNamespace="http://localhost/wsdl.com">
            Xmlns:xsd="http://myworld.xmlsoap>

<service name=".....name of service...">
      <port name="ourVision" binding="eles">
            <soap: address location=http://localhost/wsdl.com>
      </port>
      <message name="valuesWant">
            <part name="body" element="xsd:Updating">
      </message>
.......
.......
</service>
</definition>
```

Fig. 7.8 A simple example for WSDL.[1,7–9]

WSDL 1.2 is simpler to implement; however WSDL 2.0 is also released which is better for supporting web services. From these two versions, a WSDL is often used in combination with SOAP and XML Schema to provide web services over the internet. A client program connecting to a web service can read the WSDL to determine what functions are available on the server. The client can then use SOAP to actually call one of the functions listed in the WSDL.[1,8–9]

7.4 GLOBAL XML ARCHITECTURE

Vendors like IBM Corporation, Microsoft are working on a global XML Architecture. It provides the open- standard and modular model approach to the XML web services. Note that infrastructure protocols are used for building the web service applications. These applications are building upon the information set provided by the XML and transport level. All process are running above on SOAP and WSDL technologies. This architecture concentrates on issues such as reliability, addressing, transactions and security.[6–9]

What is the vision of the Global XML architecture?

The answer for this question is straight forward. It provides a functionality for maintain consistent data. It reduces the time spent on developing applications, so that application transparency duration using protocols are reduced. The main vision is it provides basic open standards based designs for interoperable messaging across multiple vendors.

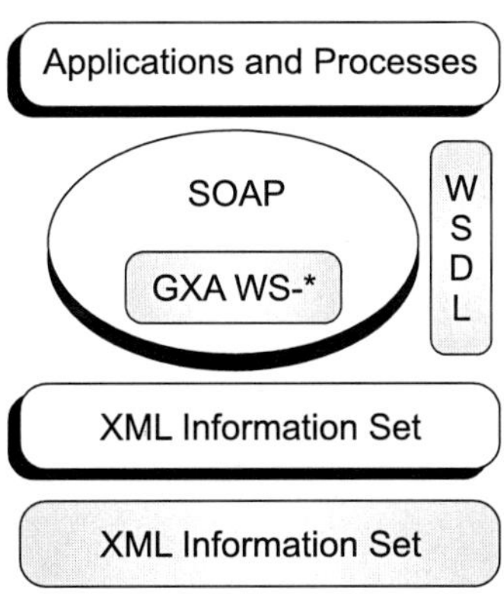

Fig. 7.7 The Global XML architecture.[1,7–9]

The main principle of GMA includes:[6–9]

(*i*) XML information set.

(*ii*) Open standards.

(*iii*) Service policy.

(*iv*) Security.

7.4.1 XML Information Set

XML information set was defined by World Wide Web Consortium (W3C) for XML specifications). Its purpose is to provide a consistent set of definitions for use in other specifications that need to refer to the information in a well-formed XML document. It defines the abstract data set. SOAP and WSDL both are coming into this category. The main parts/components in XML information set are:[6–9]

- The GXA protocols are SOAP extensions based on SOAP headers or features. SOAP is trying to adopt a transport independent wire format for XML message.
- For achieving the agreement among web services GXA maintains some conditional values/constraints between the parties. These agreements are mainly applied on semantics and syntaxes.
- *Decentralization* is a concept which allows the parties for taking their own decision while message processing includes: security, policies. *Federation* is another concept so that parties are exchange meaningful information.
- GXA doesn't dictate on the transport mechanism for message exchange. Application neutrality defines standards for XML messages that needed to be exchanged.

7.4.2 Open Standards

Standard organizations, including OASIS and W3C define almost all standard protocol definitions. These standards organizations, together with web service interoperability Organization (WS- I), can provide the desired infrastructures for the industries for developing web service in the area grid.[6–9]

The building blocks identified by the GXA includes:

- Coordination among partners using transferring messages.
- Reliable message exchange patterns
- Routing mechanisms and addressing mechanisms for dispatching messages
- Service policies for message handling
- Message level security
- Exchanging transaction-aware messages and metadata information exchange

These are the main building blocks for solving interoperability.

7.4.3 Service Policy

Service policy is a model or framework for expressing policy assertions about a web service. Policy assertions are useful for expressing grammar related things, characteristics of a service. This can be done by using WS- Policy. Policies governing the behavior of self-managing entities are derived from service level agreements (SLAs), and deployed as part of the management context under which the manageable resources are used.[6–9]

According to joseph, the components in the policy framework and model are:

(*i*) **Policy expression:** It is a mechanism to convey a set of policy assertions.

(*ii*) **Policy subject:** The policy can be bound by using some entity. This entity is described by the policy subject.

(*iii*) **Policy assertion:** An individual requirement, preference, capability or other property (ex: security, privacy and so on).

(*iv*) **Policy attachment:** It is a mechanism for associating policy with one or more subjects is called as policy attachment.

The following policy expression example explains these components:

```
<wsp:policy xmlns:wsp=”…..” xmlns:wsu=”…”
   Xml:base=http://www.w3c.com/policies
   Wsu:Id=”P”
   Name=”MyPolicy”
   TargetNamespace=http://www.w3c.com/policies”>
<wsse:SecurityTlken>
   <wsse:TokenType>wsse:binaries</wsse:TokenType>
</wsse:SecurityToken>
<wsse:Integrity>
   <wsse:Algo type:”wsse:authentication” URI=http://gridworld/../>
</wsse:Integrity>
</wsp:policy>
<wsp:policy xmlns:wsp=”…..” xmlns:wsu=”…”
   Xml:base=http://www.w3c.com/policies
   Wsu:Id=”Q”
   Name=”SecPolicy”
   TargetNamespace=http://www.w3c.com/policies”>
   ……..
</wsp:policy>
```

According to example,

Container element- <wsp:Policy>

Attributes- Id, name, preference

Operations- <wsp:all/ExactlyOne/OneorMore> defutly <wsp:all> is used.

7.4.4 Policy Expression and Assertions[6–9]

A policy expression is XML information set with a combination of container element <wsp:policy>, policy operators (see above) and some attributes. For identifying policy expression attributes like name and ID useful.

Policy expressions–AB and XY (which are names to expressions).
Assertions can be defined by standards like WS- Security, WS-Trust etc.
Policy assertion to AB- wsse:SecurityToken
Policy assertion to XY- wsse:Integrity
These two must satisfy.

Policy attachment

```
<wsp:policyAttachment>
        <wsp:......>
                <wsa:Reference>
                        .........
                </wsa:Reference>
        </wsp:.......>
        <wsp:policyReference URI="http://............./policy.xml"/>
</wsp:policyAttachment>
```

There are mainly two mechanisms one is XML- based resource- this can be achieved by global XML schema attributes. The second one is the XML definition.

SUMMARY

XML was created by the W3C using Standardized General Markup Language (SGML). XML was mainly designed for web application to simplify the tasks. So it's a web- friendly meta data language. It supports the different types of data for easy use of the existing code and supports the compatibility applications. A well- defined document is produced by using XML only especially in mark up languages.

SOAP, important component in web services, which is used to define a standard way of packaging a message for interoperability. Why we choose the SOAP. SOAP supports XML, which makes interacting application interoperable because XML transfers data in text format. The data is self-describing; therefore, the receiving applications can interpret it easily.

Web Services Description Language (WSDL) is a format for describing a Web Services interface. WSDL document contains a description of the web service's interface. WSDL defines an XML schema for describing a web service.

KNOWLEDGE TESTING

1. What is the significance of web services in grid computing? Explain the grid components in web services.
2. Explain WSDL document elements. What is the functionality of each element in grid?
3. Compare and contrast WSDL 1.1 and WSDL 1.2. Which one is better for grid services? Write four arguments related to your answer.
4. What is the role of Global XML Architecture in grid? Explain each of the components.
5. How do you provide security in grid area? Write the XML generated code for the security. What are the certificates that related to the security?
6. Suppose your are implemented any one grid service. How do you publish these services so that client can access?
7. What are the building blocks of the GXA? Explain the open standards that support the GXA.
8. How do you describe the services with the help of semantic grid information?

REFERENCES

1. Bruce Bahlmann and Diane Shired, *WSDL–Web Services Definition Language, http://www.birds-eye.net/definition/acronym/?id=1152375836.*
2. C. M. MacKenzie, K. Laskey, F. McCabe, P. F. Brown, and R. Metz, *OASIS Reference Model for Service Oriented Architecture V 1.0*, Technical report, OASIS, July 2006.
3. *OWL-S: Semantic Markup for Web Services*, *http://www.daml.org/services/owl-s/1.1/.*
4. G. M¨uhl, L. Fiege, and P. Pietzuch, *Distributed Event-Based Systems*, Springer- Verlag, 2006.
5. Dumitru Roman, Uwe Keller, Holger Lausen, Jos de Bruijn, Ruben Lara, Michael Stollberg, Axel Polleres, Cristina Feier, Christoph Bussler, and Dieter Fensel, *Web Service Modeling Ontology*, Applied Ontology, 1(1): 77–106, 2005.
6. Kunal Verma, Karthik Gomadam, Amit P. Sheth, John A. Miller, and Zixin Wu. *The METEOR-S Approach for Configuring and Executing Dynamic Web Processes, http://lsdis.cs.uga.edu/projects/meteor-s/techRep6- 24-05.pdf.*
7. Joshy Joseph, M. Ernest, C. Fellenstein, *Grid Computing*, Pearson Education, 2005.
8. Web Service Definition Language (WSDL), *http://www.w3.org/TR/wsdl.*
9. WSDL Binding for SOAP 1.2, schemas.xmlsoap.org/wsdl/soap12/soap12WSDL.htm.

PART III

GRID PLATFORMS

In part 1 and part 2 we discussed about basic concepts of grid computing, various technologies used in grid. These two parts are helpful for understanding what are grids and various technologies helpful for establishing grid services. When grid word comes into this world a number of middleware solutions were made for solving grid problem. Later technologies are improved and concept of dynamic virtualization was introduced in between heterogeneous computers.

Now part 3 will discuss about Open Grid Service Architecture (OGSA) which provides a uniform way for describing services and OGSA basic services, Open Grid Service Infrastructure (OGSI) which is a grid software infrastructure based on the web services and finally grid security including Grid Security Infrastructure (GSI). Grid specifications are defined by OGSA. The concept of OGSA evolutes the existing grid standards with the help of Service- Oriented Architecture (SOA) and web. When people knowing what SOA is sometimes they don't understand what a service is. A service is an entity that provides some specific ideas/functions/capabilities to its clients by exchanging messages. Message exchange pattern was defined with the help of operation attribute which is in portType element (later section will explain this concept).

According to Ian foster interface definition language (IDL) manipulate the services in four different aspects. Those are:

1. **Service Discovery:** Specifies the available resources and creates registers by SOA for maintaining user queries.
2. **Service composition:** It enables the code reuse and the dynamically construct the complex systems from existing components.
3. **Specialization:** Different implementations of a service on different platforms.
4. **Interface Extension:** It is one of future of Interface Definition Language (IDL) allows specific functions, add additional implementations without disturbing common interfaces.

Overall this part gives some idea about message patterns, interoperability among grid services, common management model, description of grid services, protocol bindings, service specifications and basic components of grid computing.

8

OPEN GRID SERVICE ARCHITECTURE (OGSA)

8.1 INTRODUCTION

In previous chapters we discussed about the web services, virtualization concept, interoperability, how to manage resources and services. Grid mainly provides a virtual computing environment that appears to be more powerful.[1]

In this section, we are going to discuss:

- How OGSA came into existence?
- What are the reasons that lead to OGSA creation?
- Where the OGSA creation gets started? And also OGSA platform architecture.

Grid concept mainly concentrates on how to achieve distributed resource sharing across dynamic virtual organizations and in between heterogeneous systems. Foster, Kesselman, and Tuecke describe the Open Grid Service Architecture (OGSA) as a solution to this type of problems. Key to the realization of this Grid vision is standardization, so that the diverse components that make up a modern computing environment can be discovered, accessed, allocated, monitored, accounted for, billed for, etc., and in general managed as a single virtual system. Here we will discuss about the architectural concept which describes grid standards with the emerging Service Oriented Architecture (SOA) as well as the Web.[1]

Before going to the standards and requirements of OGSA—let's see the work of Web Services. Web Services are a very general model for building applications and can be implemented for any operation system that supports communication over the Internet. Web Services use the best of component-based development and the Web. Web Service standard is an open standard mechanism for creation of services, service naming, and discovering services. We know XML is a message exchange pattern so that interoperable can be achieved between client and server through XML as the message format.[1]

OGSA needs a set of functional and non-functional requirements; these use cases cover infrastructure and application scenarios for both commercial and scientific areas.[1]

What are the requirements either functional or non-functional, needed for OGSA?

For providing uniform way to describe grid services, OGSA requires the following general requirements. These requirements are:

Name	*Requirements*
Resource Sharing	1. *Metadata services:* Allow for access to and propagation, aggregation, and management of entity metadata across administrative domains. Important for finding, invoking, and tracking entities. 2. *Resource usage data:* Mechanisms and standard schemas for collecting and exchanging resource usage. 3. *Global name space:* Resource and data access. 4. *Site autonomy:* Mechanisms are required for accessing resources across sites while respecting local control and policy.
Optimization	This is one of the technique used allocate resources effectively to meet consumer and supplier requirements. This technique applies to both suppliers and consumers of services and resources.
Interoperability, Dynamic, Heterogeneous	1. *Normal management capabilities:* Managing the resources, security in the grid environment mainly in legacy systems. 2. *Resource virtualization:* used to reduce the complexity of managing heterogeneous systems and to handle diverse resources in a unified way. 3. *Resource discovery:* While discovering resources maintain the attributes and properties. Here we use grid service mechanisms part in web services- for discovering the resources. Not only had these for achieving interoperability standard protocols also considered.

Contd...

Name	Requirements
Quality of Service	Process creations, running are the main tasks of any services. These services are should be the agreed-upon QoS. QoS dimensions include availability, security, and performance. 1. *Service level agreement*: between service requester and provider prior to service execution. 2. *Service level attainment*: issues are monitoring services quality, estimating resource utilization, and planning for and adjusting resource. 3. *Migration*: migrate executing services or applications to adjust workloads for performance or availability.
Process Execution	In grid environment job is distributed over a great number of heterogeneous resources. OGSA must provide manageability for execution of user-defined work (jobs) throughout their lifetime. 1. *Job Management*: supports manageability interfaces and these interfaces must work with various types of groupings of jobs (e.g., workflows, job arrays). 2. *Diffferent types of processes*: support simple jobs and complex jobs such as workflow and composite services. 3. *Scheduling*: supports multiple schedulers and scheduling across administrative domains. Allow the priority processes which executes first and allocate resources to them. Network also plays a important role while executing jobs. The general process execution diagram is shown in Fig. 8.1.
Information services (data level)	Any organization/scientific fields developing grid, want huge amount of data for sharing- information databases that are managed and administered independently. 1. *Data access*: efficient accessing from databases and files. 2. *Data consistency*: when cached or replicated data is modified consistency should be maintained.

Contd...

Name	***Requirements***
	3. *Data persistency*: persistency models apply to data and its association with its metadata. 4. *Integration and location management*: integrate the heterogeneous and distributed data. OGSA should allow for selection in various ways, such as transfer, copying, and caching, according to the nature of data.
Security	Controlling the services through robust security protocols and according to provided security policy. General security issues are authentication and authorization, multiple security infrastructures, perimeter security solutions, delegation, isolation, policy exchange, protection and secure logging.
Others	*Reducing cost:* Policies may include availability, performance, security, scheduling, and brokering. The complexity of administering large-scale distributed, heterogeneous systems increases administration costs and the risk of human errors. *Scalability*: systems are either hierarchical or peer-to-peer (federated/collaborative) fashion. Achieve the High-throughput by parallel executing jobs. *Availability*: high availability is often realized by expensive fault-tolerant hardware or complex cluster systems. Mechanisms used are Fault management mechanisms- It can be required so that running jobs are not lost because of resource faults.Disaster recovery mechanisms- are needed so that the operation of a Grid system can be recovered efficiently and quickly in case of natural or human-caused disaster.

Note: It is complex to predict all of the many and varied needs that users will have. Therefore, mechanism and policy must be realized via extensible and replaceable components, to permit OGSA to evolve over time and allow users to construct their own mechanisms and policies to meet specific needs.

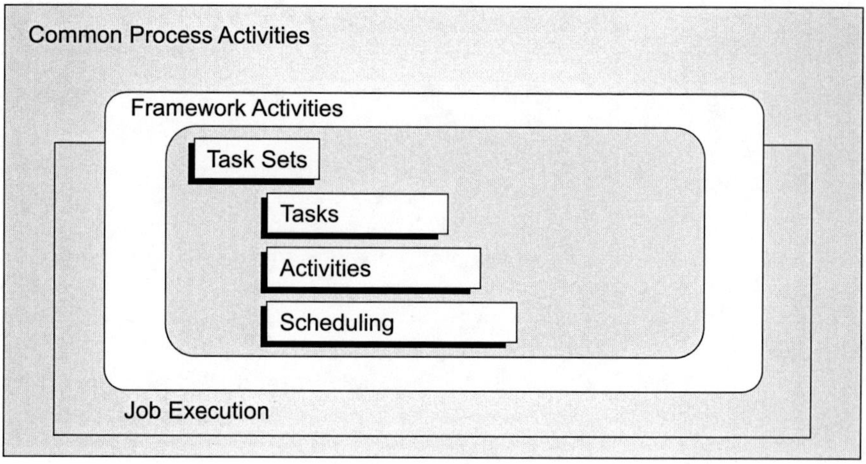

Fig. 8.1 General process diagram in grid.[1,4–5]

OGSA architecture defines behavior of grid services, service description mechanisms by using Web Service Description and protocol binding information by using web service enhancements. For forming the OGSA some core technologies are required. Those are:[1]

(*i*) **XML:** Extensible Markup language is a universal language used to define the message exchange pattern and structure.

(*ii*) **WSDL:** The WSDL defines services as collections of network endpoints, or ports. The Web Services Description Language specification provides an XML format for describing the web services; the same WSDL is used for describing grid services. Both WSDL and UDDI were designed to clearly distinguish between abstract metadata of grid and concrete services. It acts as a interface definition language. Complete details provided in web services chapter.

(*iii*) *SOAP*, XML based protocol, originally defined as *Simple Object Access Protocol*, is a protocol specification for exchanging structured information in the implementation of web services in computer networks. Mainly its work is define a set of standard message exchange patterns.

(*iv*) **UDDI:** The Universal Description, Discovery and Integration (UDDI) consist of registries that expose the information about a business or its components and technical interfaces, such as API's. It defines a way to publish and discover information about Web services. It publicly accessible set of implementations of the specification that allow businesses to register information about the Web services they offer so that other businesses can find them. Its uses in grid- easily and dynamically find the web services over the distributed networks like Internet, Intranet and mobile and ubiquity computations.[1]

We will briefly lookup these topics in next chapters. Let's see the architecture, service models, grid services and other issues.

Grid is a virtualized distributed computing environment. It enable dynamic *runtime* selection, sharing and aggregation of distributed autonomous resources based on the availability, capability, performance and also cost.[1]

8.2 OGSA ARCHITECTURE

OGSA is an extension of the Web Services architecture and the descriptive language such as Web Service Description Language (WSDL). It mainly covers the service types defined by collection of ports. It is developed by Global Grid Forum along with Open Grid Services Infrastructure (OGSI). Why we need OGSA? There are so many problems while working with the systems whose are in network, like heterogeneity, consistency, integration and virtualization. To address these challenges GGF provides an OGSA to integrate a set of well defined interfaces and standards and conventions.[1–2]

OGSA theme is collecting individual services and builds web service standards among them so that finally we have to achieve the relevant grid services (grid services are in next page). OGSA represents the services, their interfaces, and the semantics/behavior and interaction of these services. It should be noted that the software architecture driving the implementation of the internals of these services is outside the OGSA working group's scope.[1–2]

The architecture of OGSA is not layered, where the implementation of one service is built upon, and can only interact with, the layer upon which it is logically dependent; or object-oriented—though many of the concepts may seem to be object-based.[1–2]

The architecture is looking like after proposing so many grid people-looking like.

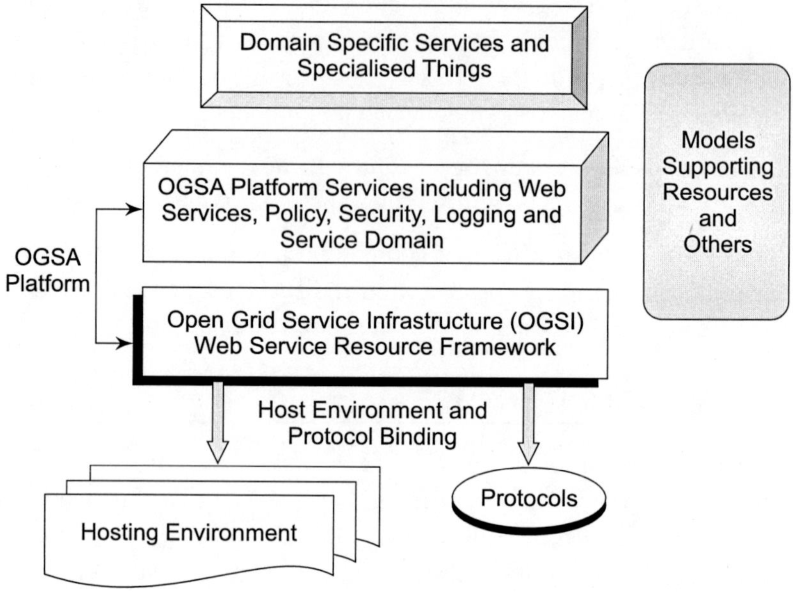

Fig. 8.2 OGSA component platform architecture.[1,4–5]

8.2.1 From Web Services to Grid Services

Web services enable you to build highly scalable, loosely coupled, and distributed applications using standard web protocols such as HTTP, XML, and SOAP. It's a programming component that implements program logic and provides functionality for discrete applications. The main feature of the XML Web services is that a client need not know the language in which XML Web service are implemented. The client just needs to know the location of a web service and the methods that the client can call on the service.[1–2]

A Web Service is designed to support interoperable in peer-to-peer communication systems over a network. It has an interface described by the WSDL. SOAP- for interacting other systems to the web service through by message level using HTTP with an XML Serialization in conjunction with other web standards. Actually message standard/exchange is defined by WSD. Web Service model is based on the SOAP, WSDL, and UDDI standards.[1–2]

Let's enter into grid services. The model of web service provides mainly two plus points to grid services.[1–2]

- WSDL is a mechanism for defining interfaces and also discovering endpoint implementation descriptions. WS supports dynamic discovery and composition of services in heterogeneous distributed computing environment.
- It allows the framework to exploit new tools and technologies such as service wire formats, directories, description processors, workflow systems, language enhancements (WS Enhancement) and hosting mechanisms.

Grid services are descriptive in nature. A grid service is a web service packaged that provides state information, objects in the state and a set of well defined interfaces and that follows specific conventional methods. It aimed to provide transparency, dynamic service creation, lifetime management, location discovery and manageability. Similar to the web services, grid services are also some of the components like:[1–2]

- Directory components: It is a central place to store published information about services in grid. It maintains the data such that you may search the information about other services.
- Discovery components: Using this process, clients locate the documents that describe services using WSDL. The discovery process enables clients to know about the presence of services and about the location of particular service.
- Description component: This component enables you to know which operations to perform on grid services. It may also includes the message pattern structures.

Following block diagram shows the various components (Fig. 8.1) and the way of communicating (Fig 8.2).

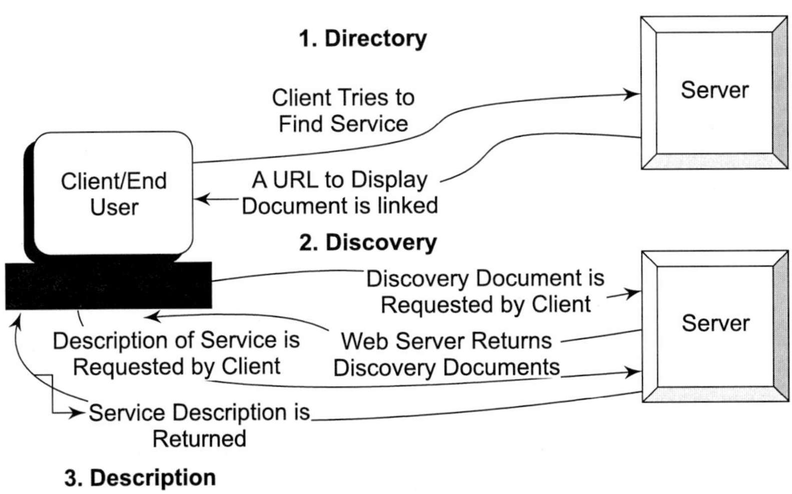

Fig. 8.3 Component diagram for grid services.[2–5]

8.2.2 Role of OGSA in Grid Service

OGSA defines standard interfaces (port Types in WSDL terminology) for basic Grid services. OGSA introduces several service concepts that need to be adopted in order to qualify as Grid services. Necessary components are *factories, registries, and handle maps*. Additional mechanisms that can be used to build our data grid are *notification* and *lifetime management*.[1–2]

From a software-design perspective, a grid can be viewed as a collection of self- contained computing services that can be described, published, located, and invoked over any type of network.[1–2]

The design principles of OGSA related to the grid services includes:[1–2]

(*i*) **Resource virtualization:** Each grid component is treated as a service.

(*ii*) **Standard interface definition mechanisms:** Enabling multiple protocol bindings and transparency between local or remote services.

(*iii*) **Standard foundation services:** Defining service semantics, reliability and security models, and core functions such as lifecycle management, or discovery.

(*iv*) **Implementation independence:** Support for multiple development languages and hosting environments including Java, COBOL, C, J2EE, CICS, and .NET.

The OGSA uses Web services technologies like WSDL, SOAP, and WSIL to abstract platform and implementation differences, giving transparent access to grid services.[1–2]

8.2.3 Grid operation Service

The Grid Operations Service operates the local Grid infrastructure and has management responsibilities for the Italian Grid facility at large. (taken from CNAF). Activities are carried out in collaboration with the Italian Grid site managers and in coordination with the operations on the European Grid infrastructure developed under the umbrella of the European project EGEE2, and in particular of the SA1 working group. The Grid Operations Service at CNAF is responsible of:[1–2]

(*i*) The collaboration to the production, test and certification of the INFN Grid release.

(*ii*) The coordination of the deployment of the INFN Grid release both locally and on the national Grid infrastructure.

(*iii*) The support to Grid site managers, new Grid Virtual Organizations, and users.

(*iv*) Site certification.

(*v*) The operation and monitoring of Grid services, including Grid information services, Grid Workload Management, Virtual Organization Management Services, File Transfer Services, monitoring (GridICE servers), accounting (HLR servers) and Local File Catalogues;

(*vi*) The management of the pre-production, preview and certification infrastructures.

(*vii*) Ticket processing management.

(*viii*) The coordination of the Italian Regional Operation Centre (ROC) activities.

(*ix*) The optimization of Grid service configurations for an enhanced high availability and reliability of the center.

(*x*) The collection and validation of accounting data.

(*xi*) The support of experimental services for stress testing of new functionalities for critical middleware components (e.g. the Workload Management System, the CREAM Computing Element, etc.).

(*xii*) The participation to international Grid standardization bodies such as the Open Grid Forum.

8.3 GRID SERVICE DESCRIPTION

Service descriptions are located and discovered using Web Services Inspection Language (WSIL). The service description defines a syntax and semantics for describing the attributes of these grid services called a Grid Service Description. The Service Description is a set of Service Attributes abstract definitions. In general, a Service Description consists of zero or more Service Attributes. There are three classes of Grid Service Description that are used in three contexts:[3–6]

- Service Description is a collection of all the Service Attributes registered and maintained on a given Grid Service Manager.
- Request Description is a collection of Service Attributes representing service requirements of a Request or agent. It is generated as a result of a Service Discovery request. Request description is included in the input parameter of SearchService( ) or QueryService( ), or in the Query Service call message.
- Reply Description is a union between the local Service Description and Request Description. It is generated as a response to a Service Discovery request. The record is included in the output parameter of QueryService( ), or in the Query Service reply.

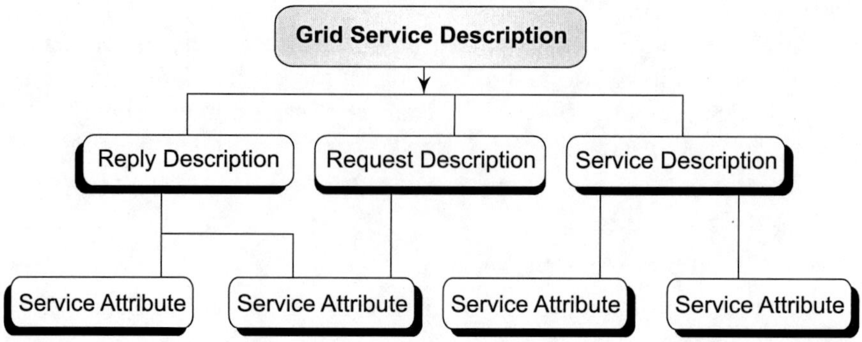

Fig. 8.4 Grid service description.[2–5]

A Service Attribute consists of an Attribute ID field, identifying the type of the attribute a result field that indicates the result of the comparison and a Value field, containing the value of the attribute. The result field is used in two ways:[3–6]

- Attribute in registered or Request Description—This field specifies the type of a function that compares the Attribute Value of the Service Description with that of the Request Description.
- Attribute in reply Service description—This field indicates the result of the comparison.

OGSA defines mechanisms to create, manage, and exchange information between Grid Services, a special type of Web service. The architecture uses WSDL extensively to describe the structure and behavior of a service. By combining elements from grid computing and Web services technologies, OGSA establishes an extensible and interoperable design and development framework for Grid Services that includes details for service definition, discovery, and life-cycle management.[3–6]

8.4 OGSA CORE SERVICES

OGSA is open-architecture. It develops the standards and specifications that address the distributed infrastructure, high- throughput computing and service mobility. The main aim is to achieve the heterogeneous environment between the virtual organizations. For achieving interoperability and distributed nature OGSA services are mainly categorized into six broad areas (proposed by smith and dave berry):[3–6]

(*i*) **Infrastructure service:** These services include common functionalities, such as naming, typically required by higher level services.

(*ii*) **Execution management services:** These services deal with issues related to starting and managing tasks, including provisioning, and life-cycle management. It includes the job work flows.

(*iii*) **Data management services:** These services handle issues such as data consistency, persistence, and integrity by providing functionality to move data to where it is needed

(*iv*) **Security services:** Security services deals the authentication, authorization, and integrity, data access etc. These services facilitate the secure policy within an organization and support safe resource sharing.

(*v*) **Resource management services:** These services provide management capabilities for grid resources: the resources themselves, resources as grid components, and the OGSA infrastructure.

(*vi*) **Information services:** These services provide physical and logical entities of efficient information, and access to, information about the grid and its constituent resources.

SUMMARY

Grid computing incorporates almost all internet services for delivering applications. For this one, web services are the general model for delivering applications and can be implemented for any operation system that supports communication over the Internet. OGSA needs a set of functional and non-functional requirements; these use cases cover infrastructure and application scenarios for both commercial and scientific areas. For providing services using grid, OGSA requires some technical concepts like resource sharing, optimization, interoperability, QoS and security.

OGSA architecture defines behavior of grid services, service description mechanisms by using Web Service Description and protocol binding information by using web service enhancements. OGSA represents the services, their interfaces, and the semantics/behavior and interaction of these services. It should be noted that the software architecture driving the implementation of the internals of these services is outside the OGSA working group's scope.

OGSA is open-architecture. It develops the standards and specifications that address the distributed infrastructure, high- throughput computing and service mobility. Following are the main core services provided by OGSA.

- Infrastructure service
- Data Management service
- Execution of services
- Security service
- And finally Information service

KNOWLEDGE TESTING

1. What is the role of OGSA in grid computing?
2. What are the requirements (functional & non- functional) OGSA needs for delivering grid services over the internet?
3. Explain the technologies which form the OGSA (Note: these technologies are core technologies).
4. Briefly explain the OGSA Platform architecture.
5. How can we derive the grid services from web services? Explain each step clearly.
6. How request-response goes in grid services (ex. In web applications)? Explain with neat diagram.
7. Explain the role of OGSA in grid services.
8. What are the core services of OGSA? Explain each of them.

REFERENCES

1. H. Kishimoto and J. Treadwell, *Defining the Grid: A Roadmap for OGSA™ Standards Version 1.0*, Open Grid Services Architecture Working Group, September 16, 2005.
2. Foster, I., Kesselman, C: *The Grid: Blueprint for a New Computing Infrastructure.* Second Edition, Morgan-Kaufman, 2004.
3. Mark Baker, Rajkumar Buyya, and Domenico Laforenza, Grids and Grid Technologies for Wide-area Distributed Computing, *Software—Practice and Experience*, 2002.
4. *http://www.gridforum.org/.*
5. *http://www.ggf.org/documents/.*
6. Joshy Joseph, M. Ernest, C. Fellenstein, *Grid Computing*, Pearson Education, 2005.

❑❑❑

9

OGSA Basic Services

9.1 INTRODUCTION

In this section, we are going to discuss how OGSA came into existence? , and what are the reasons that lead to OGSA creation? Where the OGSA creation gets started? And also OGSA platform architecture. At the end, we study basic services provided by OGSA.[1,3,5]

The Grid Infrastructure is mainly deals with the **creation**, **management**, and the **application of dynamic coordinated resources** and **services**. These dynamic and coordinated resources and services may be individual or collection of entities. These entities are complex and have short or long life span.[1,3,5]

Resources may be constituted from single or from multiple institutions so as to provide a homogeneous or heterogeneous set of functionalities. So the complexity and difference in resources and services may vary within every virtual organization. But resources and services are all agreed to deliver a set of **QoS** features including common security semantics, workflow, resource management, problem determination, failover, and service-level management. A well-defined architecture is needed to achieve the desired level quality of service (QoS). So that **OGSA** (Open Grid Service Architecture) is came into existence.[1,3,5]

OGSA is an open standard developed by GGF (Global Grid Forum). OGSA supports the **creation**, **maintenance**, and **application of services maintained by virtual organizations**. Before going to study OGSA architecture we have to know about what is a resource? And how it was defined?[1,3,5]

Resource: A resource is anything that has an URI(Uniform Resource Identifier) and also provides some services to the clients.[1,3,5]

9.2 OGSA BASIC SERVICES

The OGSA provides the following basic services:[2,4]

- Common Management Model.
- Service Domains.
- Policy Architecture.
- Security Architecture.
- Metering and Accounting.
- Common Distributed Logic.
- Distributed Data Access And Replication.

9.2.1 Common Management Model

It is an abstract representation of grid resources like physical resources (like disk), file system and operating system etc. it deals the all network elements ports and IP Addresses. The main terms in CMM are:[2,4]

- Manageability.
- Management.
- Manageable Resources.

Manageability: It is a concept and contains the resource information that can be used to manage the resource. Manageability details all the aspects of a resource that support management, including interaction with a resource from the management applications.

Management: It is a process of monitoring, modifying, and making decisions about a resource.

Manageable Resources: It is an IT entity. And it has some state to which the management operations can be performed. A manageable resource can be any entity, software components (a database), hardware(hard drives), complete applications (help desk system).

A manageable resource grid service façade contains two interfaces. They are:

- Manageability Interfaces.
- Domain-Specific Interface.

Manageability Interfaces: Every resource represented by Common management model has a grid service façade that represents the underlying resource and exposes a set of canonical interfaces and behaviors common to all the CMM services.[2,4]

Domain-Specific Interfaces: In addition to the canonical manageability interfaces for management applications, every CMM resource provides a number of domain-specific interfaces. Domain specific interfaces are tightly coupled to the domain in which these resources are defined.[2,4]

The OGSA CMM specification defines three aspects of manageability:[2,4]

(*a*) An XML schema Definition for modeling the resource manageability information.

(*b*) A Collection of manageability port types.

(*c*) Guidelines for modeling resource.

New Constructs for Resource Modelling. Modelling of resource's manageability information done by using XML schema.[2,4]

In order to better capture the data, CMM defined the following new data types: counter and gauge. In addition to these data types, CMM defined XML attributes that are classified as:[2,4]

- Versioning related
    - Version
    - Deprecated
    - Experimental
- Unit related
    - Units
- Lifecycle characteristics
    - Valid
    - Changeable
    - Volatile
    - Latency

Some of the core concepts defined in the CMM specification are as follows:[2,4]

Service data resource properties: Properties of a manageable resource are expressed as service data and grid port type operations. "findServiceData" and "setServiceData" can be utilized to access and modify these properties.

Base management port type and its behaviour: Base Manageable Resource canonical port type contains service data elements that must be implemented by all manageable resources. This port type extends the OGSI GridService port type by adding service data. Service data has valuable information about the manageable resource.

Table 9.1: Service data elements in base management port type

Service Data Name	*Description*
Life cycle model	Describes the states of the resource through the resource will transition. These are static service data values.
Current life cycle state	It deals with the current state of the resource.
Service group type	The port type of the manageable resource that provides the service group function for manageable resource of this type. This static value in WSDL and must present only with the primary apex-derived port type in the hierarchy. This helps to "locate" a service group that holds these resource instances.
Search property	Zero or more service data elements that are utilised for searching for a manageable resource. A service can use these values for caching and for searching. These are static service data values.
Related instance	Expresses the relationship between management resources instance.
Related type	Expresses the relationship between management resources type.

9.2.2 Service Domains

The OGSA service domain architecture proposes a high-level abstraction model to describe the common behaviours, attributes, operations, and interfaces to allow a collection of services to function as a single unit.[2,4]

In general, the services in a service domain can be thought of as the following:[2,4]

- Resource oriented, including CPU, storage space, and network bandwidth.
- Systems and infrastructure oriented ,including security, routing, and management.
- Application-oriented services such as purchase orders, stock transactions, insurance, etc.

9.2.3 Policy Architecture

9.2.3.1 *Policy*

It can be defined as a definitive goal, course, or method of action based on a set of conditions to guide and determine present and future decisions. Policies are implemented and utilized in a particular context such as security, workload, networking services, business processes. In the context of grid services, the OGSA policy service provides a set of rules or policies to administer, manage, and control access to any grid service.[2,4]

9.2.3.2 *Policy Service Interfaces*

The OGSA policy framework defines some core interfaces and functionalities to implement a robust, end-to-end, distributed policy management set of services. Policy framework should always include the following:[2,4]

- A canonical representation for expressing the policy (*i.e.*, the Policy Information Model).
- A management control point for defining and sustaining the policy lifecycle (*i.e.*, the Policy Service Manager Interface).
- An interface for policy consumers to retrieve policies (*i.e.*, the Policy Service Agent Interface).
- A means to ensure that a service is fully policy aware, and will validate a Policy as required (*i.e.*, the Policy Enforcement Point Interface).
- A means to effect changes on a resource (*i.e.*, utilizing the Common Management Model).

9.2.4 Security Architecture

9.2.4.1 *Grid security requirements*

We now proceed to translate the preceding general discussion of the Grid security problem into specific Grid security requirements. Recall that the goal and purpose of Grid technologies is to support the sharing and coordinated use of diverse resources in dynamic, distributed VOs: in other words, to enable the creation, from distributed components, of virtual computing systems that are sufficiently integrated to deliver desired qualities of service. Security is one of the characteristics of an OGSA-compliant component. The basic requirements of an OGSA security model are that security mechanisms be **pluggable** and **discoverable** by a service requestor from a service description. This functionality then allows a service provider to choose from multiple distributed security architectures supported by multiple different vendors and to plug its referred one(s) into the infrastructure supporting its Grid services. OGSA security must be seamless from edge of network to application and data servers, and allow the federation of security mechanisms not only at intermediaries, but also on the platforms that host the services being accessed.[2,4]

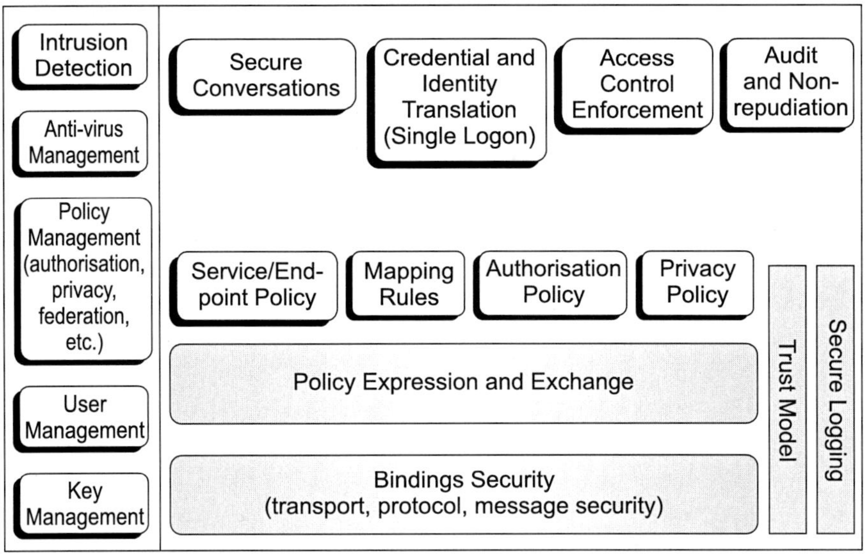

Fig. 9.1 Components of grid security model.[1–5]

The basic OGSA security model must address the following security disciplines:[2,4]

- **Authentication:** Provide plug points for multiple authentication mechanisms and the means for conveying the specific mechanism used in any given authentication operation. The authentication mechanism may be a custom authentication mechanism or an industry-standard technology. The authentication plug point must be agnostic to any specific authentication technology.
- **Delegation:** Provide facilities to allow for delegation of access rights from requestors to services, as well as to allow for delegation policies to be specified. When dealing with delegation of authority from an entity to another, care should be taken so that the authority transferred through delegation is scoped only to the task(s) intended to be performed and within a limited lifetime to minimize the misuse of delegated authority.
- **Single Logon:** Relieve an entity having successfully completed the act of authentication once from the need to participate in re-authentications upon subsequent accesses to OGSA-managed resources for some reasonable period of time. This must take into account that a request may span security domains and hence should

factor in federation between authentication domains and mapping of identities. This requirement is important from two perspectives:

(*a*) It places a secondary requirement on an OGSA-compliant implementation to be able to delegate an entity's rights, subject to policy (*e.g.*, lifespan of credentials, restrictions placed by the entity)

(*b*) If the credential material is delegated to intermediaries, it may be augmented to indicate the identity of the intermediaries, subject to policy.

- **Credential Lifespan and Renewal:** In many scenarios, a job initiated by a user may take longer than the life span of the user's initially delegated credential. In those cases, the user needs the ability to be notified prior to expiration of the credentials, or the ability to refresh those credentials such that the job can be completed.
- **Authorization:** Allow for controlling access to OGSA services based on authorization policies (*i.e.*, who can access a service, under what conditions) attached to each service. Also allow for service requestors to specify invocation policies (*i.e.*, who does the client trust to provide the requested service). Authorization should accommodate various access control models and implementation.
- **Privacy:** Allow both a service requester and a service provider to define and enforce privacy policies, for instance taking into account things like personally identifiable information (PII), purpose of invocation, etc. (Privacy policies may be treated as an aspect of authorization policy addressing privacy semantics such as information usage rather than plain information access.)
- **Confidentiality:** Protect the confidentiality of the underlying communication (transport) mechanism, and the confidentiality of the messages or documents that flow over the transport mechanism in a OGSA compliant infrastructure. The confidentiality requirement includes point–to–point transport as well as store-and-forward mechanisms.
- **Message integrity:** Ensure that unauthorized changes made to messages or documents may be detected by the recipient. The use of message or document level integrity checking is determined by policy, which is tied to the offered quality of the service (QoS).
- **Policy exchange:** Allow service requestors and providers to exchange dynamically security (among other) policy information to establish a negotiated security context between them. Such policy information can contain authentication requirements, supported functionality, constraints, privacy rules etc.

- **Secure logging:** Provide all services, including security services themselves, with facilities for time-stamping and securely logging any kind of operational information or event in the course of time - securely meaning here reliably and accurately, i.e. so that such collection is neither interruptible nor alterable by adverse agents. Secure logging is the foundation for addressing requirements for notarization, non-repudiation, and auditing.
- **Assurance:** Provide means to qualify the security assurance level that can be expected of a hosting environment. This can be used to express the protection characteristics of the environment such as virus protection, firewall usage for Internet access, internal VPN usage, etc. Such information can be taken into account when making a decision about which environment to deploy a service in.
- **Manageability:** Explicitly recognize the need for manageability of security functionality within the OGSA security model. For example, identity management, policy management, key management, and so forth. The need for security management also includes higher-level requirements such as anti-virus protection, intrusion detection and protection, which are requirements in their own rights but are typically provided as part of security management.
- **Firewall traversal:** A major barrier to dynamic, cross-domain Grid computing today is the existence of firewalls. As noted above, firewalls provide limited value within a dynamic Grid environment. However, it is also the case that firewalls are unlikely to disappear anytime soon. Thus, the OGSA security model must take them into account and provide mechanisms for cleanly traversing them—without compromising local control of firewall policy.
- **Securing the OGSA infrastructure:** The core Grid service specification (OGSI) presumes a set of basic infrastructure services, such as handleMap, registry, and factory services. The OGSA security model must address the security of these components. In addition, securing lower level components (e.g., DNSSEC) that OGSI relies on would enhance the security of the OGSI Environment As Grid computing continues to evolve to support e-business applications in commercial settings, the requirements and functions discussed in this roadmap will form the foundation for standards-based interoperability not only between real organizations within a VO (intra VO) but also across organizations belonging in different VOs (inter VO). On this foundation applications and infrastructure can be built to establish trust relationships that are required for commercial distributed computing, enterprise application integration and business-to-business (B2B) partner collaboration over the Internet.

9.2.4.2 *Relationship to Security Standards*

The Grid environment and technologies address seamless integration of services with existing resources and core application assets. As discussed in the Grid Security Model section, the Grid security model is a framework that is extensible, flexible, and maximizes existing investments in security infrastructure. It allows use of existing technologies such as X.509 public-key certificates, Kerberos shared-secret tickets and even password digests. Therefore, it is important for the security architecture to adopt, embrace and support existing standards where relevant. Given Grid services are based on web services, Grid security model will embrace and extend the Web services security standards proposed under the WS Security roadmap [WSR].[2,4]

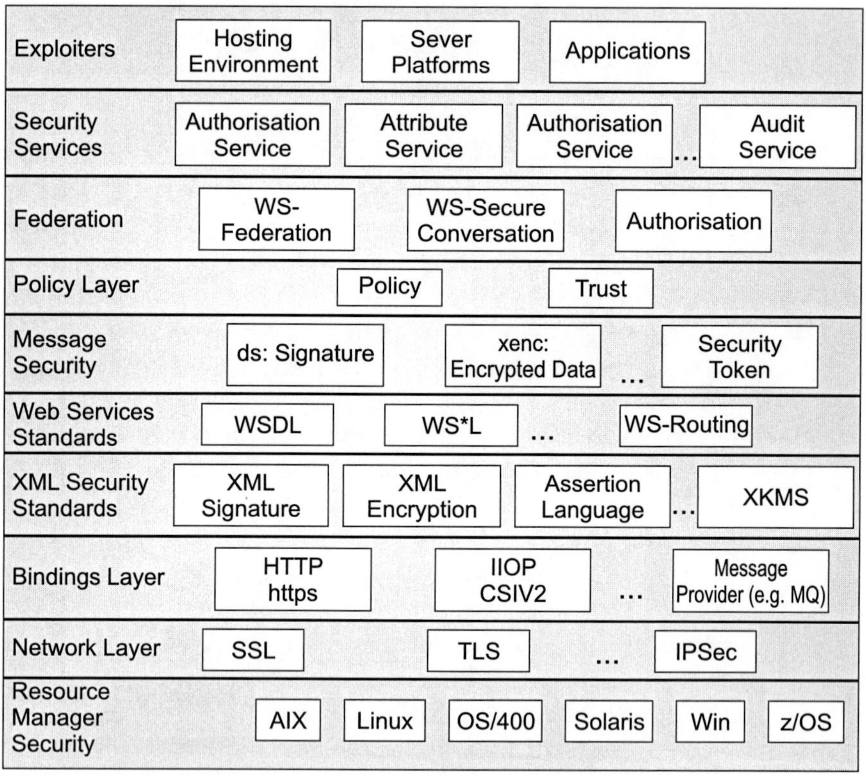

Fig. 9.2 Building blocks for grid security architecture.[1–5]

Specifically, given that OGSA is a service oriented architecture based on Web services (i.e. WSDL based service definitions), the **OGSA security model needs to be consistent with web services security model.** The web services security roadmap [security-roadmap] provides a layered approach to address web services, and also defines SOAP security bindings.

In a service-oriented environment, every decision engine should be constructed as a service. But given these services are hosted in a Grid environment, and the hosting environment itself needs to use security technologies and solutions, for bootstrapping reasons, there is a limited set of trust anchors that the system needs to start building on. Such trust anchors can be certificate authorities, trusted Kerberos domains, authorization authorities or simply minimal set of security pieces that are tied to the hosting environment. For example, if configuration is stored as files in the file system, a trust anchor can be the file system security manager itself. Therefore, the security model is based on certain resource managers provided by the hosting environment or the platforms themselves.

As discussed in previous sections, security can be an inherent part of a network and binding layer. In the case of the network layer, IPSec, SSL [SSL] or TLS [TLS] can provide it. In the case of the binding layer, it can be provided by HTTPS; in the case of IIOP, it can be provided by CSIv2. In a messaging environment, the message provider (e.g., MQ) can provide end-to-end message security.

Given the increasing use of XML, the security standards in the XML space play an important role: XML Digital Signature, XML Encryption, XML Key Management Service (XKMS), and assertion languages (*e.g.*, SAML). Built on top of XML standards are the Web services standards, including WSDL.

Message level security provides means to achieve end-to-end security instead of depending on underlying hop-by-hop security technologies like SSL. In the case of SOAP payloads, security is based on WS-Security and the areas it addresses: digital signature, encryption and security tokens. As described in the Grid security model, the policy layer and the federation layer will be built based on the underlying security layers and technologies.

A number of security functions can be provided through a service oriented approach as well. Security services can be built based on the core underlying technologies and solutions. These services can be built from scratch and exposed, or alternatively existing security functionality (*e.g.*, authorization function embedded in an operating system) can be exposed as an authorization service. Such security services can be exposed as Web services themselves – so that they can be discovered, bound to and invoked. Components that can exploit these services can be broadly categorized to be the platforms (*e.g.*, an AIX platform can use the Kerberos service hosting in a z/OS platform), hosting environment (*e.g.*, a J2EE application server such as IBM's Web Sphere can use an external security service through its pluggable authorization framework), or applications themselves (*e.g.*, a financial application may have its own payload digitally signed using a digital signature service).

9.2.5 Metering and Accounting

There is a general requirement that resource utilization should be monitored for cost allocation, capacity analysis, grid-service pricing, dynamic provisioning, fraud and intrusion detection, and billing. The OGSA platform architecture is defining a common set of interfaces and behaviors for these metering and accounting requirements.[2,4]

The OGSA metering and accounting service contains following Interfaces:[2,4]

- **Metering Service Interface:** Grid services often consume multiple resources shared by multiple service instances. The OGSA metering service provides access to systems providing aggregated utilization data. This aggregated data is exposed through a metering service data element. Metering involves the capability to measure the resource consumption in a workflow model executing on widely distributed, loosely coupled servers, storages, and network resources.
- **Rating Service Interface:** A rating interface is responsible for the following:
    (*i*) Converting the metered resource information into financial measurements.
    (*ii*) Providing valuable financial information to the business service (*i.e.*, financial advice) including the cost of the components utilized to deliver the service. This helps the service to advertise its estimated cost and usage pricing schemes, and enables customers to make the best economic decision.
- **Accounting Service Interface:** Accounting services can make use of the rated financial information retrieved through rating servicers in order to calculate the user subscription costs over a specific period of time.
- **Billing/Payment Service Interface:** These services work in collaboration with the accounting service to collect the payments, provide mediation capabilities, and a wide variety of financial interface requirements.

9.2.6 Common Distributed Logging

The distributed logging capability can be viewed as typical messaging applications where message producers generate log messages (*i.e.*, informational, trace, error, or debug messages), and which may or may not be consumed by the interested message consumers over a period of time.[2,4]

9.2.7 Distributed Data Access and Replication

Distributed data forms a complexity of data access and management on a grid arises from the scale, dynamism, autonomy and the geographical distribution of the data sources. These complexities should made transparent to grid applications through a layer of grid data virtualization services. These services provide location transparency and easier data management techniques.[2,4]

SUMMARY

OGSA is an open standard developed by GGF (Global Grid Forum). OGSA supports the creation, maintenance, and application of services maintained by virtual organizations. The Grid Infrastructure is mainly deals with the creation, management, and the application of dynamic coordinated resources and services. These dynamic and coordinated resources and services may be individual or collection of entities.

Mainly there are seven basic services are available in OGSA. Out of seven services, Common Management Model, Domain services, Policies and Security are important. Almost all management issues are comes under the category of CMM. Domain issues also handle by CMM (Please study CMM part). Service Domains can handle the high-level abstraction model to describe the common behaviors, attributes, operations, and interfaces to allow a collection of services to function as a single unit.

Policies are implemented and utilized in a particular context such as security, workload, networking services, business processes.

The basic requirements of an OGSA security model are that security mechanisms be **pluggable** and **discoverable** by a service requestor from a service description.

KNOWLEDGE TESTING

1. What is the use of OGSA basic services? What are they?
2. Explain the following:
   - Common Management Model (CMM)
   - Policy Assertions
   - Security Architecture
3. Differentiate between Manageability, management and Manageable resources.
4. What are the two interfaces provided by manageable resource? Explain them.
5. Explain briefly about service data elements.
6. What are the requirements we need to consider in grid security? Explain with neat diagram.

REFERENCES

1. J. Joseph, M. Ernest, C. Fellenstein, Evolution of Grid Computing Architecture and Grid Adoption Models, *IBM Systems Journal*, Vol. 43, No.4, pp. 624–645, January 2004.
2. Joshy Joseph, M. Ernest, C. Fellenstein, *Grid Computing*, Pearson Education, 2005.
3. *www.wikipedia.org/Open_Grid_Service_Infrastructure.html.*
4. Mary Thompson (LBNL), Von Welch (NCSA), Markus Lorch (IBM), Rebekah Lepro (NASA Ames), David Chadwidk (University of kent), Vincenzo Ciaschini (INFN CNAF). *Attributes used in OGSI Authorization, www.ggf.org/documents/GFD.57.pdf.*
5. S. Tuecke (ANL), K. Czajkowski (USC/ISI), I. Foster (ANL), J. Frey (IBM), S. Graham (IBM), C. Ksselman (USC/ISI), T. Maquire (IBM), T. Sandholm (ANL), D. Snelling (Fujitsu Labs), P. Vanderbilt (NASA) "Open Grid Service Infrastructure (OGSI), Version 1.0", *Global Grid Forum*, June 27, 2003.

❑❑❑

10

OPEN GRID SERVICES INFRASTRUCTURE (OGSI)

10.1 INTRODUCTION

Grid computing has evolved into ubiquitous computing with the evolution of Business on Demand computing and Autonomic computing. So, it became a challenge to achieve efficient coordinated resource sharing, ensuring the required quality of service. In this regard, Global Grid Forum (GGF) was in search of introducing a set of architectural standards and framework activities. With all its efforts, GGF first introduced OGSA (discussed in previous chapter). But OGSI is the base which laid the foundation for OGSA.[3–4]

OGSI (Open Grid Service Infrastructure) was introduced by GGF (Global Grid Forum) in July 2003. OGSI defines a set of conventions and extensions, which uses Web Service Description Language (WSDL) to express a Grid service as a stateful Web Service. Grid services provide controlled management as well as long time state which is useful in complex distributed applications. It provides approaches for creating, naming and maintaining subset of services, for defining and verifying service state data, to inform improper service state change, for handling in-service faults and for discovering grid services.[3–4]

Obsolescence...

*"OGSI, which was the former set of extensions to Web services to provide stateful interactions — I would say at this point is **obsolete**, i.e., that was the model which was used in the Globus Toolkit 3.0, but it's been replaced by WSRF, WS-Security, and the broader set of Web services standards. But OGSA, which focuses on specific service definition in the areas of execution components, execution modeling, grid data components, and information virtualization, still has an important role to play in the evolution of standards and open source tool kits like Globus".*

—Jay Unger

10.2 OGSI AUTHORIZATION AND ATTRIBUTES

The implementation of OGSI, involves an authorization service conducted by Grid community. For this authorization purpose, OGSI needs to consider some attributes and assertions. The need for considering these attributes and assertions is to facilitate compatibility between issuers of attribute assertions and the authorization systems that consume them. We know that, in a Grid environment the major issue is 'security'. There is no guarantee for the user data to be secure and protected. The same problem arises in the case of attribute assertions also. So, some specific semantics and conventions must be followed in assigning these authorization attributes.[1–2]

10.2.1 Attribute Requirements

Attributes are used to describe entities that are used as identities in making authorization decisions. Attributes are defined in a descriptive form, associated with a characteristic of an entity. These attributes are used in assigning access permissions to the resources. Like these, each and every attribute is classified based on the characteristic associated with it. In general, there are three types of attributes:[1–2]

- **Subject attributes:** Responsible for starting of an activity (e.g., defining a policy).
- **Resource attributes:** attributes that are used for defining resources.
- **Environmental attributes:** attributes that define environmental information.

Basic requirements of all these attributes are, first the attribute assertion should restrict the caching of the attribute. Second, extensibility in defining attributes names, values and conditions. Finally, the attribute assertions must allow the interoperability between different Grid Services.[1–2]

10.2.2 Standards and Specifications of Attributes

There are many standards available for attribute specifications, but here only five standards have been specified. They are:[1–2]

- **x.509 Attribute Certificate:** Responsible for assigning attributes to a holder followed by Digital signatures from the authority.
- **SAML Attribute Assertions:** Security Assertion Markup Language provides an XML-based protocol for handshake, authentication, attribute and authorization assertion about principals.
- **XACML Attributes:** Extensible Access Control Markup Language is responsible for defining access control policy and the context attached with an initiator, when requesting an authorization.

- **Shibboleth:** The architecture of Internet-2 for sharing web resources with access control, defines attributes about its users to sites.
- **EDG VOMS:** The Virtual Organization Membership Service, developed by the European Data Grid, has an attribute that defines groups, roles and capabilities of its members.

10.3 OGSI COMPONENTS

Open Grid Services Infrastructure acts as base interface for providing web services. The main intention of OGSI is to provide interoperability among the components of OGSA. The figure below shows various components of OGSI existing as layers in a Web Service with interfaces and behaviours.[2]

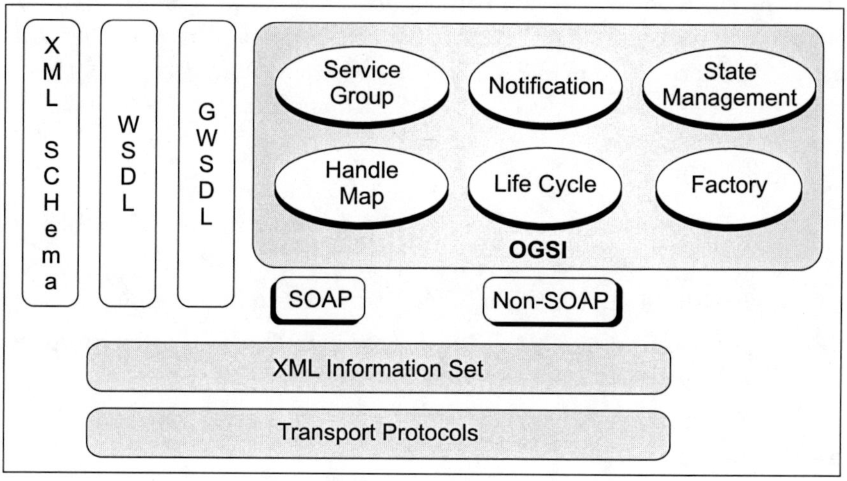

Fig. 10.1 OGSI architecture and its components.[1–5]

(*i*) WSDL is the description language for the web service provided by the OGSI.

(*ii*) GWSDL (Grid WSDL) is the extension properties of WSDL, which provides port type for particular web service.

(*iii*) SOAP protocol is used to send messages which are built using xml schema, among the components or outside environment.

(*iv*) Along with this, OGSI provide some interesting services such as life-cycle management, service state data, state-change notifications, factory services, etc using an OGSI description model.

10.4 WSRF (WEB SERVICE RESOURCE FRAMEWORK)

Web Service Resource Framework is set of standards that support grid services and other stateful services. The components of WSRF help define open standards to the grid architectures and there by increasing quality of the service. Using this alignment and with the help of Web services stack, grid services can avail the Web Service standards such as WS-Notification, WS-addressing, WS-security, etc., and there by extending the capabilities such as service state data, lifetime, grouping and reference management.[4–5]

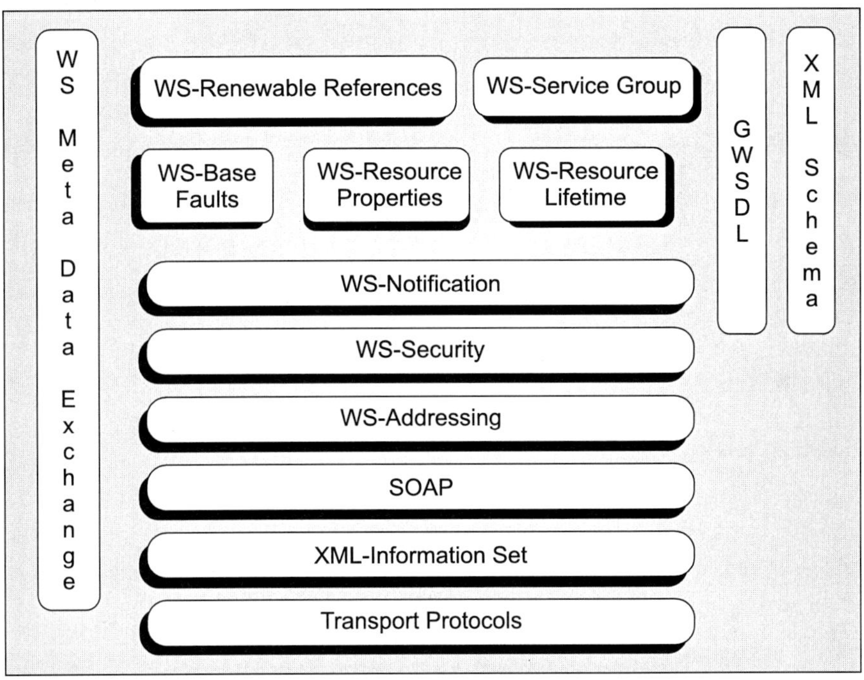

Fig. 10.2 WSRF with web services specifications.[1–5]

10.4.1 WSRF-Components

The main intention of WSRF is to merge grid services and web services. The OGSI specifications of WSRF mainly use XML schemas, but in some cases it may not use them. Another important factor of WSRF, is to converge the grid services with the existing programming languages, models, tools and technologies of Web Services.[4–5]

10.4.2 WS-Addressing

This ability enables to locate and access web services. When the OGSI specifications are enabled with flexible and extensible constructs and some SOAP message headers, then it helps header elements to easily locate the addresses of the web services and access them.[4–5]

Generally, web services are invoked using the port type information provided by the WSDL. This port type specifies the address of the web services. But in order to access the web service using port type information, client needs a primary key and an unique identifier. No current existing mechanisms provide the details of keys. This problem can be resolved using WS-Addressing, as it provides the port type information and binding mechanism of the SOAP message headers. In this WS-Addressing enable a WSRF to provide stateful web services and available grid services.[4–5]

A WS-addressing specification provides WS-Addressing EPR which is xml version of the network wide pointer to a web service. An EPR contains address of the service (wsa: serviceAddress), description of the web service (WSDL), web service policy (wsp: policy) and reference properties (wsa: Reference Properties) which are used to uniquely identify stateful resources at a particular endpoint address.[4–5]

10.4.3 WS-Resource

Any resource such as processor, storage, system, OS, cache, etc that are available on service provider side are referred to as WS-Resource, when they are involved in providing a Web Service. A WS-Resource is involved both in all the details of the identity information for the WS-Resource depend on the binding and the service consumer should not modify the content.[4–5]

A WS-Resource can maintain multiple interfaces and can associate multiple web service facades with different ERPs. The service state data of the stateful resource is open to service requestor via WS-Reference Properties. Every stateful resource has a well defined lifecycle for creation and destruction, with identity of the resource attached to it. a stateful service and a web service.[4–5]

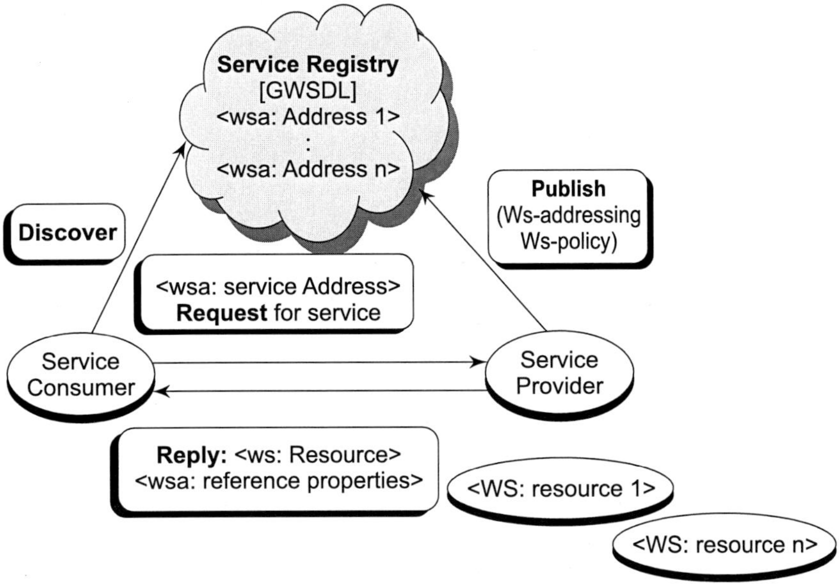

Fig. 10.3 Accessing WS-Resource in web service resource framework.[1–5]

In the above figure, we can see *service provider* is submitting all the port type definitions to the *service registry* and consequently, *service consumer* accessing that WS-Resource using port type information provided by service registry.[4–5]

10.4.4 WS-Notification

This is a notification given when the events occurred in the inter-object communication. WS-Notification is a set of specifications to define a standard for the intimation in a message service. It involves exchange of messages by service providers, notification-broker service provider and operational requirements with prior to service providers and requesters who participate in WS-Notifications and an XML model.[4–5]

WS-Notifications typically will have three notifications: WS-Base Notification, WS-BrokerNotification and WS-Topics. *WS-Base Notification* provides interfaces for notification producers as well as consumers. But this is enabled when there exists a message exchange by service provider in the notification scenario. *WS-BrokerNotification* provides interface for notification broker, but it includes message exchange by notification broker in a standard WS-Notification scenario. A notification broker is one, who acts as a mediator between service provider and service consumer and responsible for the publication of messages from a service provider. WS-Topics provide a mechanism for organizing and classifying. It provides three topic expressions which are used for subscription in a message request for subscription.[4–5]

10.4.5 WS-Resource Properties

Every grid resource may have properties such as form and state associated with it. In general, these characteristics in Web services are referred to as WS-Resource Properties. These resource properties enhance web services to form interfaces with other resources and will form a part of the resource state. Description of a resource and its state information may be available on the request. The specifications of the web service cannot explain how the values are been assigned to the properties. These values can be found inside the resource or outside the resource, but the properties are defined in xml documents.[4–5]

On the other hand, the specifications define a set of message exchange patterns that enable users to update, query and insert additional resource properties. In the earlier discussion (WS-Resource), we have seen that a client could get port type definitions from the service registry as published by a service provider. Using that port type (end-point) information, a client can access a resource and modify these resource properties.[4–5]

A service requestor can get the details of the modifications (update, insert, etc.) performed by him to the values of the resource-properties. In this way a client can participate in a web service notification scenario.[4–5]

10.4.6 WS-Resource Lifetime

Web service is created with a limited lifetime and so it is temporary (meaning that it is changing or updating every time). Generally, clients are interacting with the web services, so they are able to control the resources using a clean-up mechanism provided by resources. The specifications enables to customer to specify time (lifetime) to a resource, beyond which the resource expires and no longer available. These resource destruction capabilities are given to the customer for a particular resource he is accessing. This controlled destruction is attached with some policies and rules.[4–5]

WS-ResourceLifetime specifies set of service properties and two messages for service destruction:[4–5]

(*i*) The properties are *Initial Termination Time*, *Current Time* and *Termination Time*.

(*ii*) The Destruction Messages are:

- *Immediate Destruction*: This message warns a Web Service to immediately destroy the particular resource after receiving the message.
- *Scheduled Destruction*: This message is also a warning signal to the Web Service, but it specifies a time period after which the particular resource that is specified must be destroyed by the web service.

The WS-Notifications provide customer some notifications for subscribing for a notification to destroy a resource.[4–5]

10.4.7 WS-ServiceGroup

A WS-ServiceGroup is formed by combining some set of web services in order to provide a domain specific solution. A Web ServiceGroup specifies a set of references for WS-Resources and enables to manage the group. WS-ServiceGroup uses some web service standards to uniquely identify its resources as WS-Resources and properties such as lifetime, notification and addressing.[4–5]

10.5 WSRF VS OGSI

The functionalities of OGSI and WSRF may be identical, but some factors will differentiate them:[4–5]

(*i*) The resource pattern defines the idea of stateful resource (WS-Resource) and also this pattern defines an interface for Grid Service as directed by OGSI. This makes all the resources and grid services to be handled by some specified Web Service tools.

(*ii*) WS-Addressing of WSRF replaces the concepts of Grid Service Handle (GSH) and Grid Service Routine (GSR) of the OGSI specification using an EPR and reference properties.

(*iii*) The notification framework of WSRF enables Web Services and Grid Services to provide notifications. The framework acts as an interface for subscription for a notification, message exchange pattern, negotiation with a web service, etc. In other words, it serves as a broker between client and the service.

The comparisons made difference in the functionalities and methods of OGSI and WSRF and so the following observations can be made if we see clearly the properties and characteristics of them. In general, these differences say that the properties of one entity are replaced by other properties in the other entity.[4–5]

Table 10.1: The difference between components of OGSI and WSRF

OGSI	*WSRF*
Grid service interface	WS-Addressing endpoint reference
Grid service handle	WS-Addressing endpoint reference
Handle resolver port type	WS-Renewable references
Service data definition and access	WS-Resource Properties
Grid service lifetime management	WS-Resource Life cycle
Notification port type	WS-Notification
Factory port type	Factory pattern concept
Service group port type	WS-Service Group
Base fault type	WS-Base faults

10.6 OGSI PORT TYPE MODEL

OGSI port type model typically has four layers. All the layers intend to define basic port types for accessing a grid service. In the first layer OGSI defines a port type which is a base port type for the grid service. In the next layer it defines base management resource port type used for managing meta-O.S. Third layer is meant for user defined port types such as Operating System service port type and Operating System Factory service port type. Then the last is concerned about the service implementation. Here we have Operating System services and Factory services.[1–2]

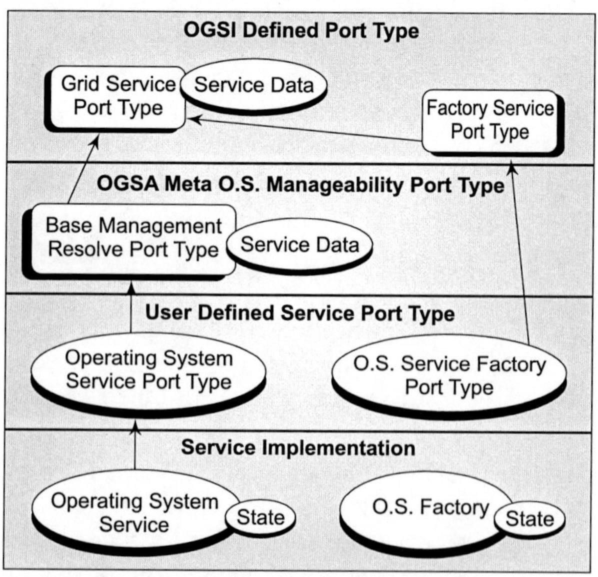

Fig. 10.4 OGSI-Port type inheritance model.[1–5]

The figure shows the layers involved in OGSI (Open Grid Service Infrastructure framework. In the figure, we can see how a client service acquires a grid service port type and access the required grid service through the OGSI framework.[1–2]

OGSI is responsible for providing common interface and common port type with prior to a grid service. Base Manageable resource port type is the port type of the base resource. For this, it needs state data to be added to it. With this framework OGSI is providing a service called *interface flattening*. Interface flattening is concept of transforming WSDL into GWSDL and vice versa. This concept can be well explained with the following example, where a client is intending to access an XML WebService. For this purpose he can use protocols such as Simple Object Access Protocol (SOAP), Hyper Text Transfer Protocol (Http), IFOP, etc.[1–2]

If this web service needs to be accessed as a Grid service, the description of that WebService WSDL is transformed into GWSDL, where the functionalities are changed according to OGSI. After changing into GWSDL, the web service can have service state data and hence it is being called as *Stateful WebService* or *Grid Service*. After this transformation, a client will have a webservice along with OGSI. The following figure provides a pictorial view about the interface flattening.[1–2]

In the below figure we can see the visualization of interface flattening. If we closely observe the above diagram, the dotted line between the GWSDL and WSDL shows the flattening of the two interfaces into a single narrow interface resulting into a deliverance of stateful web service.[1–2]

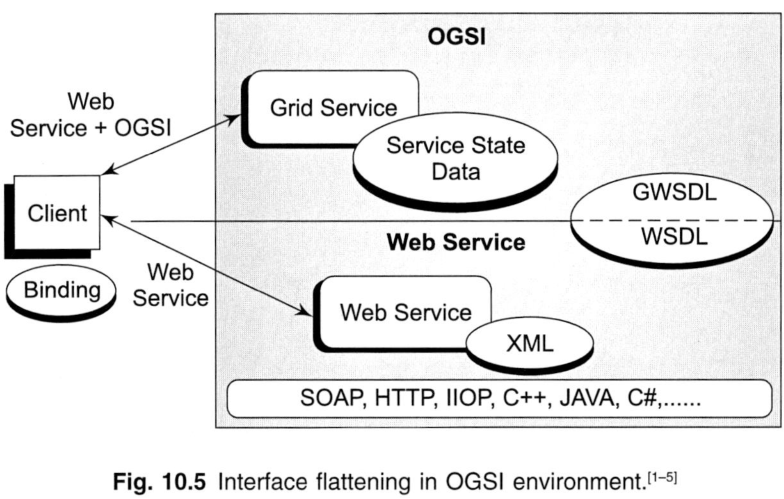

Fig. 10.5 Interface flattening in OGSI environment.[1–5]

10.6.1 Roles played by OGSI[1–2]

- Acts as an interface for providing Grid Services.
- Responsible for providing port type model.
- Uses WSDL 1.2 to define GWSDL.

10.7 SERVICE DATA CONCEPTS

OGSI introduces grid services which are nothing but stateful web services. For a webservice to be a grid service, it needs to define some service state data which we call *Service Data Concepts*. The main objective of these concepts is to define a stateful WebService (Grid Service). In general, there are four service data concepts. To know the complete state information of the webservice, it is required to describe the service state elements:[3]

- Service Data Declaration (SDD).
- Service Data Elements (SDE).
- Service Data Values (SDV).
- Service Data Set.

10.7.1 Service Data Elements

The XML Data elements defined in a GWSDL port type definition that are accessed from interface of the stateful webservice are referred as Service Data Elements (SDE).[3]

10.7.2 Service Data Declaration

Service Data Declaration is a functionality to define the elements of the service state data of a stateful web service. The elements which are defined using these declarations are only accessible via the interfaces defined in this specification but the declarations which are private to the specification cannot be accessed. These declarations can be seen in following code fragment.[3]

Code:

```
<gwsdl: portType name= " CPU Scheduling">
    <wsdl: operation name="schedule">
    ............................................................
    </wsdl:operation>
    ............................................................
    ............................................................
```

```
<sd:serviceData name="Round-Robin CPU Scheduling algorithm"
                    type="Round-Robin Scheduling"
                    minOccurs="1"   //default value is 0
                    maxOccurs="1"   //deault value is 1
                    nillable="true"
                    mutability= "static" />
<sd:serviceData name="SJF CPU scheduling algorithm"
                    ...............................
                    ...............................
                    ............................... />
......................................................................
</gwsdl:portType>
```

Service data will have attributes such as 'name' and 'type', using which we can identify service data. Apart from these two it also has attributes such as *minOccurs*, *maxOccurs, nillable*, *mutability*,etc. Based on the service we can have any number of service data elements. In the above we have two SD declarations Round-Robin and SJF. Service data is the only element that differentiates a Grid Service from a WebService, where a Grid Service contains Service Data but the Web Service do not. Webservice need not have a Service Data Element, because there is no need for it to maintain the state data. As it don't have state data, it is a stateless service. Hence, Grid service is called as a Stateful Web service.[3]

10.7.3 Service Data Values (SDV)

Service Data values are the values assigned to the Service Data Elements of a grid service. In general, these values are defined as XML code fragments and they certainly follow an XML schema which is specified by the type attribute of the service data. Based on the mutability attribute of the service data there are two type of Service data values. They are:[3]

(*a*) **Static:** The values that are declared as a part of GWSDL port type definition are static values. Generally these values will have the value of mutability attribute as 'static'.

(*b*) **Dynamic:** These values are assigned to the Service Data Elements dynamically and their behavior is based on the implementation. The client invoking these values may obtain from a third part or through some meta data exchange or else message exchange.

10.7.4 Service Data Set

The Data set is an aggregation or collection of service data elements and their values for a specific service instance. These Service Data sets can be accessed by clients through the interfaces available in a Grid Service Port type definition. The SDE's involved here belongs to all the port types defined in a interface hierarchy of service implementation.[3]

10.7.5 Service Data Structures

Service Data Structures are the attributes that uniquely identify a service data element. They define the properties for an SDE. The following are some of the data structures available:[3]

- *Name*: This attribute uniquely identifies a service data element in a target namespace.
- *Type*: This attribute defines the XML schema type of the service data element.
- *maxOccurs*: this attribute specifies how many times this SDE is reffered at the Maximum.
- *minOccurs*: this attribute specifies how many times this SDE is reffered at the Minimum.
- *Nillable*: This attribute indicates whether the Service Data value may have a nil value or not.
- *Modifiable*: This attribute indicates whether the service data element is readable or writable or both.
- *Mutability*: This is a crucial attribute which specifies how the service data values are changed. The behavior of change can be in four fashions like 'static','constant','extendable','mutable'.

10.8 NAMING IN GRID SERVICE INSTANCES

Grid services have a global name, named by Grid Service Handle (GSH). GSH just indicates URI of the grid service but it cannot provide entire information for the client to communicate with the service. To resolve this problem a client communicates using another component called as Grid Service Reference (GSR). GSR provides every required information to the client, which a GSH don't provide to communicate with a client.[3]

10.8.1 Grid Service Handle (GSH)

Like all the URIs, Grid Service Handle (GSH) also has a scheme and scheme specific data to resolve GSH into a GSR.A client at an instance can choose either the service Handle or any Handle resolver port type. A typical GSH will have the following properties:[3]

- Must be a valid URI.
- Must not refer to more than one Grid service instance.
- A grid service must define atleast one GSH.
- A grid service can have multiple GSH's with multiple schemes or multiple GSH's with single shceme.
- If multiple GSH's are included in one Grid service instance, then the Service Data Element values corresponding to them must refer to that service instance only.
- Grid Service may have multiple GSR's that refer to that instance itself.
- Service resolver may return return different GSR's for the same GSH or different GSR's to same GSH as resolved by the client.
- For a grid service instance there may be an unresolvable GSH before, during or after the instance.
- The resolution of the GSH into GSR can be guaranteed or cannot be guaranteed based on the client's choosing of the service instance.

10.8.2 Grid Service Reference (GSR)

GSR is basically a reference to a Grid Service in a Grid Service hosting network/ environment. Using these GSR's only the Grid services are being accessed by the clients. With all the communication protocol bindings, a GSR will have entire information for a client to interact with the grid service instance. Using this GSR information, a client can directly negotiate with a service instance at the specified service port type.[3]

The encoding of GSR is crucial for the client to communicate. Along with Operational message, encoding format of the GSR is binded together and is used by the client to communicate with the grid service instance. The lifetime of the GSR is associated with the lifetime of the grid service instance. We say that a GSR is valid when it is existing with the grid service instance and is accessed through it.[3]

The binding of the grid service is implemented using an attribute called Expiry Time, which states that the time after which the associated grid service instance may no longer available. If the grid service needs to be accessed it should be done within this Expiry time. So, the clients are required to refresh their session with the grid service at regular time intervals, rather than waiting for its expiry time to over. As the GSH is valid for the entire lifetime of the grid service instance and the GSR may become invalid, it is better to resolve a GSH into a valid GSR.[3]

SUMMARY

Open Grid Service Infrastructure (OGSI) acts as an interface between client and the service. It provides the specifications to the clients to communicate with the web service and access its resources. The clients who use these specifications are the authorized users to access the resources. OGSI provides the description of the grid service it offers in the form WSDL written in XML code fragments. OGSI protocol inheritance model shows the core functionality of the OGSI and the services provided by the OGSI.

OGSI provides port type definition of a service using which a client can negotiate with a grid service and access the resources. OGSI also provides service state data of a grid service instance which differentiates a grid service from a web service. Hence, OGSI helps in developing a stateful web service or a grid service. Two components of OGSI, Grid Service Handle (GSH) and Grid Service Reference (GSR) serves as references for grid services. Using these references, clients can access the grid service instances they required.

Finally, OGSI along with OGSA forms as an interface between the client and the grid services. Both of them form as basic platform of the Grid Computing to access the grid services and resources provide by a Grid.

KNOWLEDGE TESTING

1. What is OGSI? How it differs from OGSA? Compare and Contrast between OGSA an OGSI.
2. Name some attributes of OGSI. How they are helpful in accessing a Grid service using OGSI.
3. What is a Web Resource Framework? Explain in detail using an architectural diagram of WSRF.
4. Compare and Contrast between OGSI and WSRF. Which one you prefer more advantageous in providing a Grid Service?
5. Give the OGSI port type Inheritance model for operating system service and the operating system factory service sample.
6. "OGSI helps in providing stateful web services." Comment on this statement using the Service state data.
7. What is the role played by OGSI in providing a Grid service instance? Justify your answer using Interface inheritance model.
8. How naming is implemented in OGSI? What are the components involved in it?

Contd...

9. Observe the following code sample:

```
<gwsdl: portType name= "Memory management Techniques">
        <wsdl: operation name="Memory Management">
            .............................................
        </wsdl:operation>
            .............................................
            .............................................
<sd:serviceData name="Virtual memory implementation"
                type="virtual memory"
                minOccurs="1"   //default value is 0
                maxOccurs="1"   //deault value is 1
                nillable="true"
                mutability= "extendable" />
<sd:serviceData name="Dynamic patitioning"
                type = "partitioning"
                minOccurs="1"
                maxOccurs="1"
                mutability="dynamic"  />
.......................................................................
</gwsdl:portType>
```

Explain the above code fragment using service data concepts. (*****)

10. What are various standards and specifications involved in authorization attributes of OGSI?

REFERENCES

1. S. Tuecke (ANL), K. Czajkowski (USC/ISI), I. Foster (ANL), J. Frey (IBM), S. Graham (IBM), C. Ksselman (USC/ISI), T. Maquire (IBM), T. Sandholm (ANL), D. Snelling (Fujitsu Labs), P. Vanderbilt (NASA) "*Open Grid Service Infrastructure (OGSI), Version 1.0*", *Global Grid Forum*, June 27, 2003.
2. Mary Thompson (LBNL), Von Welch (NCSA), Markus Lorch (IBM), Rebekah Lepro (NASA Ames), David Chadwidk (University of Kent), Vincenzo Ciaschini (INFN CNAF) "*Attributes used in OGSI Authorization*", *www.ggf.org/documents/GFD.57.pdf.*
3. J. Joseph, M. Ernest, C. Fellenstein, Evolution of Grid Computing Architecture and Grid Adoption Models, *IBM Systems Journal*, Vol. 43, No. 4, pp. 624–645, January 2004.
4. Joshy Joseph and C. Fellenstein, *Grid Computing*, Pearson Education, 2005.
5. *www.wikipedia.org/Open_Grid_Service_Infrastructure.html.*

PART IV

GRID IMPLEMENTATIONS

Up to now we discussed concepts and technologies in grid computing. But actual implementations and configurations are not come in previous chapters. This part mainly concentrates on configuration of Globus toolkit.

Chapter 11 discusses almost all security concepts in grid computing. These concepts will also useful in cloud computing technology also. Security fundamentals, Authentication schemes, some standard protocols, Grid taxonomy, web service security and Grid Security Infrastructure (GSI) are discussed in Chapter 11. Some important security diagrams also included in this chapter.

Chapter 12 concentrates on globus toolkit. The Globus Toolkit provides a set of services to enable the secure sharing of resources across corporate, institutional and geographic boundaries. More information about toolkit provided in Chapter 12.

11

GRID COMPUTING SECURITY

11.1 INTRODUCTION

In today's world grid computing is a buzzword in both industries and academics/organizations. The evolution pattern of grid technologies is very similar to the growth and evolution of Internet technologies. Similar to the Internet, the initial grid computing technologies were also developed mostly in the universities and research labs to solve unique research problems and to collaborate between different researchers across the globe.[1–2]

After completing this chapter you would be able to understand the topics like:[1–2]

- Types of securities in web services and grid.
- Why grid require the security.
- Security mechanisms applied in grid.
- Taxonomy of grid security issues.
- Grid security architecture, infrastructure and models.
- Message level security, service level security and network security.

According to Foster and Kesselman a grid is a system that conforms to three specific categories:[1–2]

- It coordinates resources that are not subject to centralized control.
- It uses standard, open, and general purpose protocols and interfaces.
- It delivers non-trivial quality of service.

Kon *et. al.*, define grid computing as "*coordinated resource sharing and problem solving in dynamic, multi-institution virtual organizations*".[1–2]

The first generation of Grid computing middleware implemented their own interfaces, the introduction of the service- oriented computing paradigm and the corresponding web service standards such as WSDL and SOAP in the field of Grid computing through the Open Grid Services Architecture (OGSA). Since grid is on-demand business the software contains the third party persons should provide a authentication mechanisms for allowing. Grid software is somewhat complex; grid middleware faces number of security problems.[1–2]

The basic security components within the Globus Toolkit provide the mechanisms for authentication, authorization, and confidentiality of communication between grid computers. Without this functionality, the integrity and confidentiality of the data processed within the grid would be at risk. A grid is highly complex and dynamic, making its management extremely challenging. Classical Grid computing relies fully on standard operating system security mechanisms to protect users from each other. Let us we go one by one topic in gird security.[1–2]

11.2 SECURITY FUNDAMENTALS

Security threats—any system should be concerned about security threats. Threads may be in the form of interruption, interception, modification and replication. Characteristics of security system are:[1–2]

- **Confidentiality:** Sensitive information must be secure from the third part persons unless otherwise he/she has permission. Data confidentiality is often also referred to as privacy.
- **Integrity:** In grid environment, integrity is in terms of messages like message level integrity.
- **Authentication:** Authentication is the process of verifying the validity of a claimed individual and identifying who is he/she. Authentication applied to services and applications also.
- **Single Sign on:** In a grid environment, there may be instances where requests may have to travel through multiple security domains. Therefore, there is need for single sign-on facility in the grid infrastructure.
- **Delegation:** There may be a need for services to perform actions on the user's behalf. A computational job may require accessing database many times. In that case there is a need to delegate the authority to some service which will perform the action on the user's behalf.

Not only these key management and access control are also part in grid computing.[1–2]

11.3 AUTHENTICATION SCHEMES

Authenticating a system based on mainly three mechanisms- shared secret, public key and based on third party.[2]

- **Shared secret:** System would be to share a password between the authenticator and the user. In this type of system, the authenticator asks the user for a password which when disclosed will allow the user to enter the system. These systems are simple to implement and are computationally inexpensive.[2]
- **Public key:** It is maintained by representatives (like HR managers in the organizations) who are controlling grid. In this type of scheme the user has a public and private key pair and the authenticator knows the public key of the user. The user encrypts standard information with his private key.[2]
- **Third party:** the user gets a digital certificate from a Certificate Authority (CA) which is a known third party. Certificates are nothing but information about the user hashed and then signed by the CA's private key.[2]

11.4 STANDARD PROTOCOLS

We will concentrate on some of the standard protocols and mechanisms used in grid computing systems. We will discuss public key infrastructure, Secure Socket Layer (SSL), Kerberos, and IP security.[4–5]

11.4.1 Public Key Infrastructure

An infrastructure which supports the public key based authentication and encryption is called the Public Key Infrastructure (PKI). It has a concept called 'certificates'.[4–5]

- **Certificates:** Certificates are credentials of a specific user containing the user details which is signed by the CA. Different types of certificates are available. The most popular and commonly used certificate format is called X.509 format . A typical X.509 certificate consists of the following information:[4–5]
  - Versioning.
  - User's information.
  - Signatures algorithm.
  - Validity of the certificate.
  - The public key information.
- **Certification Authority (CA):** The CA's are responsible for certifying the public keys of different users who subscribe to the CA.[4–5]

11.4.2 Secure Socket Layer

It is most popular protocol to secure the transport layer. The best example of this layer protocol is Transport Layer Security (TLS). It provides security in managing sessions over the transport channel.[4–5]

11.4.3 Kerberos

For providing authentication at network level Kerberos useful. It is one of the examples of a third party authentication.[4–5]

11.4.4 IPSec

This is a method applied in the network layer. It support a variety of application scenarios is that it can encrypt or authenticate all traffic at the IP level. Thus, all distributed applications, including remote login, client/server, e-mail, file transfer, Web access, and so on, can be secured.[4–5]

11.5 GRID TAXONOMY

The grid security taxonomy mainly characterized into three groups:[3–5]

- Architecture.
- Infrastructure.
- Management.

11.5.1 Architecture Taxonomy

It concerns the grid system as a whole. It deals the information security, authorization, and service level security. There is a Grid Security Infrastructure (GSI) layer of OGSA which addresses most of the information security challenges.[3–5]

11.5.2 Infrastructure Taxonomy

The combination of grid nodes plus communication network is nothing but infrastructure security. Main issues in infrastructure security are host security, data protection, network security (deals multicasting, accessing like VPN's and routing).[3–5]

11.5.3 Management Taxonomy

We know grid is heterogeneous in nature and may consist of multiple entities, components, users, domains, policies, and stakeholders. Management taxonomy is generally either trust or resource monitoring.[3–5]

Up to here we see just basic elements/issues in security. Now let us discuss about the concept of Grid Security Infrastructure (GSI).[3–5]

11.6 GRID SECURITY INFRASTRUCTURE (GSI)

GSI enabling secure authentication and communication over an open network provides a number of useful services for Grids, including mutual authentication and single sign-on. Resource sharing among heterogeneous virtual organization participants is a complex process because of the challenges faced in integration, interoperability and trust relationship. There are numerous security framework, standards and implementations available today.[4–5]

Using GSI components we have to create a set of keys for public key cryptography and request your certificate from the Certificate Authority and a copy of the public key of the CA. For establishing GSI communication does the following steps:[4–5]

(*i*) Copy the Certificate Authority's public key to your grid host with which you set up GSI.

(*ii*) Create your private key and a certificate request.

(*iii*) Send your certificate request to CA by e-mail or another more secure way if you are running a production system and need to positively identify the sender.

(*iv*) CA signs your request to make your certificate and sends it back to you.

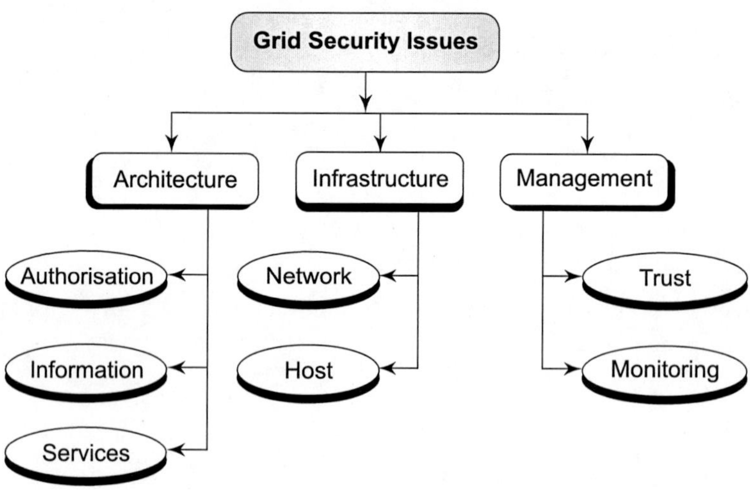

Fig. 11.1 Grid security taxonomy.[1–5]

When that procedure has been completed and you have received your signed digital certificate, you will have three important files on your grid host. They are:[4–5]

- The CA's public key.
- The grid host's private key.
- The grid host's digital certificate.

GSI based on public key encryption, X.509 certificates, and the Secure Sockets Layer (SSL) communication protocol. An extra layer of security was added to the private key, which includes a secret passphrase that must be used when using your private key along with your digital certificate. This is to prevent someone from stealing your digital certificate and private key and being able to automatically use them to access grid resources. The host key is protected by the local operating system privileges within the grid server.[4–5]

The procedure for preparing GSI is a shown in diagram.

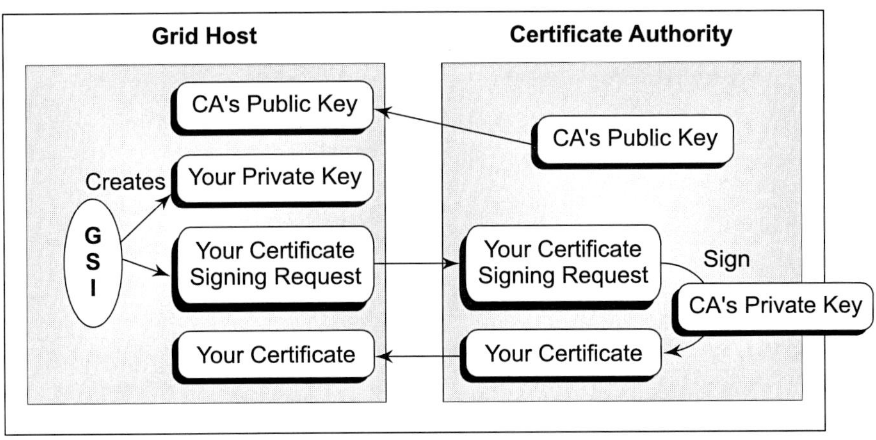

Fig. 11.2 Preparation procedure for GSI.[1–5]

Some points about GSI[4–5]

Basic Globus grid security is a two-step process:

(*a*) Verify a user's identity.

(*b*) Verify that the identified user has permission to use the grid resources he is trying. Step 2 is dependent on Step 1.

Four functions implemented by GIS are:

- Single/Mutual Authentication.
- Confidential Communication.

- ❒ Authorisation.
- ❒ Delegation.

11.7 SECURITY

There are mainly two types of mechanisms are there in security- either point-to point security or end-to-end security.[1–2]

11.7.1 Point-to-Point

Point-to-point security can be achieved with the help of SSL/TLS and IPSec etc. requester maintain direct contact to the intermediate shown below:[1–2]

Fig. 11.3 Point-to-point security.[1–5]

11.7.2 End-to-End Security

This type of message security applied between sender and final receiver of the message in web services. Many intermediaries are involved while messages are delivering. It includes end- point authentication, integrity, confidentiality trust and federation etc.[1–2]

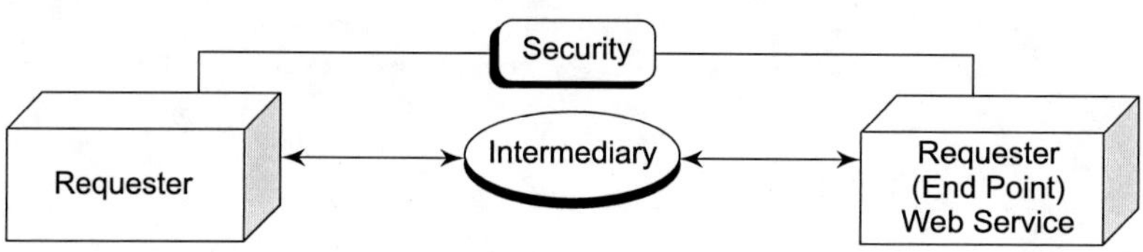

Fig. 11.4 End-to-end security.[1–5]

> For achieving end-to-end security the following points must be accomidated.
>
> - ❒ A web service requester can ask the requester to submit the necessary claims.
> - ❒ A requester can send the message along with proof of the claim, which is normally called "security tokens" such as user name and password, Kerberos and X509 certificates.
> - ❒ If requester doesn't have claims, he/she will take claims from other trusted agencies. These trusted authorities are called *"security token services".*
>
> —Joshy Joseph

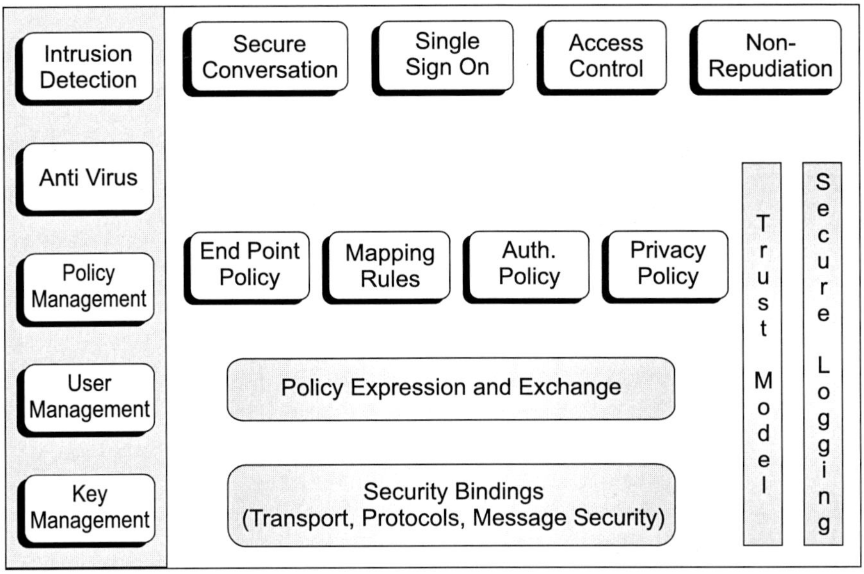

Fig. 11.5 Components of the grid security model (by Anirban Chakrabarti).[1–5]

11.8 WEB SERVICES SECURITY[2]

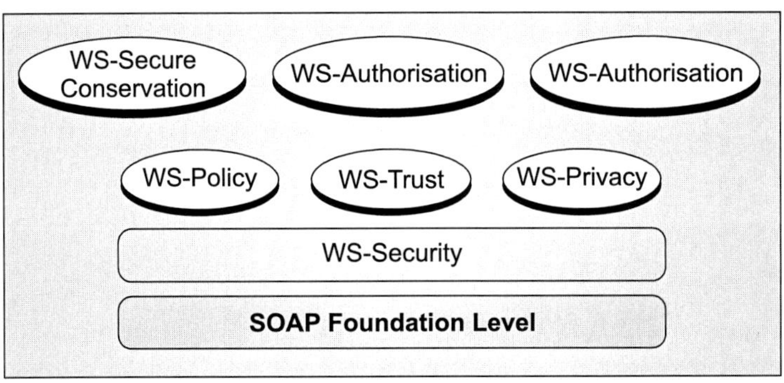

Fig. 11.6 Web services security architecture.[1–5]

11.8.1 WS-Security

WS-Security is a standard released by OASIS. There are mainly three levels of security namely Secure Socket Level (SSL), Message Level Security (MLS) and Transport level security (TLS) (for more information read web services security). It is a set of standards that describe the security mechanisms in a Web services scenario through the extensions of SOAP header to provide message integrity and confidentiality. For securing this is the flexible one which provides models like Public Key Infrastructure, Kerberos and SSL.[2]

Following are the WS-Security requirement as a web service security standard:[2]

(*a*) User name, password, X.509 Certificates, Kerberous- all these are security tokens.

(*b*) Multiple trust domains.

(*c*) Different encryption technologies.

(*d*) Message level security (point-to-point/end- to-end) generally prefer end-to-end.

The WS-Security core specification also defines the application of XML encryption and XML digital signatures to provide end-to-end messaging integrity and confidentiality without the support of the underlying communication protocol.[2]

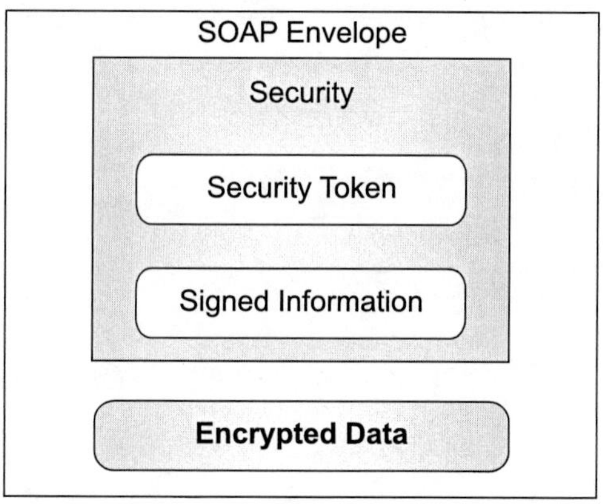

Fig. 11.7 WS-security message structure.[1–5]

The above structure shows the WS-Security message. It consists of the SOAP envelope which specifies routing of a message. The <Security> header contains the security information for receiver. The receiver may be the ultimate receiver or am intermediary. The header consists of a security token which is associated with the message.[2]

In the above structure WS-Security allows two types of security tokens in the message, one is a simple username and password and the other is a binary security tokens which can be of the form Kerberos tokens and X.509 certificates. The message integrity is provided by XML signature which helpful for security tokens to ensure that messages are transmitted without modifications.[2]

In general, WS- Security can addresses *security credential exchange, signatures* and *encryption.*[2]

```
<? Xml version="1.0" encoding="……"?>
<soap:envelope   xmln: s=http://......
            Xmlns: wsse=http://....../ws/.....>
   <soap:Header>
            <wsse:Security>
                    <wsse:userToken>
                         <wsse: Username>Ramesh</wsse: Username>
                         <wsse: pwd>999</wsse:pwd>
                    </wsse:userToken>
            </wsse:Security>
   </soap:Header>
   <soap:body>
   ………..
   </soap:body>
</soap:evvelope>
```

WS- Security header in SOAP message and passing username token.

> **Note:** The requester must possess a secure token to establish a secure message to the web service end point.

11.8.2 WS-Policy

WS-Policy defines a base set of constructs that can be used and extended by other Web services specifications to describe a broad range of service requirements, preferences, and capabilities.[2]

11.8.3 WS-Trust

WS-Trust deals the different aspects of secure token services. It includes:[2]

- How to request a token and
- Issuing of tokens in trusted manner.

Request for token, security tokens and trust relationship management aspects are specified in the WS-Trust.[2]

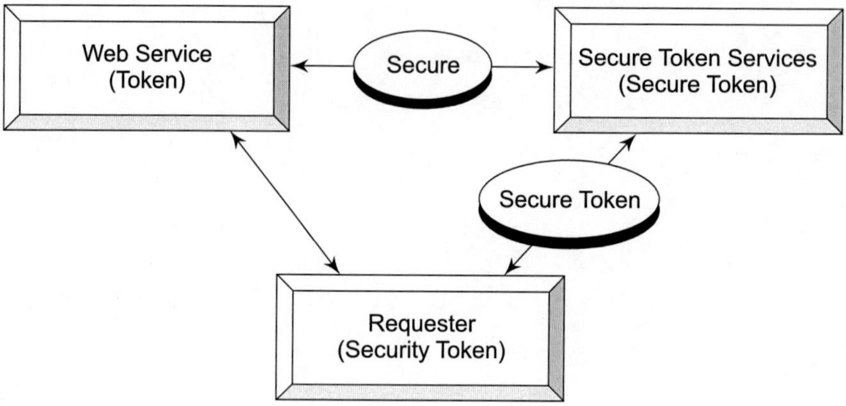

Fig. 11.8 Token services and exchange.[1–5]

11.8.4 WS-Secure Conservation

It deals the sharing security contexts and deriving session tokens from secure context.[2]

11.8.5 WS-Federation

It defines mechanism used to enable identity, attribute, authentication and authorization across different trusted environment.[2]

11.9 DIFFERENT EMERGING SECURITY TECHNOLOGIES IN GRID[1–2]

- XML-based security protocols.
- Message-level security.
- Group authentication and key exchange.
- X.509/PKIX enhancements.
- Multiple policies.
- Identity and credential federation.
- OGSA security.

11.10 STANDARD DIAGRAMS[3–5]

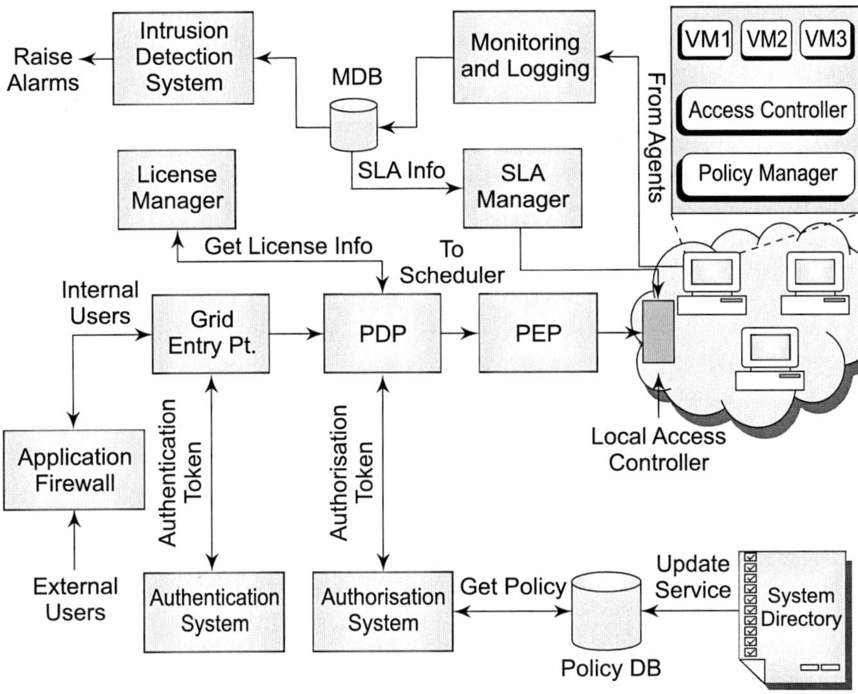

Fig. 11.9 Grid security architecture (by Anirban Chakrabarti).[1–5]

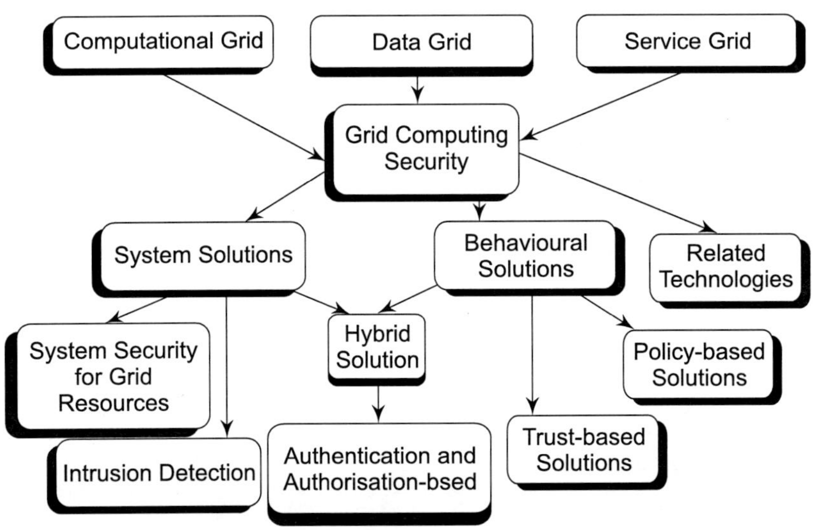

Fig. 11.10 Grid security model diagram (by Erin Cody).[1–5]

SUMMARY

This chapter mainly concentrates on security mechanisms and issues in grid. GSI part is also included in this chapter.

A grid is a system that conforms to three specific categories: it coordinates resources that are not subject to centralized control, it uses standard, open, and general purpose protocols and interfaces, and it deliver nontrivial quality of service. The basic security components within the Globus Toolkit provide the mechanisms for authentication, authorization, and confidentiality of communication between grid computers. A grid is highly complex and dynamic, making its management extremely challenging. Classical Grid computing relies fully on standard operating system security mechanisms to protect users from each other.

KNOWLEDGE TESTING

1. For achieving security in grid area what are the issues you are proposed. Discuss each one of them.
2. Discuss the standard protocols for achieving grid security.
3. Write a short notes on:
   - Grid taxonomy.
   - GSI.
4. Prepare your own procedure for achieving Grid Security Infrastructure. Discuss each one of them in the procedure.
5. What are grid security issues? Write a short note on it.
6. What are the public key and private key in GSI? What are the functionalities implemented by GSI.
7. Write a short note on:
   - Point-to-point security.
   - End-to-end security.

   What is the importance of these two in grid security?
8. Discuss the message structure in WS-Security.
9. What are security standards in grid? Write a short note on each one of them.

REFERENCES

1. Anirban Chakrabarti, *Grid Computing Security*, Springer, 2007.
2. Erin Cody, Raj Sharman, Raghav H. Rao and Shambhu Upadhyaya, *Security in Grid Computing: A Review and Synthesis*, *Decision Support Systems* 44(4): pp. 749–764, 2008.
3. M. Smith, M. Schmidt, N. Fallenbeck, T. Dörnemann, C. Schridde and B. Freisleben *Secure on-demand grid computing*, *Future Generation Computer Systems*, Vol. 25 , Issue 3, pp. 315–325, 2009.
4. Joshy Joseph and C. Fellenstein, *Grid Computing*, Pearson Education, 2005.
5. Ian Foster and Carl Kesselman (Eeds), *The Grid: Blueprint for a New Computing Infrastructure*, Morgan Kaufmann, July 1998.

❑❑❑

12

GLOBUS TOOLKIT

There are two main software's in the grid world namely GLOBUS and CLUSTER implementation. This chapter provides background information on the main components of globus. We discussed here:

- Basic concepts in the Globus, its structure and its architecture.
- A collection of installation packages required for the globus and cluster like software prerequisites etc.
- Steps for installing globus.

The Globus Toolkit is an open source software toolkit to build computational grids and grid-based applications. Globus is one of the core-level middlewares. The Globus Toolkit provides a set of services to enable the secure sharing of resources across corporate, institutional and geographic boundaries. Globus Toolkit has three pyramids of support built on top of a security infrastructure.

- Data Management.
- Resource Management.
- Information Services.
- Security.

12.1 DATA MANAGEMENT

The data management pyramid provides support to transfer files among machines in the grid and for the management of these transfers. It can able to handle terabytes and petabytes of data.

12.2 RESOURCE MANAGEMENT

The resource management pyramid provides support for:

- Resource allocation.
- Submitting jobs: Remotely running executable files and receiving results.
- Managing job status and progress.

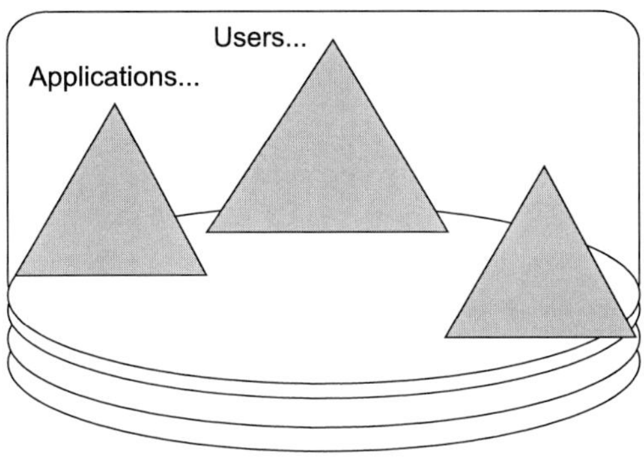

Fig. 12.1 Globus toolkit with three pyramids.[1–4]

Globus Toolkit does not have its own job scheduler to find available resources and automatically send jobs to suitable machines. Instead, it provides the tools and interfaces needed to implement schedulers and is often used with third-party schedulers. It focuses on the uniform and scalable mechanisms for computational resources and remote systems.[4]

12.3 INFORMATION SERVICES

The information services pyramid provides support for collecting information in the grid and for querying this information, based on the Lightweight Directory Access Protocol (LDAP). It discusses what type of protocol algorithms used for implementing grid applications.[1]

- Grid Middleware consists of two levels:
  - User-level Middleware and
  - Core-level Middleware.
- User-level Middleware
  - Examples are Nimrod-G and Gridbus Broker.
  - Provide a easy way to access remote Grid resources (run one of the core-level middlewares).
  - Does not actually execute jobs.
- Core-level middleware
  - Examples are Aneka, Achemi, Unicore etc.

- Shows the complexity of the Grid system, not very easy to use.
- Provides a Grid environment for executing jobs.

12.4 SECURITY

Establishes security policies in the administrative domains and plays a important role in the security objects. Security mainly applied at transport-level.

The Globus Toolkit 4.2.1, there are a few things you should consider. The toolkit contains many subcomponents. There are non-web services implementations of:

- Security (Non-WS Authentication and Authorization).
- File Transfers GridFTP.
- Resource Management (GRAM2).
- Replica Location Service.
- And Information Services (MDS2).

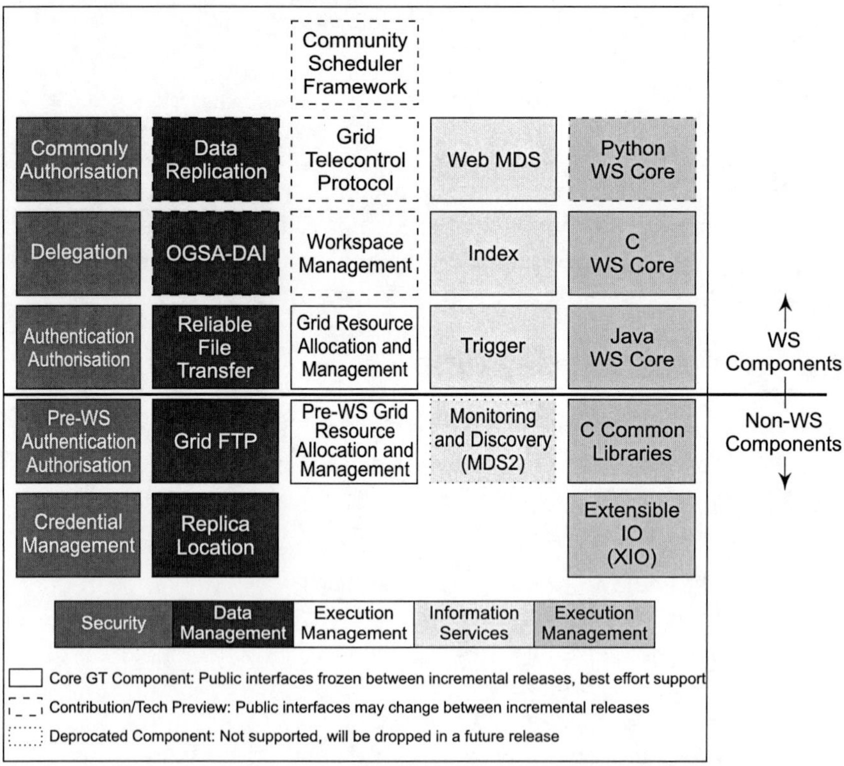

Fig. 12.2 Basic Components of Globus toolkit (GT4).[1–4]

This diagram shows the basic components in the globus which as mainly divided into web service components and Non-web service components. All management and security policies are placed at lower level.[1–2, 5]

12.5 ARCHITECTURE

The Globus [GT4] software concept based on the open standard resource sharing and interoperability in grid computing. The architecture of the GT4 is almost similar to the GT3. The GT4 architecture is divided into three main parts:

(*i*) Core part.

(*ii*) Globus base services.

(*iii*) User-defined services.

Globus toolkit provides a strong, clear and standard- based security model; modular functions providing all of the core grid functions. The data in the globus can be virtualized. Grid software beyond that provided by these suites are being defined and implemented by many organizations and universities.[5]

(*i*) **Core part:** Core part mainly consists of OGSI reference implementation. The recently released version of globus 4.0 provides a complete implementation of OGSI and it has defined interfaces, messages and globus behaviors. Globus core part provides discovery of services, program execution jobs and submission and monitoring information's. This part is base for creating base services.

Security services—which include end-to-end and message level services. It also includes authentication and authorization. Other services like data delivery, replication of data and location etc.. WS- Security specifications are also included here.

System point of view services are system- level services. Network routing services, logging services, administrative services and problem resolver services all are sub parts in user- defined services.

The globus toolkit provides the basis for an open source OGSA implementation and supports API's as well as WSDL interfaces. These services are lie under the bottom of the core architecture. However all these services are lie under hosting environment.[4–5]

(*ii*) **Globus base services:** These are built upon the GT4 core. Data management services, information services and process execution and job submission are the main services that are part in base services:

- Data management services include parallel data transfer, third party control of data transfer, file and reliable transfers. It manages the maximum bandwidth with TCP/IP While the data can be travelled via network.

- Information services are also known as monitoring and discovery services (MDS). Resource discovery, selection of process and optimization all are handled by information services. The other services are modeling data, collecting data, aggregation, queries and security. Some of the information models are Grid service Handler (GSH), Grid service reference (GSR) and registry services.
- Job management services provide a way of submitting and monitoring jobs remotely that is, submitting jobs in the Grid. It follows the interfaces defined in OGSI by using WSDL, which is based on XML. Job management services provide a client-side command called managed-job-globus run that invokes the Master Managed Job Factory Service (MMJFS) to submit a job.[4]

How do you describe the job arrivals in grid with mathematical point of view?

Job arrivals can be described as a point process, which is defined as a mathematical Construct that represents individual events as random points at times {Tn}. The inter arrival time process {In} is a real valued random sequence with and it completely describes the point process.

In = Tn " Tn"1

However, it eliminates the direct correspondence between the absolute time and the index number therefore it only allows rough comparisons with correlations in the point process.

(*iii*) **User defined services:** User defined services are application level services that are created by the users and exploit the OGSI reference implementations. For better improvement in the behavior of the resources and working procedures these services are work with the high- level services. Resource Scripting Language (RSL) can be used for job submissions because it uses the XML Schema.

Grid service container was included in the GT4 software, which forms an abstract notion of a runtime environment. This runtime environment provides capabilities for grid service persistence management, lifecycle management and instance management. J2EE EJB container manages the lifecycle objects. The current GT4.0 can be implemented by J2SE/L2EE web container.[4–5]

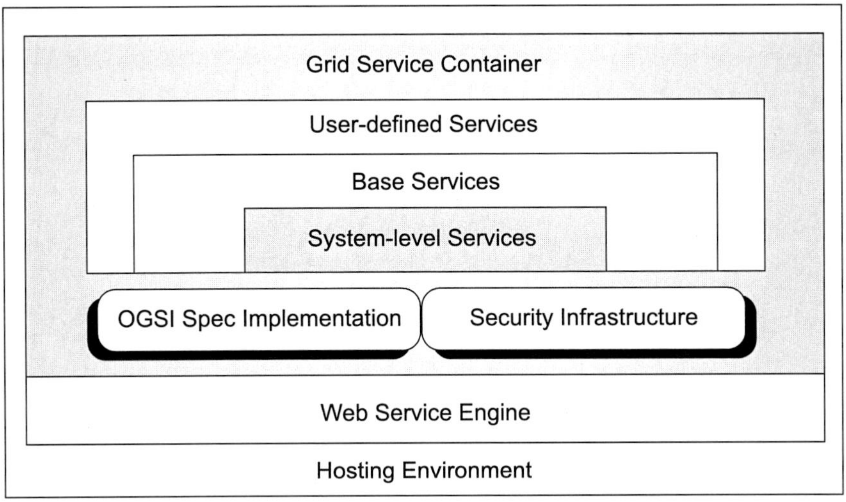

Fig. 12.3 GT4 core architecture.[1–4]

A hosting environment is one in which GT4 runs. It is the server environment, such as an operating system or an application server. Currently, GT4 supports the following types of hosting environments associated with GT4 Service Containers that can be selected during the installation/configuration time:

- Embedded Container.
- Stand-alone Container.
- J2EE Web Container (Servlet).
- J2EE Enterprise JavaBeans Container (EJB).

The layers in the hosting environment are implementation layer, transport/binding layer and interface layer. Implementation layer provides the OGSI specifications and web engine such as Apache AXIS. The AXIS engine is responsible for managing SOAP over HTTP communication. It acts as a SOAP message listener and performs the SOAP request/response serialization and de-serialization, service configuration, and deployment. The layers diagram is shown in next page.

GT4 provides a set of predefined services, which we list briefly here and of course describe in far more detail in online documentation. GT4 provides libraries and tools to assist with the development of custom Web services (the white boxes in the "server" domain) in Java, Python, and C.

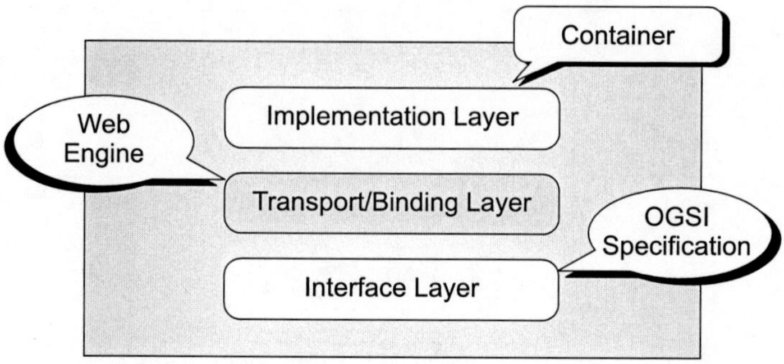

Fig. 12.4 Hosting environment layers.[1–4]

> **Note:** An embedded hosting environment is a hosting environment used mainly on clients or on lightweight servers to allow creation and management of Grid services.[1–4]

12.6 GT4 SOFTWARE PREREQUISITES

12.6.1 Required Software

- Globus Toolkit installer, from Globus Toolkit download page
- Make sure Java is installed: J2SE 1.5.0+ SDK from Sun2, IBM3, HP4, or BEA5 (do not use GCJ6).
- Ant 1.6.2+7.Do not use the Ant distributed with Fedora Core2,or other recent RedHat/Fedora distributions (RHEL3, Scientific Linux 3.0.x, FC3/4).
- C compiler. If gcc8,avoid version 3.2. Versions 3.2.1 and 2.95.x are okay.
- GNU tar9
- GNU sed10
- zlib 1.1.4+11
- GNU Make12
- sudo13 for basic GRAM4 functionality. For a more complete list of prerequisites, see Prerequisites for installing GRAM4.
- Openssl 0.9.7 or later. For linux systems, this includes the -devel version of the package.
- gpt-3.2autotools2004 (shipped with the installers, but required if building standalone GPT bundles/packages).[4]

12.6.2 Optional Software

1. IODBC14 (compile requirement for RLS) For a more complete list of RLS prerequisites, see Prerequisites for RLS.
2. A Relational Database Server (RDBMS) that supports ODBC (we provide instructions for both PostgreSQL and MySQL [olink to appendix]):
   - If you use PostgreSQL, you'll also need psqlODBC (the ODBC driver for postgreSQL).
   - If you use MySQL, you'll also need the MyODBC (Connector/ODBC) packages.
   - MySQL's top level installation directory must be specified. By default these are assumed to be in $GLOBUS_LOCATION.
   - The package is used to interface to the ODBC layer of the RDBMS. The location of iODBC and the odbc.ini file must be specifed before installing the RLS server.
   - Tomcat15 (required by Web MDS, optional for other services)– Make sure to download it directly from the Apache web site.
   - gLite16 Java VOMS parsing libraries - binary available17 (compile requirement for Workspace Service).[4]

12.7 STEPS TO INSTALL GLOBUS

Step1: Create a user named "Globus" (Optional but recommended):[4]

- It is recommended to create a user named "globus" and execute the installation as this user.
- Exception to the above will happen when you have to set up server services.

Step2: Create a location to install Globus:[4]

- Create two directories, one where you want to install GTK and the other to install GPT. They should be owned by user "globus".
- Set up the Globus environment variables: {csh} setenv GLOBUS_LOCATION <globus_install_dir> {bash} export GLOBUS_LOCATION=<globus_install_dir>.
- Set up GPT environment variables: {csh} setenv GPT_LOCATION <gpt_install_dir> {bash} export GPT_LOCATION=<gpt_install_dir>.

Step3: Installing GPT[4]

- What is GPT (Grid Packaging Tool)?
  - GPT is a multi-platform packaging system used to deploy Grid middleware, developed by NCSA.
- GPT was designed to re-implement the deployment requirements of Globus plus shared libraries.
  - Most of Globus is libraries.
  - Globus has deployment requirements for client tools, service daemons, and development/build environments.
  - Globus wants to release individual components separately.
  - Globus wants to add outside software (ie. openssl, openldap) to these deployments.
  - Globus wants to work on multiple platforms.
- GPT requires Perl 5.005 or greater and GNU tar and GNU make.
- In the directory where you downloaded the tarballs, do the following:
  1. tar -xzvf gpt-2.2.9-src.tar.gz
  2. cd gpt-2.2.9.
  3. ./build_gpt.

Step 4: Binary Bundle Installation[4]

- To install the binary bundle on Intel i686 platform, run the following commands:
  - $GPT_LOCATION/sbin/gpt-install globus-all-2.4.0-i686-pc-linux-gnu-bin.tar.gz.
  - {csh} source $GLOBUS_LOCATION/etc/globus-user-env.csh or {sh} $GLOBUS_LOCATION/etc/globus-user-env.sh
  - $GPT_LOCATION/sbin/gpt-postinstall.
  - If you install any sdk bundle, you have to run the following command:
    $GPT_LOCATION/sbin/gpt-build <flavor> -nosrc
  - You have to run the following command for each source bundle you downloaded: $GPT_LOCATION/sbin/gpt-build <bundle> <flavors> \- logdir=<log directory>.
  - You need to source the following file before we finish our install. So that all the required environment and the library paths will be set. To do so, run the following command depending on your shell:
    {csh} source $GLOBUS_LOCATION/etc/globus-user-env.csh
    {sh} $GLOBUS_LOCATION/etc/globus-user-env.sh
  - Lastly, run the following command:
    $GPT_LOCATION/sbin/gpt-postinstall.

Step 5: Obtaining Certifictaes[4]

- Security is at the heart of Globus. As such, you will not be able to test Globus until you get a certificate for yourself.
- Currently, Globus has three different types of certificates:
  - User Certificate.
  - Host Certificate.
  - LDAP Certificate.
- I will describe here how to obtain a Globus Certificate. However, be aware that there are CA, which will involve the configuration step of adding trusted CA into Globus.

Obtaining Globus Certificates[4]

- Make sure you are running as your normal user account.
- Run grid-cert-request.
- grid-cert-request will ask for a password to protect your key, and give you a set of instructions for how to mail your request to the CA.
- Three files will be generated into ~/.globus: usercert_request.pem, userkey.pem and usercert.pem.
- Send the usercert_request.pem to CA for signing.
- When you receive your signed certificate from Globus, place it into ~/.globus directory.

Obtaining HOST Certificate[4]

- Very important: The certificate must be for a machine that has a consistent name in the DNS; it should not run on a machine where a different name could be assigned to it.
- Become root and run the following command:
  - grid-cert-request host -host <your-hostname-here>
- Then, using your regular, user mail agent, send an email to ca@globus.org and copy and paste the contents of the request into it. grid-cert-request will output the location of the request. Please do not include this file as an attachment. Do not send this mail from the root account.
- After receiving signed certificate, move it to /etc/grid-security/ location.

Obtaining LDAP Certificate[4]

- Become root and run the following command:
  - grid-cert-request -service ldap -host <FQDN>
- Then, using your regular, user mail agent, send an email to ca@globus.org and copy and paste the contents of the request into it. grid-cert-request will output the location of the request. Please do not include this file as an attachment.
- When you receive the certificate, save the entire email to
  - /etc/grid-security/ldap/ldapcert.pem and to /etc/grid- security/ ldap/ldapkey.pem.

Step 6: Creating Grid-Map file[4]

- Once you get your user certificate, you must create the grid-mapfile, which must contain the pair subject name as an user account of all user allowed to access your Grid services.
- Run grid-proxy-init to create a user proxy and afterwards run: grid-proxy-info -subject to get your subject name.
- Become root. Create a file named: /etc/grid-security/grid-mapfile and add an entry like this: "/O=Grid/O=Globus/OU=tau.ac.il/ CN=Itzhak Ben-Akiva" benakiva.(User name).

  *When ever some grid job comes from the user who uses this certificate, then that particular job would be running under the mapped user account(benakiva).

Step 7: Configuring your Installation[4]

- Now, you have to become root to run the command to set up GSI.
- Run $GLOBUS_LOCATION/setup/globus/setup-gsi.This will install GSI files into /etc/grid-security.
- If you do not have root on the system run $GLOBUS_LOCATION/ setup/globus.

/setup-gsi -nonroot to install the security information into $GLOBUS_LOCATION/etc instead of /etc/grid-security.The -nonroot option is aimed at client-side installs.

Step 8: Testing your Installation for:[4]

(*i*) **GRAM (Grid Resource Allocation Manager):** GRAM is the module that provides the remote execution and status management of the execution. When a job is submitted by a client, the request is sent to the remote host and handled by the gatekeeper daemon located in the remote host. Then the gatekeeper creates a job manager to start and monitor the job. When the job is finished, the job manager sends the status information back to the client and terminates.[1, 4]

- As your normal user run the following command to create a proxy: grid-proxy-init -debug –verify.
- Start your personal gatekeeper by running:
  - globus-personal-gatekeeper -start

  This will generate a contact string like:

  alzt1.tau.ac.il:39705:/O=Grid/O=Globus/OU=tau.ac.il/CN=benakiva.
- Run globus-job-run <contact> /bin/date. Substitute the contact string by the one generated by globus-personal-gatekeeper.
- Stop the personal gatekeeper and destroy the proxy by running:
  - globus-personal-gatekeeper -killall.
  - grid-proxy-destroy.

(*ii*) **MDS (Monitoring and Discovery Service):** MDS provides access to static and dynamic information of resources. Basically, it contains the following components:

- Grid Resource Information Service (GRIS)
- Grid Index Information Service (GIIS)
- Information Provider
- MDS client
- By default, MDS allows anonymous access, which we will use for the purpose of this test..
- Start MDS by running the command:
  - GLOBUS_LOCATION/sbin/globus-mds start
- Send a test query on a local host by running the command:
  - GLOBUS_LOCATION/bin/grid-info-search -anonymous -L.[1, 4]

(*iii*) **Grid FTP:** Grid FTP provides a secure and reliable data transfer among grid nodes. The word Grid FTP can referred to a protocol, a server, or a set of tools. Grid FTP is a protocol intended to be used in all data transfers on the grid. It is based on FTP, but extends the standard protocol with facilities such as multistreamed transfer, auto-tuning, and Globus based security. This protocol is still in draft level.

- First, create a user proxy:
  - grid-proxy-init.

- Create a file named ~/.gridmap and add an entry with your subject, like:

  "/O=Grid/O=Globus/OU=tau.ac.il/CN=Itzhak Ben-Akiva" your-username
- Start the GridFTP server:
  - $GLOBUS_LOCATION/sbin/in.ftpd -S -p 5678
  - S leaves the daemon in the background
  - p specify the port
- Create a file name /tmp/file1 and run the following command:
  - globus-url-copy -s "`grid-cert-info -subject`" \
    gsiftp://localhost:5678/tmp/file1 file:///tmp/file2
- Check to make sure that /tmp/file2 now exists.

> **Note:** Please see the complete installation in Chapter 13.

Developing service using Globus toolkit (GT4) in Windows Environment:[4]

Perquisites:

Toolkit	:	GT4_WS_Core.4.0.5
Server	:	Apache Ant, ApacheTomcat 5.0
Programming Language	:	Java-jdk1.4 above versions
Script	:	Python Version in windows Os

12.8 INSTALLATION

12.8.1 Preparation: Download GT4, and ANT

Download the WS-core service of GT4

- www.globus.org/toolkit/downloads/4.0.4/#wscore_bin/
- Decompress the compressed file.

Download the Ant version 7

- http://ant.apache.org/bindownload.cgi/
- Decompress the compressed file.

12.8.2 Preparation: Setting up your Environment

Define & set the environment variable

- ANT_HOME

$ export ANT_HOME=$HOME/<ANT_dir>/

- GLOBUS_LOCATION

$ export GLOBUS_LOCATION=$HOME/<WS-CORE_dir>/

- JAVA_HOME

$ export JAVA_HOME=/usr/java/<jdk_dir>

PATH:

$ export PATH=$JAVA_HOME/bin: \

$ANT_HOME/bin: \

$GLOBUS_LOCATION/bin:$PATH

12.8.3 Preparation: Test if it Works

Start the container:

$ globus-start-container –nosec

Watch your screen carefully spot any Error message

Stop the container:

$ globus-stop-container

12.8.4 Preparation: Finally Download the Tutorial

http://gdp.globus.org/gt4-tutorial/

This is a very important step:

- If you don't want to re-write everything from scratch
- Decompress the compressed file.

12.9 OGSA, WSRF AND GT4

- Open Grid Services Architecture (OGSA), developed by The Global Grid Forum.
- aims to define a common, standard, and open architecture for grid-based applications.

- Web Services Resource Framework, a specification developed by OASIS.
- WSRF specifies how we can make our Web Services stateful, along with adding a lot of other cool features.

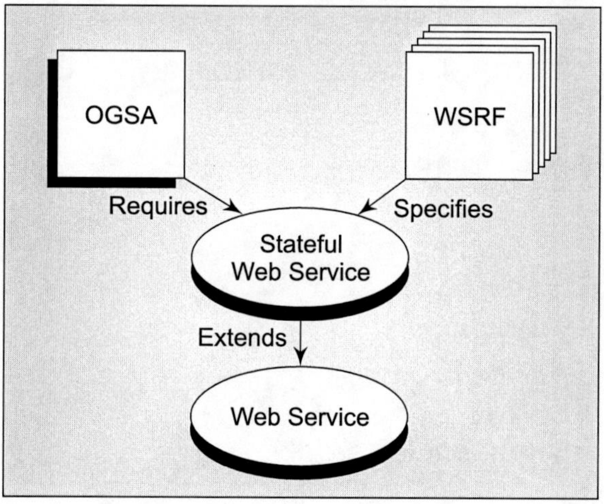

Fig. 12.5 Relationship of OGSA, WSRF and web service.[1–4]

Introduction: How does this relate to GT4?

- GT4, includes quite a ***few high-level services*** that can be used to build Grid applications
- These services, ***meet most*** of the ***abstract requirements*** set forth in OGSA
- GT4 includes a ***complete implementation*** of the WSRF specification.
- GT4 ***isn't*** the ***only WSRF implementation***. Another ***complete implementation*** of the WSRF specification is WSRF.NET.

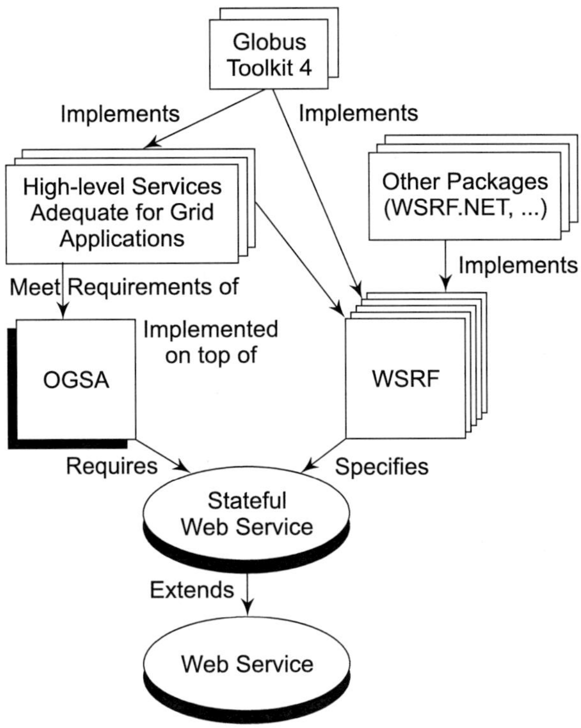

Fig. 12.6 GT4 service model.[1–4]

Introduction: The mandatory layered diagram

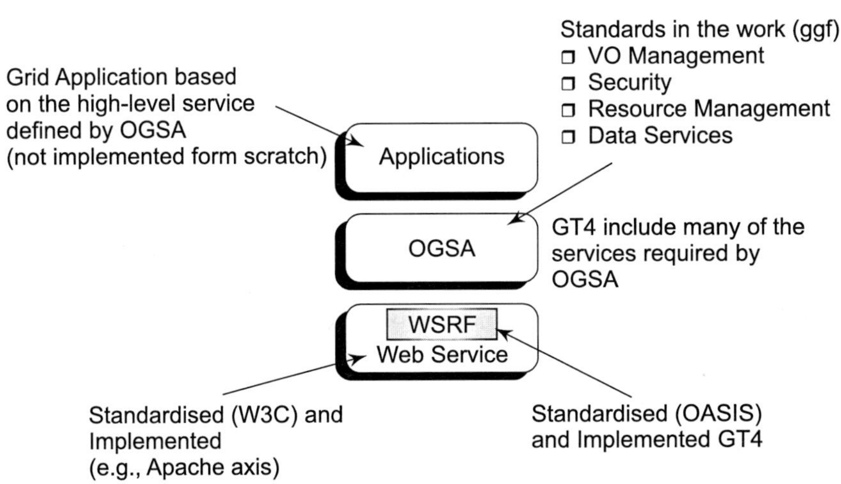

Fig. 12.7 GT4 layered architecture.[1–4]

Tutorial starts: The first web service

- The first web service is an extremely simple ***Math Web Service***, which we'll refer to as ***MathService***.
- It will allow users to perform the following operations:
  - Addition
  - Subtraction
- MathService will have the following ***resource properties*** (**RP**s for short):
  - Value (integer)
  - Last operation performed (string)
- The MathService example
- 5 steps to implement GT4 MathService:
  - **Step1:** Define the Interface in the WSDL.
  - **Step2:** Implement the MathService in java.
  - **Step3:** Configure the deployment (**WSDD & JNDI**).
  - **Step4:** Create the deployement File.
  - **Step5:** The client application.

The ***MathService*** web service

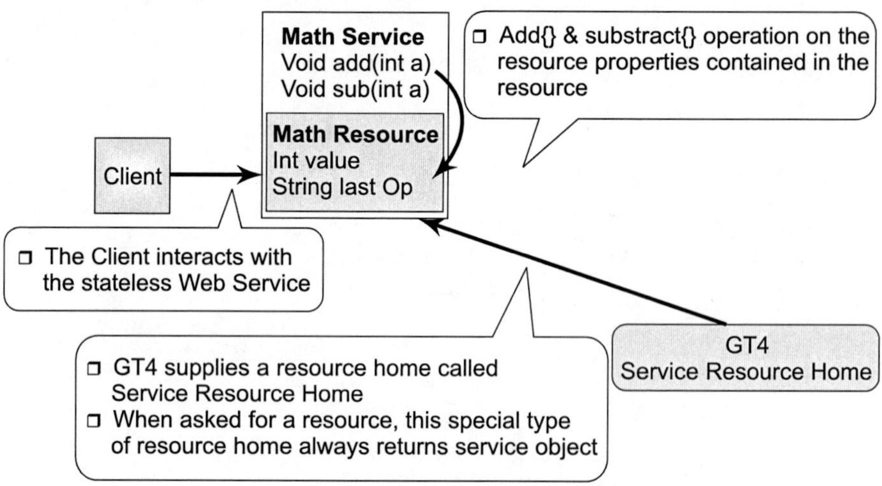

Fig. 12.8 Structure of Math Service.[5]

Step 1: Define the Interface in WSDL

- WSRF and GT4-specific features of WSDL
  - Resource properties
  - The WSDL Preprocessor
  - **No bindings**: Bindings are an essential part of a normal WSDL file. However, we don't have to add them, they are generated automatically by a GT4 tool that is called when we build the service
- Namespace mappings
  - WSDL is that it's *language-neutral*. Because we need to refer to the interface defined in WSDL from some specific language we need to:
    - map **WSDL namespaces** to specific language (Java packages)
    - **$EXAMPLES_DIR/namespace2package.properties**

Step 2: Implementing the Service

- The QNames interface
  - QNames includes a namespace and a *local name*.
  - For example, the QName of the **Value** RP is:
    - **{http://www.globus.org/namespaces/examples/core/MathService_instance}Value**
    - **$EXAMPLES_DIR/org/globus/examples/services/core/first/impl/MathQNames.java**
- The service implementation
  - **$EXAMPLE_DIR/org/globus/examples/services/core/first/impl/MathService.java**

Step 3: Configuring the deployment in WSDD and JNDI

Step 4: Create and deploy a GAR file

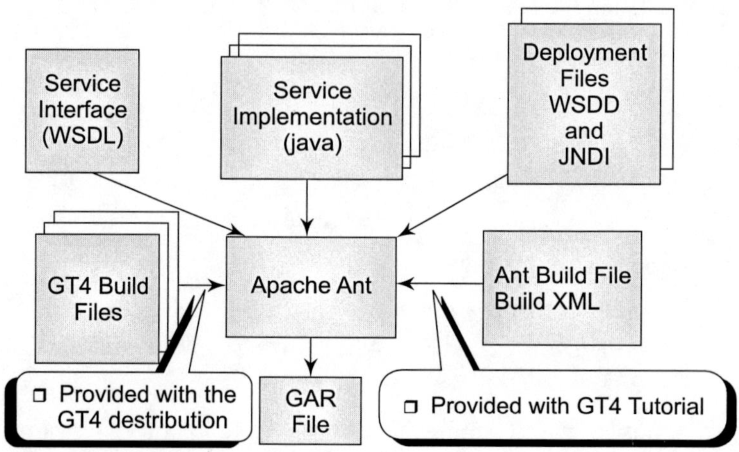

globus-deploy-gar $EXAMPLES_DIR/org globus examples services core first gar
globus-undeploy-gar org. globus examples services core first.

Step 5: Compile and run the Simple Client[4]

(*i*) Set the environment for the client[4]

```
$ source \
$GLOBUS_LOCATION/etc/globus-devel-env.sh
```

(*ii*) Compile the simple client

```
$ javac –classpath \
    ./build/stubs/classes/:$CLASSPATH
org/globus/examples/clients/MathService_instance/Client.java
```

(*iii*) run the simple client

```
$ java \ -classpath \
    ./build/stubs/classes/:$CLASSPATH
org.globus.examples.clients.MathService_instance.Client
http://127.0.0.1:8080/wsrf/services/examples/core/first/MathService
```

Now, Any user program can make use of MathService for counting purposes. More details on MathService may be obtained from *http://gdp.globus.org/gt4-tutorial/.*

SUMMARY

Globus is one of the core-level middleware's. The Globus Toolkit provides a set of services to enable the secure sharing of resources across corporate, institutional and geographic boundaries. The data in the globus can be virtualized. Grid software beyond that provided by these suites are being defined and implemented by many organizations and universities. The first main part in globus,

Core part consists of OGSI reference implementation. This part also concentrates on security services.

Base services Data management services, information services and process execution and job submission are base services in globus.

User defined services are application level services that are created by the users and exploit the OGSI reference implementations.

The globus toolkit provides the basis for an open source OGSA implementation and supports API's as well as WSDL interfaces. These services are lie under the bottom of the core architecture. However all these services are lie under hosting environment.

KNOWLEDGE TESTING

1. Explain the pyramid diagram of a globus toolkit and what are services provided by the globus?
2. Explain the following:
   (*i*) Information services
   (*ii*) Data management services
   (*iii*) Resource management
   (*iv*) Security
3. Draw the core architecture of globus and explain each part of them.
4. How do you describe the job arrivals in grid with mathematical point of view?
5. What is meant by hosting environment? Explain the layers in hosting environment.
6. Write short notes on "steps for installing globus".
7. Write a short note on:
   (*i*) LDAP
   (*ii*) MDS
   (*iii*) GRAM
   (*iv*) gridFTP
8. How do you install the Globus in windows? Write a few steps and explain with an example.

REFERENCES

1. D. G. Feitelson. *Workload Modeling for Computer Systems Performance Evaluation.* Draft Book Version 0.7, 2006. *http://www.cs.huji.ac.il/home/feit/wlmod/.*

2. A. Iosup, C. Dumitrescu, D. Epema, H. Li, and L. Wolters. How are Real Grids Used? The Analysis of Four Grid Traces and its Implications. In proceedings of 7th IEEE/ACM Intl. Conference on Grid Computing (Grid06), 2006.

3. N. H. Kapadia, J. A. B. Fortes, and C. E. Brodley. Predictive Application-Performance Modeling in a Computational Grid Environment. In IEEE International Symposium for High Performance Distributed Computing (HPDC), 1999.

4. *http://gdp.globus.org/gt4-tutorial/.*

5. *http://gdp.globus.org/gt4-tutorial/singlehtml/progtutorial_0.2.1.html#pre_docs .*

❑❑❑

PART V

GRID APPLICATIONS

Part V mainly discusses running globus toolkit on Linux platform with some simple web service.

Chapter 13 will discuss Tools to build applications that exploit Grid infrastructures.

Open Source and open standards Provides Grid development environment where we can develop new OGSA-compliant Web Services, new applications using Java or C/C++. Very implementation details are provided in Chapter 13.

Chapter 14 discuss about cluster implementations. Generally, a cluster is designed to work combined on a particular problem, so that the cost of computation reduces and performance increases. A computer cluster is a small group of computers that work together and seems to be working on a single computer. More details about cluster we'll see on cluster chapter.

Chapter 15 about latest technologies in grid, systems and scheduling parts.

13

GT4 in Linux and Running Sample Web Service

This part will discuss about:

- Tools to build applications that exploit Grid infrastructures.
- Open source and open standards.
- Provides Grid development environment where we can develop new OGSA-compliant Web Services, new applications using Java or C/C++.
- A set of basic grid services we can allow here e.g. Job submission/ management, File Transfer (individual, queued), Database access, Data management (replication, metadata), Monitoring/Indexing system information.

13.1 INSTALLING GLOBUS TOOLKIT 4.0.7

13.1.1 Requirements[5–9]

S.No.	***Tools***	***Version***
1.1	Operating System	Fedora Core X with all utilities supported
1.2	Globus Toolkit	4.0.X all source installer
2.1	Postgresql Database	... (check for in-built or rpm pkg)
2.2	GCC compiler	... (check for in-built or rpm pkg)
2.3	GCC C++ Compiler	... (check for in-built or rpm pkg)
2.4	Tape Archiver (tar)	... (check for in-built or rpm pkg)

Contd...

S.No.	Tools	Version
2.5	Streams Editor (sed)	... (check for in-built or rpm pkg)
2.6	Sudo	... (check for in-built or rpm pkg)
2.7	Zlib Libraries	... (check for in-built or rpm pkg)
2.8	OpenSSL	... (check for in-built or rpm pkg)
2.9	Make Tool	... (check for in-built or rpm pkg)
2.10	Perl XML Parser	... (check for in-built or rpm pkg)
2.11	Xinetd	... (check for in-built or rpm pkg)
3.1	Java	1.4.2 or later
3.2	Apache-ant	1.5.1 or later
3.3	Junit	3.8.1 or later
3.4	Jakarta-tomcat	5.0.27 or later
4.1	Torque(for PBS)	2.0.0 or later
4.2	Or SGE	6 or later

13.2 DETAILS STEPS FOR INSTALLATION ALONG STARING FROM OPERATING SYSTEM SET-UP

13.2.1 Installing Operating System

Install Fedora Core-X(Fedora Core-9) with all utilities supported, Configure system name (e.g.grid2.vitgrid) and then set i.p address (e.g. 192.168.31.2), Continue installation with setting time, date, username, password….[5–9]

13.2.2 Checking for Dependant Softwares

(If any package is not installed then install it using command::rpm -ivh <software_package_name>

.rpm)

(*i*) For Postgresql:(code given below)

```
[root@grid2 ~]# rpm -q postgresql
postgresql-8.3.1-1.fc9.i386
[root@grid2 ~]# /etc/init.d/postgresql restart
Stopping postgresql service: [FAILED]
Starting postgresql service:  [  OK  ]
```

```
[root@grid2 ~]# /sbin/service postgresql status
postmaster (pid 3602 3601 3600 3599 3597 3592) is running...
```

(*ii*) For GCC Compiler (gcc):(code given below)

```
[root@grid2 ~]# rpm -q gcc
gcc-4.3.0-8.i386
```

(*iii*) For GCC C++ Compiler (gcc-c++):(code given below)

```
[root@grid2 ~]# rpm -q gcc-c++
gcc-c++-4.3.0-8.i386
```

(*iv*) For Tape Archiver (tar):(code given below)

```
[root@grid2 ~]# rpm -q tar
tar-1.19-3.fc9.i386
```

(*v*) For Streams Editor (sed):(code given below)

```
[root@grid2 ~]# rpm -q sed
sed-4.1.5-10.fc9.i386
```

(*vi*) For Sudo:(code given below)

```
[root@grid2 ~]# rpm -q sudo
sudo-1.6.9p13-4.fc9.i386
```

(*vii*) For Zlib:(code given below)

```
[root@grid2 ~]# rpm -q zlib
zlib-1.2.3-18.fc9.i386
```

(*viii*) For Openssl:(code given below)

```
[root@grid2 ~]# rpm -q openssl
openssl-0.9.8g-6.fc9.i686
```

(*ix*) For Make Tool: (code given below)

```
[root@grid2 ~]# rpm -q make
make-3.81-12.fc9.i386
```

(*x*) For Perl XML Parser: (Code given below)

```
[root@grid2 ~]#rpm -q perl-XML-Parser
perl-XML-Parser-2.36-3.fc9.i386
```

(*xi*) For Xinetd: (Code given below)

```
[root@grid2 ~]#rpm -q xinetd
xinetd-2.3.14-20.fc9.i386
```

13.3 INSTALLATION OF PREREQUISITES SOFTWARE[5–9]

13.3.1 Installation of Java[5–9]

(*a*) Obtain suitable java package for example jdk1.5.0 from necessary URL,

(*b*) Install JDK by the following steps:

(*i*) Change current working directory to /usr/local & copy source file there

(*ii*) run the command: rpm -q jdk1.5.0.fc9.i386.rpm

(*iii*) set environment variable JAVA_HOME to /etc/profile

[root@grid2 ~]vi /etc/profile

JAVA_HOME=/usr/java/jdk1.5.0

PATH=$JAVA_HOME/bin:$PATH

[root@grid2 ~]. /etc/profile

(*iv*) To check installation,execute the command

[root@grid2 java]# java -version

java version "1.5.0"

Java(TM) 2 Runtime Environment, Standard Edition (build 1.5.0-b64)

Java HotSpot(TM) Server VM (build 1.5.0-b64, mixed mode.

13.3.2 Installation of APACHE ANT[5–9]

(*a*) Obtain suitable java package for example apache-ant-1.6.4-bin.tar from necessary URL

(*b*) Install Apache-ant by the following steps

(*i*) Change current working directory to /usr/local & copy source file there

(*ii*) run the command: tar -xvf apache-ant-1.6.4-bin.tar

(*iii*) set environment variable ANT_HOME to /etc/profile

[root@grid2 ~]vi /etc/profile

ANT_HOME=/usr/local/apache-ant-1.6.4

PATH=$ANT_HOME/bin:$PATH

[root@grid2 ~]. /etc/profile

(iv) To check installation,execute the command

[root@grid2 java]# ant

Buildfile: build.xml does not exist!

Build failed

> **Note:** This step is failed because a build.xml file is missing, but this output means that Apache Ant is working.

13.3.3 Installation of JUNIT-3.8.1[5–9]

(a) Obtain suitable java package for example junit-3.8.1 from necessary URL

(b) Install Junit by the following steps

(i) Change current working directory to /usr/local & copy source file there

(ii) Unzip Junit source file juint3.8.1.zip by executingthe command:

unzip junit3.8.1.zip

(iii) set environment variable JUNIT_HOME to /etc/profile

[root@grid2 ~]vi /etc/profile

JUNIT_HOME=/usr/local/junit3.8.1

PATH=$JUNIT_HOME/bin:$PATH

[root@grid2 ~]. /etc/profile

(iv) To check installation,execute the command

[root@grid2 java]# echo $JUNIT_HOME

/usr/local/junit3.8.1

13.3.4 Installation of JAKARTA-TOMCAT[5–9]

(a) Obtain suitable java package for example jakarta-tomcat-5.0.27.tar.gz from necessary URL

(b) Install Jakarta-Tomcat by the following steps

(i) Change current working directory to /usr/local & copy source file there

(ii) run the command: tar -xzvf jakarta-tomcat-5.0.27.tar.gz

(iii) set environment variable CATALINA_HOME to /etc/profile

[root@grid2 ~]vi /etc/profile

CATALINA_HOME=/usr/local/jakarta-tomcat-5.0.27

PATH=$CATALINA_HOME/bin:$PATH

[root@grid2 ~]. /etc/profile

(*iv*) To check installation,execute the command

[root@grid2 java]# echo $CATALINA_HOME

/usr/local/tomcat-5.0.27

13.4 INSTALLATION OF LOCAL RESOURCE MANAGEMENT SYSTEM (LRMS)[5–9]

Check if LRMS_TYPE is PBS go for PBS Installation otherwise go for SGE Installation.

13.4.1 Installation of PBS[5–9]

(*a*) First Install Scheduler Torque:

(*i*) Obtain suitable Torque for example torque-2.0.0p8.tar.gz from necessary URL

(*ii*) Create a new user by the name torque and set password

[root@grid2 ~]useradd torque

[root@grid2 ~]passwd torque

(*iii*) Change current working directory to /usr/local & copy source file there

(*iv*) run the command: tar -xzvf torque-2.0.0p8.tar.gz

(*v*) Change current working directory to /torque-2.0.0p8 and make another directory and enter into that by execuing the commands

[root@grid2 ~]mkdir head

[root@grid2 ~]cd head

(*vi*) run installation by using the commands

[root@grid2 ~]./configure —disable-gui —set-server-home=/var/spool/PBS –set- default-server=$SERVER

[root@grid2 ~]make

[root@grid2 ~]make install

(*b*) Create PBS node description file

touch /var/spool/PBS/server_priv/nodes

echo “$SERVER np=1” > /var/spool/PBS/server_priv/nodes

(*c*) Configure PBS mom

touch /var/spool/PBS/mom_priv/config

echo "$""logevent 0x0ff" >> /var/spool/PBS/mom_priv/config

echo "$""clienthost $SERVER" >> /var/spool/PBS/mom_priv/config

echo "$""restricted $SERVER" >> /var/spool/PBS/mom_priv/config

(*d*) Configure PBS server

/usr/local/sbin/pbs_server -t create
echo "# Create queues and set their attributes" > $QMGR
echo "create queue workq" >> $QMGR
echo "set queue workq queue_type = Execution" >> $QMGR
echo "set queue workq max_queuable = 50" >> $QMGR
echo "set queue workq enabled = True" >> $QMGR
echo "set queue workq started = True" >> $QMGR
echo "set server scheduling = True" >> $QMGR
echo "set server default_queue = workq" >> $QMGR
echo "set server log_events = 511" >> $QMGR
echo "set server mail_from = adm" >> $QMGR
echo "set server query_other_jobs = True" >> $QMGR
echo "set server resources_default.neednodes = 1" >> $QMGR
echo "set server resources_default.nodect = 1" >> $QMGR
echo "set server resources_default.nodes = 1" >> $QMGR
echo "set server scheduler_iteration = 600" >> $QMGR
echo "set server node_check_rate = 150" >> $QMGR
echo "set server tcp_timeout = 6" >> $QMGR
echo "set server node_pack = False" >> $QMGR
/usr/local/bin/qmgr < $QMGR

(*e*) Enable PBS on startup

cp /usr/local/pbs_startup.sh /etc/init.d/pbs

chkconfig pbs on

(*f*) Testing PBS

/sbin/service pbs stop

/sbin/service pbs start

/sbin/service pbs status

13.4.2 Installation of SGE[5–9]

(*a*) Change current working directory to /usr/local & copy source file there

(*b*) set SGE_ROOT=/usr/local/sge and run the command:

tar -xzvf /usr/local/sge61u5_linux24-i586_targz.tar.gz

(*c*) follow the commands:

mv sge6_1u5 $SGE_ROOT

cd $SGE_ROOT

tar -zxvf sge-6_1u5-bin-linux24-i586.tar.gz

tar -zxvf sge-6_1u5-common.tar.gz

(*d*) creating sge configuration file

echo "# SGE default configuration file" > /usr/local/sge.conf

echo "SGE_ROOT=\"/usr/local/sge\"" >> /usr/local/sge.conf

echo "SGE_QMASTER_PORT=\"5536\"" >> /usr/local/sge.conf

echo "SGE_EXECD_PORT=\"5537\"" >> /usr/local/sge.conf

echo "CELL_NAME=\"default\"" >> /usr/local/sge.conf

echo "ADMIN_USER=\"\"" >> /usr/local/sge.conf

echo "QMASTER_SPOOL_DIR=\"/usr/local/sge/default/spool\"" >> /usr/local/sge.conf

echo "EXECD_SPOOL_DIR=\"/usr/local/sge/default/spool\"" >> /usr/local/sge.conf

echo "GID_RANGE=\"20000-20100\"" >> /usr/local/sge.conf

echo "SPOOLING_METHOD=\"berkeleydb\"" >> /usr/local/sge.conf

echo "DB_SPOOLING_SERVER=\"none\"" >> /usr/local/sge.conf

echo "DB_SPOOLING_DIR=\"/usr/local/sge/default/spool/spooldb\"" >> /usr/local/sge.conf

echo "PAR_EXECD_INST_COUNT=\"20\"" >> /usr/local/sge.conf

echo "ADMIN_HOST_LIST=\"`/bin/hostname`\"" >> /usr/local/sge.conf

echo "SUBMIT_HOST_LIST=\"`/bin/hostname`\"" >> /usr/local/sge.conf

echo "EXEC_HOST_LIST=\"`/bin/hostname`\"" >> /usr/local/sge.conf

```
echo "EXECD_SPOOL_DIR_LOCAL=\"\"" >> /usr/local/sge.conf
echo "HOSTNAME_RESOLVING=\"true\"" >> /usr/local/sge.conf
echo "SHELL_NAME=\"ssh\"" >> /usr/local/sge.conf
echo "COPY_COMMAND=\"scp\"" >> /usr/local/sge.conf
echo "DEFAULT_DOMAIN=\"none\"" >> /usr/local/sge.conf
echo "ADMIN_MAIL=\"none\"" >> /usr/local/sge.conf
echo "ADD_TO_RC=\"false\"" >> /usr/local/sge.conf
echo "SET_FILE_PERMS=\"true\"" >> /usr/local/sge.conf
echo "RESCHEDULE_JOBS=\"wait\"" >> /usr/local/sge.conf
echo "SCHEDD_CONF=\"1\"" >> /usr/local/sge.conf
echo "SHADOW_HOST=\"\"" >> /usr/local/sge.conf
echo "EXEC_HOST_LIST_RM=\"`/bin/hostname`\"" >> /usr/local/sge.conf
echo "REMOVE_RC=\"true\"" >> /usr/local/sge.conf
echo "WINDOWS_SUPPORT=\"false\"" >> /usr/local/sge.conf
echo "WIN_ADMIN_NAME=\"Administrator\"" >> /usr/local/sge.conf
echo "WIN_DOMAIN_ACCESS=\"false\"" >> /usr/local/sge.conf
```

(*e*) Modify the Configuration of Qmaster

```
sgeinstall=./util/install_modules/inst_qmaster.sh
sge_conf="reporting=false"
sge_newconf="reporting=true"
sed "s/$sge_conf/$sge_newconf/g" $sgeinstall > sge_inst_qmaster.sh
echo "Copying sge_inst_qmaster.sh to $sgeinstall"
cp sge_inst_qmaster.sh $sgeinstall
sge_conf="joblog=false"
sge_newconf="joblog=true"
sed "s/$sge_conf/$sge_newconf/g" $sgeinstall > sge_inst_qmaster.sh
cp sge_inst_qmaster.sh $sgeinstall
./inst_sge -m -x -auto /usr/local/sge.conf
```

(*f*) SGE Startup Services Configuration

```
cp default/common/sgemaster /etc/init.d/
cp default/common/sgeexecd  /etc/init.d/
chkconfig sgeexecd on
chkconfig sgemaster on
echo "sge_qmaster     5536/tcp          # Grid Engine Qmaster
Service" >> /etc/services
echo "sge_execd       5537/tcp          # Grid Engine Execution
Service" >>                             /etc/services
service xinetd reload
touch default/common/reporting
source $SGE_ROOT/default/common/settings.sh
qconf -as 'hostname'
qhost
```

13.5 INSTALLING GLOBUS

I. Pre-Installation Task: There are some pre-installation task such as Time settings, Firewall settings[5–9]

(*a*) Time setting: For all machines in a grid environment it is necessary that all nodes must have accurate and synchronized time setting

(*i*) On all machines in grid environment login as root user & edit the file /etc/ntp.conf file

[root@grid2 java]# vi /etc/ntp.conf

make the following two lines uncommented and ensure that all other lines are commented with leading # character

server 127.127.1.0 # local clock

driftfile /var/lib/ntp/drift

(*ii*) To configure ntp server to run on the next boot:

In all nodes login as root user & configure the ntp daemon so that the ntp setting is ensured and runs on the next boot

[root@grid2 java]# chkconfig ntpd on

(*iii*) In all the hosts login as root user and start the ntp server by:

[root@grid2 java]# service ntpd start

(*iv*) login as root user in client nodes and check if time is synchronized with ntp server by the ntpq command, if you get an * before, then your ntp service is properly configured

[root@grid2 java]# ntpq -p

remote	refid	st	t	when	poll	reach	delay	offset	jitter
*LOCAL(0)	.LOCL.	5	1	3	64	377	0.000	0.000	0.001

(*b*) Firewall Setting: If you are in a firewall environment, you must openTCP ports listed below such that you can use the service or components of globus toolkit.

TCP port Number	Application
2811	GridFTP
8080	Globus Container(non-secure mode)
8443	Globus Container(secure mode)

II. Installation of gobus from source package of gt4.0.7-all-source-installer.tar.gz[5–9]

(*a*) Create a user named globus:This non-privileged user will be used to perform administrative tasks such as starting and stopping the globus container, deploying services etc.

[root@grid2 ~]useradd globus

[root@grid2 ~]passwd globus

(*b*) Give the permission to globus as the owner

[root@grid2 ~]chown -R globus.globus /usr/local/globus-4.0.7

[root@grid2 ~]chown -R globus.globus $/home/globus/gt4.0.7-all-source-installer.tar.gz

(*c*) Change login as globus & run the commands:

[globus@grid2~]tar -zxvf gt4.0.7-all-source-installer.tar.gz

(*d*) Check if LRMS_TYPE is PBS set LRMS_ENABLE=—enable-wsgram-pbs & run the command:

[globus@grid2~]./configure —prefix=$GLOBUS_LOCATION —disable-rls $LRMS_ENABLE —enable-i18n –disable-drs

(*e*) Change the directory to /home/globus/gt4.0.7-all-source-installer

(*f*) Run the commands:

[globus@grid2~]make | tee installer.log

[globus@grid2~]make install.

13.6 CONFIGURING GLOBUS

Globus is using a security infrastructure with certificates per user, so users or processes running for this user can be identified using this certificate. A user can generate a certificate for him/her self, but to really use it,the certificate must be signed by someone else, a certificate authority (CA). You can visualize this as a hierarchy of people signing for other people.[5–9]

For demo and easy installation purposes, they offer us a way to avoid the above procedures, but you should definitely consider an official certificate for production systems.[5–9]

13.6.1 Creating a simple CA[5–9]

The globus installation provides a simpleCA option for demo purposes and we will use this.

Normally the following should be generated once per grid.

[globus@grid2~]$GLOBUS_LOCATION/setup/globus/setup-simple-ca

You must answer series of yes or no type questions, which will be default. Except pass phrase, in our case it is "camanager".

The following process generates and stores the CA in

/home/globus/.globus/simpleCA/globus_simple_ca_c7881362_setup-0.17.tar.gz

And the c7881362 is a short identification hash for your certificate.

[globus@grid2~]su –

root # /usr/local/globus/setup/globus_simple_ca_c7881362_setup/setup-gsi -default

The next step is to generate and sign a certificate for your host machine.

13.6.2 Generating a Host Certificate

The name of our host "grid4" is used to request a certificate for it. Check your hostname and do the same.[5–9]

root # echo $HOSTNAME

grid2.vitgrid

grid-cert-request -host 'grid2.vitgrid'

The above command would generate three files in the "/etc/grid-security/" location namely "hostkey" - A private key for your host, "hostcert_request.pem" - The certificate request for your host and "hostcert"- The signed certificate for your host.

Before signing the certificate the size of hostcert file will be zero,since it's just a certificate request. Sign the hostcert_request.pem file using the Simple CA which was generated in the previous section.

[globus@grid2~] cd /etc/grid-security/

[globus@grid2~]grid-ca-sign -in hostcert_request.pem -out hostsigned.pem

Enter password for the CA key:

The new signed certificate is at: /home/globus/.globus/simpleCA//newcerts/ 01.pem

ERROR: Cannot create the requested output certificate file

hostsigned.pem

Now overwrite the empty "hostcert" file with the signed host certificate request.

[globus@grid2~] su -

root # cd /etc/grid-security/

cp /home/globus/.globus/simpleCA//newcerts/01.pem hostcert.pem

The signed certificate will be placed some where else, move the signed file to /etc/grid-security folder and change the file permission as owned by root and read-only for others.

The host certificate is now fully ready.

13.6.3 Generating User Certificate

Now we have "globus" user acting as a certificate authority, a root user with the host certificate, and the next step is to generate the user certificate.[5–9]

Let us say the user name is "logicacmg" and was created already. Now login as "logicacmg" and request for a user certificate.[5–9]

The following command will generate three files in "/home/logicacmg/ .globus/" location, they are "userkey.pem" ,"usercert_request.pem" and "usercert.pem".The procedure is same like generating the host certificate.[5–9]

[logicacmg@grid2~] grid-cert-request

The "userkey" is private for the user, the "usercert_request.pem" will be sent to the CA to sign. After signing, the signed host certificated should be overwritten with usercert.pem file.[5–9]

This signed certificate will be the public certificate for the logicacmg user.

[logicacmg@grid2~] pwd

/home/logicacmg/.globus

$ ll

total 8

-rw-r—r— 1 logicacmg logicacmg 0 Oct 22 17:18 usercert.pem

-rw-r—r— 1 logicacmg logicacmg 1412 Oct 22 17:18 usercert_request.pem

-r——— 1 logicacmg logicacmg 951 Oct 22 17:18 userkey.pem

Because of user permissions the globus user has to be in this "/home/logicacmg/.globus/" folder to sign the usercert_request. Again, like with signing the host certificate, there will be an error but we will copy the resulting file later ourselves. Enter the passphrase for the CA to sign the certificate.[5–9]

[logicacmg@grid2~] su globus

[globus@grid2~] Password:

$ pwd

/home/logicacmg/.globus

$ grid-ca-sign -in usercert_request.pem -out signed.pem

Enter password for the CA key:

The new signed certificate is at:

/home/globus/.globus/simpleCA//newcerts/02.pem

ERROR: Cannot create the requested output certificate file

signed.pem

Instead manually copy and rename the new signed certificate at

/home/globus/.globus/simpleCA//newcerts/02.pem

Now the certificate is signed and placed in the 02.pem file. This file needs to be copied to the /home/logicacmg/.globus/usercert.pem file, but this cannot done directly by the globus or logicacmg user. So the root user is used for this. Note that you have to enter this on one single line and it will overwrite an existing empty file.[5–9]

root cp

/home/globus/.globus/simpleCA//newcerts/02.pem

/home/logicacmg/.globus/usercert.pem

This way, the permissions and ownership of the file stays the same, and no chmod or chown has to be changed.

This results in the "/home/logicacmg/.globus/" folder containing:

[logicacmg@grid2~] $ ll

total 12

-rw-r—r— 1 logicacmg logicacmg 2738 Oct 28 10:09 usercert.pem

-rw-r—r— 1 logicacmg logicacmg 1412 Oct 22 17:18 usercert_request.pem

-r———— 1 logicacmg logicacmg 951 Oct 22 17:18 userkey.pem

You are now finished creating signed certificates.

Test your user certificate

To verify that you did the right thing, you can verify your certificate with your key with your CA.

[logicacmg@grid2~] $ pwd

/home/logicacmg/.globus

$ grid-proxy-init -debug -verify

User Cert File: /home/logicacmg/.globus/usercert.pem

User Key File: /home/logicacmg/.globus/userkey.pem

Trusted CA Cert Dir: /etc/grid-security/certificates

Output File: /tmp/x509up_u500

Your identity: /O=Grid/OU=GlobusTest/OU=simpleCA-

localhost.localdomain/OU=localdomain/CN=logicacmg

Enter GRID pass phrase for this identity:

Creating proxy ....++++++++++++

....................................++++++++++++

```
Done
Proxy Verify OK
Your proxy is valid until: Thu Oct 28 22:17:03 2004
```

13.6.4 Run Permission Script[5–9]

This script will change permissions on globus executables.

```
root    # $GLOBUS_LOCATION/bin/setperms.sh
```

13.6.5 Connect Users to Certificates[5–9]

The root user now has to edit a file and add all users, in our case only the "logicacmg" user with its certificate and username. But first, let's see what should be entered in that file later.

```
[logicacmg@grid2~] $ whoami
        logicacmg
        $ grid-cert-info -subject
        /O=Grid/OU=GlobusTest/OU=simpleCA-
localhost.localdomain/OU=localdomain/CN=logicacmg
```

Root can edit the file and add this certificate and username on a single (!) line.

```
root    # vi /etc/grid-security/grid-mapfile
```

Open the grid-mapfile with root user, and place the user certificate subject along with the user name. The user certificate subject should be quoted.

```
"/O=Grid/OU=GlobusTest/OU=simpleCA-
localhost.localdomain/OU=localdomain/CN=logicacmg"
        logicacmg
```

The system is now ready to be started!

13.6.6 Start Environment[5–9]

As we did in the first chapter we have to start the database and the globus container if they are not already started.

```
root    # /etc/init.d/postgresql start
        ...
globus  $ cd $GLOBUS_LOCATION
  $ globus-start-container
        ...
```

13.7 BUILD A GRID APPLICATION

13.7.1 Project Introduction

To build this example, several tasks need to be done of which the first one is the creation of a folder structure and some files. You can find these files in the appendix. All are related to the project folder located in the path[1–2]

"/home/logicacmg/dev/HelloProject/".

build.properties

build.xml

interface-source/hello/HelloWorld.java

server-source/hello/HelloWorldImpl.java

wsdd-source/server-deploy.wsdd

client-source/helloc/HelloWorldClient.java

We will work with these files in the rest of this chapter.

13.7.1.1 *Ant script*

The Apache Ant tool is used for building our project. We created two build files for our project, a property file and a script-like file. These are the build.properties and build.xml files you can find in the appendix.[1–2]

Create these two files now, see appendix.

13.7.2 Interface Template

An interface template is written with only one method, this is used to generate the grid service files on later stages by using the ant scripts.[1–2]

Create the "interface-source/hello/HelloWorld.java" file, see appendix.

13.7.2.1 *Server implementation*

An interface template created in the previous section can be seen as a agreement between server and client implementations. Our Ant build script will use this template to generate a new java interface class, named.[1–2]

HelloWorldPortType.java. this is the stub and we have to import and implement this class in our server implementation that does the work for our Grid service.[1–2]

Create the "server-source/hello/HelloWorldImpl.java" server implementation, see appendix.

The HelloWorldImpl class extends a generic grid service GridServiceImpl and implements our generated stub[1–2]

interface HelloWorldPortType.

13.7.3 First Build Steps

Now we are ready to run our first step in building the example. The first step is creating a file structure besides the structure we created ourself.[1–2]

```
logicacmg    $ cd
             $ cd dev/HelloWorld/
             $ ant step0
```

Then we generate the grid webservice (gwsdl) file.

```
logicacmg    $ ant step1
```

The gwsdl is generated using Java2WSDL, an axis tool. The resulting file is not a normal wsdl file, but it is decorated with information specifically for Grid purposes. You might want to edit the gwsdl file manually.[1–2]

The next step generates the stub and skeleton classes using the GSDL2Java tool.[1–2]

```
logicacmg    $ ant step2
```

13.8 BUILDING A GRID ARCHIVE

"Till now, we have written all the Java code our Grid Service needs. We Java [1–2]

(*i*) A service interface.

(*ii*) A WSDL file.

(*iii*) A bunch of stub files.

(*iv*) An implementation of the service.

Now, we somehow have to put all these pieces together, and make them available through a Grid Services enabled web server! This step is called the deployment of the Grid Service.[1–2]

The most important element of deployment is the deployment descriptor. That file contains information about publishing the service on the grid, for example, it contains the URL to access the service.[1–2]

Create the "wsdd-source/server-deploy.wsdd" file, see appendix.

Build the gar file.

```
logicacmg    $ ant step2
```

The Grid archive (gar) file is a kind of jar file containing the following files;[1–2]

File: hellogrid.gar (contents might have a different name)

File: hello-stub.jar (contents might have a different name)

File: hello.jar (contents might have a different name)

File: hello-client.jar (contents might have a different name)

13.8.1 Deployment of the Grid Archive

After the development and build steps, the gar can be deployed. Now, login as the globus user, go to the[1–2]

/usr/local/globus/ folder and enter;

```
globus    $ cd /usr/local/globus
          $ chmod o+w gars
```

Then the logicacmg user is able to copy the file to the globus folder.

```
logicacmg    $ cp lib/hellogrid.gar /usr/local/globus/gars
```

And now it is possible to deploy the gar file using the globus user.

```
globus    $ cd $GLOBUS_LOCATION
          $ ant deploy -Dgar.name=/usr/local/globus/gars/hellogrid.gar
```

Note that globus is using different Ant build scripts than the one we where using earlier.[1–2]

The globus container needs to be restarted when ever some new service deployment is made, then only the deployed service will be visible to use. Then container can stop using CTRL+C and start using command which is mentioned already.[1–2]

Our Grid service is now deployed and running!

13.8.2 Build and Run the Grid Client

The next step is to build the Grid client software and run it.[1–2]

Create the "client-source/helloc/HelloWorldClient.java" file, see appendix.

This client uses generated classes to find and use the Grid service. Build the client;[1–2]

```
logicacmg    $ ant step3
```

Now you might want to change the "build.xml" file. It contains the URL of the Grid service.

<arg

value="http://127.0.0.1:8080/ogsa/services/hello/HelloWorldService"/>

And then run the client.

logicacmg $ ant run.client

Congratulations!

13.8.3 Grid network Setup

This chapter contains a short description about our "minigrid" Grid network. It needs some verification.[1–2]

13.8.3.1 *Infrastructure*

Servers: The Grid network contains three servers running Globus and one server running file services and a Tomcat web server. Also some laptop clients can be connected to this grid to use Grid services.[1–2]

Name	*IP*	*Description*
Grid 1	192.168.31.1	The NFS file server, CA manager and Tomcat web-container
Grid 2	192.168.31.2	Globus framework + grid services
Grid 3	192.168.31.3	Globus framework + grid services
Grid 4	192.168.31.4	Globus framework + grid services

The grid1 server can be connected to the LogicaCMG intranet using its second network adapter and a dynamic.[1–2]

IP using DHCP.[1–2]

We use the name "guest" for the laptop that can be connected to this grid network.[1–2]

13.8.4 Users and Groups[1–2]

Machine	userID	groupID	Password	Activities
grid1,grid2,grid3	Root	root		Super user needs
grid2,grid3	globus	globus	globus	Globus Toolkit environment
grid2,grid3	logicacmg	logicacmg	logicacmg	End-user environment

13.8.5 Fileserver Setup[1–2]

To make it easier for repeated globus installations we created a shared NFS folder called '/mnt/shared/installs/' on grid1. Read 'http://nfs.sourceforge.net/nfs-howto/intro.html' for more information to create a NFS share.

At grid1, server-side, there are three configuration files used for NFS. These are /etc/exports, /etc/hosts.allow

and /etc/hosts.deny. Then the service needs to be started, use the start-nfs-daemons script

At client side you create a folder and mount the shared NFS folder to it.

```
root    # mkdir /mnt/grid1
        # mount 192.168.0.1:/mnt/shared/ /mnt/grid1
```

In case you would like to start this mount automatically at a boot, add the following line to the /etc/fstab.

```
'10.16.0.1:/mnt/shared /mnt/grid1      nfs    ro    0 0'
```

```
rpc.portmap, rpc.mountd, rpc.nfsd, rpc.statd, rpc.lockd, rpc.rquotad
exportfs -ra
```

13.9 APPLICATION INTERFACE (HELLOWORLD.JAVA)[3–4]

```
// HelloWorld.java
// Interface used for generating
package hello;
public interface HelloWorld {
public String sayHello(String name);
}
```

13.9.1 Application Server (HelloWorldImpl.java)[3–4]

```
// HelloWorldImpl.java
package hello;
import hello.HelloWorld.HelloWorldPortType;
import java.rmi.RemoteException;
import org.globus.ogsa.impl.ogsi.GridServiceImpl;
public class HelloWorldImpl extends   GridServiceImpl
implements HelloWorldPortType {
   private int n; // to demo a state
   // Constructor
   public HelloWorldImpl() {
      super("a HelloWorld service");
   }
   // Interface implementation
   public String sayHello(String name) throws RemoteException {
      n++;
      return "Hello "+name+"! (for the "+n+" time)";
   }
}
```

13.9.2 Application Client (HelloWorldClient.java)[3–4]

```
// HelloWorldClient.java
package helloc;
import hello.HelloWorld.HelloWorldPortType;
import hello.HelloWorld.HelloWorldServiceGridLocator;
import java.net.URL;
public class HelloWorldClient {
   // Static
public static void main(String[] args) {
```

```
//
try {
   // Use command line arg
   URL GSH = new java.net.URL(args[0]);
   String name="Your Highness"; // args[1];
   // Get a reference to the Service instance
   HelloWorldServiceGridLocator helloworldLocator =
     new HelloWorldServiceGridLocator();
   HelloWorldPortType helloworld =
     helloworldLocator.getHelloWorldService(GSH);
   // Call remote method
   String result = helloworld.sayHello(name);
   System.out.println (result);
} catch (Exception e) {
   System.out.println("Exception:\n");
   e.printStackTrace();
   }
} // main
}
```

13.9.3 Application Webservice (server-deploy.wsdd)[3–4]

```
<?xml version="1.0"?>
<deployment name="defaultServerConfig" xmlns="http://xml.apache.org/
axis/wsdd/"
   xmlns:java="http://xml.apache.org/axis/wsdd/providers/java">
<!—
   service name=xxx
   This is where you define the remotely accessible name for your
   service. Your service factory URL will have the form of
```

```
    [hosting environment URL]/xxx, where hosting environment
    URL typically is http://[host]:[port]/ogsa/services
...>
      <service name="hello/HelloWorldService" provider="Handler"
      style="wrapped">
      <parameter name="name"
      value="HelloWorldService"/>
      <parameter name="className"
      value="hello.HelloWorld.HelloWorldPortType"/>
      <parameter name="baseClassName"
      value="hello.HelloWorldImpl"/>
      <parameter name="schemaPath"
      value="schema/hello/HelloWorld/HelloWorldService.wsdl"/>
      <!— Start common parameters —>
      <parameter name="allowedMethods" value="*"/>
      <parameter name="persistent" value="true"/>
      <parameter name="handlerClass"
      value="org.globus.ogsa.handlers.RPCURIProvider"/>
    </service>
</deployment>
```

13.10 ANT PROPERTIES (BUILD.PROPERTIES)[1–4]

```
// — build.properties
// — A build properties file for ant, used for globus service
// — Some settings are strange, but needed...
// PROJECT SOURCE FOLDERS
// these contain server and client packages and sources
project.server=./server-source
project.client=./client-source
```

```
project.interface=./interface-source/${package}
project.wsdd=./wsdd-source
// GENERIC SETTINGS FOLDERS
// service/
// service/src/
// service/src/interface/hellogrid/
// service/src/implementation/
// service/build/
// service/build/interface
// service/build/implementation
// lib/
// etc/
service.dir=./service
service.src.dir=${service.dir}/src
service.src.interface.dir=${service.src.dir}/interface/${package}
service.src.implementation.dir=${service.src.dir}/implementation
service.build.dir=${service.dir}/build
service.build.interface.dir=${service.build.dir}/interface
service.build.implementation.dir=${service.build.dir}/implementation
lib.dir=./lib
etc.dir=./etc
// SETTINGS
ogsa.root=/usr/local/globus/
java.interface=true
// CUSTOM PROJECT SETTINGS
// interface.name=Java class containing the interface definition
// package=The package containing interface.name
// services.namespace=Use the same as package, HelloWoldPortType is produced in
```

```
there
package=hello
interface.name=HelloWorld
services.namespace=hello
// amk:added
service.name=Hello
// SETTINGS
// /usr/local/globus/schema
// /usr/local/globus/build-services.xml
// /usr/local/globus/build-packages.xml
schema.origin=${ogsa.root}/schema
build.services=${ogsa.root}/build-services.xml
build.packages=${ogsa.root}/build-packages.xml
mapping.file=namespace2package.mappings
src.dir=${service.src.interface.dir}
build.lib=${lib.dir}
build.dest=${service.build.interface.dir}
schema.dest=./schema
// here the .java files relative to the schema dest are planned:
stubs.dest=./stubs
//here the compiled stubs will come
service.build.stubs.dir=${service.build.dir}/stubs
// CUSTOM PROJECT SETTING
// name of the grid archive file
gar.filename=hellogrid
// CUSTOM PROJECT SETTING
// locations of the grid client
client.dir=./client
client.mainclass=helloc/HelloWorldClient
```

```
client.src.dir=${client.dir}/src
client.build.dir=${client.dir}/build
client.lib.dir=${client.dir}/lib
```

13.10.1 Ant build File (build.xml)[1–4]

```
<?xml version="1.0"?>
<!— build.xml file for ant —>
<project name="HelloWorldGridService" default="all" basedir=".">
<property file="build.properties"/>
<property file="${ogsa.root}/ogsa.properties"/>
<path id="classpath">
<pathelement location="${java.home}/../lib/tools.jar"/>
<pathelement location="./"/>
<fileset dir="${lib.dir}">
<include name="*.jar"/>
</fileset>
<fileset dir="${ogsa.root}/lib">
<!— BORJA
The following line should fix the "why don't my stubs get generated??"
problem
when you try to recompile a service that is already deployed —>
<include name="*.jar"/>
<exclude name="${interface.name}-stub.jar"/>
</fileset>
</path>
<target name="clean" description="cleans everything except srcs">
<delete dir="${service.build.dir}"/>
<delete dir="${client.build.dir}"/>
<delete dir="${schema.dest}"/>
   <delete dir="${lib.dir}"/>
```

```
<delete dir="${service.dir}"/>
<delete dir="${client.dir}"/>
<delete dir="./tmp"/>
</target>
<target name="prepare" description="creates the necessary directories and files">
<echo message="package: ${package}"/>
<echo message="interface.name: ${interface.name}"/>
<echo message="service.name: ${service.name}"/>
<!—
<echo message="*** The following dirs must already be there: ***"/>
<echo message="${service.dir}"/>
<echo message="${client.dir}"/>
<echo message="${src.dir} (containing the interface)"/>
<echo message="${service.src.dir} (containing the service implementation)"/>
<echo message="${client.src.dir}"/>
...>
<echo message="Copying interface source to ${service.src.interface.dir}"/>
<mkdir dir="${service.src.interface.dir}"/>
<copy toDir="${service.src.interface.dir}">
<fileset dir="${project.interface}"/>
</copy>
<echo message="Copying server source to ${service.src.implementation.dir}"/>
<mkdir dir="${service.src.implementation.dir}"/>
<copy toDir="${service.src.implementation.dir}">
<fileset dir="${project.server}"/>
</copy>
```

```
<echo message=”Copying client source to ${client.src.dir}”/>
<mkdir dir=”${client.src.dir}”/>
<copy toDir=”${client.src.dir}”>
<fileset dir=”${project.client}”/>
</copy>
<mkdir dir=”${lib.dir}”/>
<mkdir dir=”${service.build.dir}”/>
<mkdir dir=”${service.build.interface.dir}”/>
<mkdir dir=”${service.build.stubs.dir}”/>
<mkdir dir=”${service.build.implementation.dir}”/>
<!— client stuff —>
<mkdir dir=”${client.build.dir}”/>
<mkdir dir=”${client.lib.dir}”/>
<!— SEBASTIEN
Create build tree and copy all OGSA/GT3 schema files over so that they can be accessed from our GWSDL files.
Explicitly exclude the schema matching the service being built, so that an old version is not copied over.
...>
<copy toDir=”${schema.dest}”>
<fileset dir=”${schema.origin}”>
<exclude name=”**/${service.name}/**”/>
</fileset>
</copy>
</target>
<!— shortcuts !! —>
<target name=”step0" depends=”clean,prepare” description=”shortcut for clear and
prepare”/>
```

```
<target name="step1" depends="generateWSDLfromJava" description="shortcut for task
'generateWSDLfromJava'"/>
<target name="step2" depends="gar" description="shortcut for task 'gar'"/>
<target name="step3" depends="compile.client" description="shortcut for task
'compile.client'"/>
<target name="generateWSDLfromJava" description="provides the service interface
WSDL file">
<echo message="Using ${interface.name}.java from ${src.dir}"/>
<property name="schema.file" value="${interface.name}Service.wsdl"/>
<ant antfile="${build.services}" target="generateWSDL">
<property name="interface" value="${interface.name}.java"/>
<property name="interface.package" value="${package}"/>
<!—<property name="interface.dir" value="${src.dir}/${package}"/>...>
<property name="interface.dir" value="${src.dir}"/>
<property name="generated.dir" value="${package}"/>
</ant>
</target>
<!— Generate, compile and jar stubs. —>
<target name="generateStubs">
<echo message="generateStubs. Destination relative to schema dir."/>
<ant antfile="${build.services}"
target="generateStubs">
<property name="schema.file.dir" value="${package}/${interface.name}"/>
<property name="schema.file" value="${interface.name}Service.wsdl"/>
```

```
<reference refid="classpath"/>
</ant>
</target>
  <target name="compileStubs" depends="generateStubs">
<javac srcdir="${schema.dest}/${stubs.dest}"
destdir="${service.build.stubs.dir}"
debug="${debug}"
deprecation="${deprecation}"
classpathref="classpath">
</javac>
<jar jarfile="${lib.dir}/${interface.name}-stub.jar"
basedir="${service.build.stubs.dir}" />
</target>
<!—
Compile and jar service.
...>
<target name="compileService" depends="compileStubs">
<echo message="Compile the service itself,
srcdir=${service.src.implementation.dir}                    to
${service.build.implementation.dir}" />
<javac srcdir="${service.src.implementation.dir}"
destdir="${service.build.implementation.dir}"
debug="${debug}"
deprecation="${deprecation}"
classpathref="classpath">
</javac>
<jar jarfile="${lib.dir}/${interface.name}.jar"
basedir="${service.build.implementation.dir}" />
</target>
```

```
<!— Gar stubs and service compileStubs,compileService—>
<target name="gar" depends="compileStubs,compileService">
<copy toDir="${service.dir}">
<fileset dir="${project.wsdd}">
</fileset>
</copy>
<!— IMPORTANT: make gar.name is an absolute path —>
<ant antfile="${build.packages}" target="makeGar">
<property name="gar.name" value="${lib.dir}/${gar.filename}.gar"/>
<property name="garlib.dir" value="${lib.dir}"/>
<property name="garserverdeployment.file" value="${service.dir}/
server-
deploy.wsdd"/>
<property name="garschema.origin" value="${schema.dest}/
${package}"/>
<property name="garschema.path" value="${package}"/>
<property name="build.lib" value="${lib.dir}"/>
</ant>
</target>
<!— CLIENT —>
<path id="client.classpath">
<pathelement location="${java.home}/../lib/tools.jar"/>
<pathelement location="./"/>
<fileset dir="${lib.dir}">
<include name="*.jar"/>
</fileset>
<fileset dir="${ogsa.root}/lib">
<include name="*.jar"/>
<!— <exclude name="${interface.name}-stub.jar"/> —>
```

```
</fileset>
</path>
<target name="compile.client" description="compiles the (test) client">
<javac srcdir="${client.src.dir}"
destdir="${client.build.dir}"
debug="${debug}"
deprecation="${deprecation}"
classpathref="client.classpath">
</javac>
<copy toDir="${client.build.dir}">
<fileset dir="${client.src.dir}">
<include name="**/*.properties"/>
</fileset>
</copy>
<jar jarfile="${lib.dir}/${interface.name}-client.jar"
basedir="${client.build.dir}"/>
</target>
<target name="run.client" description="runs the (test) client">
<java classname="${client.mainclass}" classpathref="client.classpath"
fork="yes">
<!— <jvmarg value="-Dlog4j.configuration=t.t"/> —>
<arg value="http://127.0.0.1:8080/ogsa/services/hello/HelloWorldService"/
>
</java>
</target>
<target name="all" depends="step0,step1,step2,step3" description="does
it all">
<echo message="*** complete HelloWorld project ***"/>
</target>
</project>
```

SUMMARY

GTK4.0.1 is very complex software unless understood carefully from the basics of every step. They are many pre-requested software that are to be installed very carefully by setting there paths according to the gtk4.0.1 requirements. Some of the pre-requested software are:

(*i*) Apache Ant.

(*ii*) postgre sql.

(*iii*) jakarta tomcat.

(*iv*) junit.

(*v*) xineted.

any error in setting the path of these software will lead to errors during the installation of the gtk4.

Hence it is suggested to have a perfect basic knowledge of the gtk4 installation.

Suggestions:

To verify the Globus installation it is assumed that a Globus grid infrastructure has been installed and configured. You can perform the following tests to verify your Globus pre-WS installation, and to ensure that it will work with GridWay: (GridWay relies on Globus services).

(*i*) Authorization test:

$ globusrun -a -r localhost

You should receive the message "GRAM Authentication test successful".

(*ii*) Submission test: $ globus-job-run localhost /bin/uname –a

You should see the output of the "/bin/uname -a" command.

(*iii*) File transfer test:

$ globus-url-copy file:///etc/hosts gsiftp://localhost/tmp/hosts1

$ globus-url-copy gsiftp://localhost/tmp/hosts1 file:///tmp/hosts2

The contents of files /etc/hosts, /tmp/hosts1 and /tmp/hosts2 should be identical.

(*iv*) Information retrieval test: $ grid-info-search –x

You should see a lot of information in LDIF format.

Contd...

Change localhost to the name of the host your want to test.

You can perform the following tests to verify your Globus WS installation, and to ensure that it will work with GridWay:

(*i*) Submission test:

$ globusrun-ws -submit -F localhost -s -c /bin/uname -a

You should see the output of the "/bin/uname -a" command (along with other information about submission progress).

(*ii*) File transfer test:

$ globus-url-copy file:///etc/hosts gsiftp://localhost/tmp/hosts1

$ globus-url-copy gsiftp://localhost/tmp/hosts1 file:///tmp/hosts2

The contents of files /etc/hosts, /tmp/hosts1 and /tmp/hosts2 should be identical.

(*iii*) Information retrieval test:

$ wsrf-query -x -s https://localhost:8443/wsrf/services/DefaultIndexService

You should see a lot of information in XML format.

Note: XML documents from wsrf-query should not contain any DEBUG messages. SOAP Message Logging for the client tools has to be disabled in $GLOBUS_LOCATION/log4j.properties.

Change localhost to the name of the host your want to test.

If a binary distribution of the Globus Toolkit is installed, you may be required to manually install *globus_core* (used to detect the compiler and platform settings of the computer that the Toolkit is installed on). The following command can be used to perform this operation:

$GLOBUS_LOCATION/sbin/gpt-build -nosrc <flavor>

KNOWLEDGE TESTING

1. Try to configure and implement Globus toolkit in your organization. Mainly try on UNIX components only like Linux, Solaris, AIX etc.
2. What are the requirements for implanting GT4.
3. Write down steps how do you implement globus toolkit?

REFERENCES

1. Joshy Joseph and C. Fellenstein, *Grid Computing*, Pearson Education, 2005.
2. J. Joseph, M. Ernest, C. Fellenstein, Evolution of Grid Computing Architecture and Grid Adoption Models, *IBM Systems Journal*, Vol. 43, No. 4, pp. 624–645, January 2004.
3. *www.gridforum.org.*
4. *www.ogf.org.*
5. *www.dutchgrid.nl/install/.../HowTo-GlobusInstallationExperience.pdf.*
6. *www.globus.org/toolkit/docs/4.0/admin/docbook/ch04.html.*
7. *www.annauniv.edu/care/GTAI-1.0.1_Userguide.pdf.*
8. *www-unix.globus.org/toolkit/docs/4.0/security/.../admin-index.html.*
9. *www.globusconsortium.org/tutorial/ch1.*

❑❑❑

14

CLUSTER

14.1 INTRODUCTION

A collection of computers that work concurrently on a particular problem and connected by a network (LAN) is known as a *cluster*. Generally, a cluster is designed to work combined on a particular problem, so that the cost of computation reduces and performance increases. In general, there are several types of clusters such as Clusters of Workstations (COW)[1], Networks of Workstations (COW)[1], Workstation Clusters (WCs)[1], Clusters of PCs (CoPs)[1], Wireless Cluster, etc. A workstation cluster is formed by connecting various systems in an office to a local area network. Workstation cluster is not only meant for hardware, but it also includes some middleware which allow computers to act as a distributed or parallel system and the applications designed to run on it.[1]

A computer cluster is a small group of computers that work together and seems to be working on a single computer. In general, a cluster uses a local area network to connect its components. Every single computer in a cluster provides more performance and availability than a single individual computer. But cluster is cost-effective compared to an individual computer.[1]

14.2 HISTORY OF CLUSTERS

The history of cluster began in the decade of 1950s and 60s. Greg Pfister provides a quote in his book '*In Search of Clusters*' that, "Virtually every Press release from DEC mentioning clusters says 'DEC, who invented clusters. IBM didn't invent them either. Customers invented clusters, as soon as they couldn't fit all their work on one computer, or needed a backup. The date of the first is unknown, but it would be surprising if it wasn't in the 1960s, or even late 1950s".[1]

Gene Amdhal of IBM, laid foundation for cluster computing by means of a post-work to parallel computing. He published a paper in 1967, Amdhal's Law, that describes the 'speed' on can expect via parllelizing a task on parallel architecture. This article provides basic difference between multi-processor computing and cluster computing, where inter-process communication is done 'inside' the computer in the former case and 'outside' the computer in the later case(via LAN).[1]

The history of clusters started with the invention of networks. Because the aim of forming a cluster is same as that of a network. World's first network was invented by RAND corporation in 1962 (based on the concept of packet switching), which was developed into ARPANET(1969), which is computer cluster based commodity network (linking 4 different computer centers). This project grew into Internet by grouping different computer clusters (which can be thought of as 'mother of all computer clusters'). This laid foundation for further developed clusters using packet switching concept to introduce inter process communication among the processors of a cluster.[1]

Fig. 14.1 Pleiades—New Penn State Computer cluster.[1–4]

The development of cluster preceded with further researches inventing various operating systems and protocols for cluster and hence cluster became a commercial shared file system. The first commercial clustering product is ARCNET [developed by DataPoint in 1977]. ARCNET as a failure, DEC [Digital Equipment Corporation, USA] released VAX cluster product in 1984 is the successful cluster project. Both ARCNET provide parallel computing and shared file systems along with data reliability and uniqueness. These clusters are still available on Open Systems from HP running on Alpha and Itanium systems.[1]

Two more commercial clusters Tandem Himalaya (a circa 1994 high-availability product) and the IBM S/390 Parallel Sysplex (also circa 1994, primarily for business use). Every cluster is developed with the help of Parallel Virtual Machine (PVM) software in 1989. Use of this software enhances the cluster with more performance, high throughput in FLOPS , etc. A cluster with these type of characteristics can only be seen in big supercomputers. The invention of "Beowulf –cluster" in 1995, was the top commodity network built for purpose of 'being a supercomputer' capable of doing all High Performance computations. With the invention of this cluster 'Grid computing' has been evolved with UNIX operating system and Arpanet clusters.[1]

14.3 CLUSTER ORGANIZATIONS

14.3.1 High Availability (HA) Clusters

The name itself specifies that they are implemented for High Availability of the resources and services of the cluster. This is implemented with the concept of redundancy, i.e., they maintain redundant nodes and they are operated when any system component fails. In many cases the size of HA clusters will be 2 nodes, which is the minimum requirement of redundancy. The redundancy in HA cluster helps to eliminate single point of failures. There are many commercial implementations of High-Availability clusters for many operating systems. The Linux-HA project is one commonly used free software HA package for the Linux OS.[3–5]

14.3.2 Load Balancing Clusters

Load Balancing clusters accept workload through one node and then the work is distributed to a collection of back-end servers. Load Balancing clusters not only improve performance but also high availability, so that a cluster of computers is sometimes referred to as a server-farm. There are many commercial load balancers available including Platform LSF HPC, Sun Grid Engine, Moab Cluster Suite and Maui Cluster Scheduler. The Linux Virtual Server project provides one commonly used free software package for the Linux Operating System.[3–5]

14.3.3 High Performance Computing (HPC) Clusters

High performance computing clusters are implemented to improve performance by dividing the assigned task into subtasks and process-ing the tasks parallely on different nodes available in a cluster. These clusters are designed to run some complex programs, exploiting the parallelism available on HPC's. HPC clusters.[3–5]

Communicate with each other and optimize their workloads, with the clusters that require jobs and processes happening.[3–5]

One of the implementations of High Performance computing is '*Beouwulf*' cluster, which is build on Linux Operating System and a free software to implement parallelism. Competing with the Linux, Microsoft introduced a Windows Computing Cluster Server as a High Performance Computing cluster. Many software programs running on High-performance computing (HPC) clusters use libraries such as MPI which are specially designed for writing scientific applications for HPC computers.[3–5]

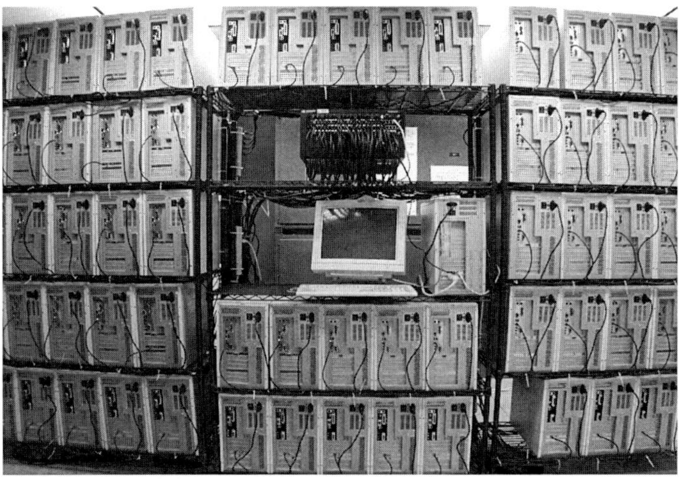

Fig. 14.2 NASA-128 processor Beowulf cluster.[5]

14.3.4 HPC cluster Implementations

The main concept of *Beowulf cluster* is to produce a cost-effective alternative to a supercomputer by using commercial off-the-shelf computers (for e.g. the project of Stone Super-computer). It is noticed that FLOPs is not always the best metric for measuring Supercomputer speed. Because Cluster will have very high FLOPs, but they cannot access the whole data at once.[3–5]

Therefore, clusters are very much preferred for parallel computation, at the same time they less performance compared supercomputer at non-parallel computation.[3–5]

14.4 IMPLEMENTATION OF CLUSTER IN LINUX ENVIRONMENT

Implementation of cluster is cost effective, when construction is started without proper plan. Cluster can be easily implemented in Linux environment by the following steps:[3–5]

14.4.1 Step A: Hardware Considerations

Building of a cluster definitely needs some machines for computing purpose. So, cluster implementation requires well configured computers (minimum two for interaction between them). It should be ensured that the computers must be homogeneous systems *i.e.*, all are Intel systems or AMD systems but not the mixture of them. Hence the Hardware requirement of a cluster is at least two computers of same type of architecture and the performance may not be equivalent.[3–5]

In order to enhance the performance of the cluster, the hardware must be configured efficiently. In general, all the nodes except master node must have identical configuration to give optimal performance. This is because a node which takes up large work may slow down, which lead to the slow down of entire network. All the remaining nodes must wait for the slowed down node to catch up, which is a block hole in the performance of a cluster and hence the cluster must be configured in the above specified way.[3–5]

14.4.1.1 *Building Master Node*

There are four characteristics to be maintained in order to build a master node. They are processor speed, disk speed, network speed, RAM.[3–5]

(*a*) **Processor speed:** When cluster is performing a computation, it is master node that will have maximum work to do. So the speed of the processor of the master node must be very high so that it may not slow down at any point of time during the computation process. If the master node slows down, then the entire cluster will be affected and the remaining slave nodes keep waiting for the next instruction.[3–5]

(*b*) **Disk speed:** Lots of amount of data needs to be stored on disk drive of master node while a computation is performed by cluster. All the slave nodes will access this stored data, if needed during the computation. So, the disk speed of master node can never be slow. A faster SCSI drive will perform better, a RAID array of types 5 /1 or an IDE drive may give better performance.[3–5] (*c*) **Network speed:** Time should not be consumed while transmitting data through the network, since the transmitting speed may alter the performance of the cluster. This may not be a problem until the programmer extremely uses the network to transfer the data from node to node. Hi-speed Ethernet is recommended for a cluster, Gigabit Ethernet is ideal. It is better to use a switch rather than a hub to design and control a cluster network.[3–5]

(*d*) **RAM:** RAM of the master node is important in two cases. First can run more processes without accessing the hard disk. Second, in the case of Linux kernel can cache more disk writes into the memory and keep them until they must be written into the disk. Both of these cases increase the speed of the master node as well as the performance of the cluster.[3–5]

14.4.1.2 *Building Slave Nodes*

Slave nodes are meant for doing two tasks mainly. First, they must perform the work assigned to them by master node and send the data to the destination. As there is no need of the disk for slaves in doing these activities, they are not equipped with a hard disk. As a result, these diskless nodes reduce the cost of building a cluster and save an amount of time in setting up a cluster. There are there important aspects need to be considered in building these slaves processor speed, Network speed and RAM:[3–5]

(*a*) **Processor speed:** The slave nodes in order to give better performance, they require powerful processors. The better the processor, the more the performance of the slave. Intel Pentium III/IV may yield good performance with no added risks in the configuration. Compared to this AMD processors will provide excellent performance but they will emit more heat and consume more power. Multiple processors for a slave node will create another risk resulting in more complexity in programming a slave node. Hence, a best suitable processor is selected according to the problem domain.[3–5]

(*b*) **Network speed:** The result that is computed at the slave node must be transmitted as quickly as possible to the master node. Otherwise, there will be performance degradation in master as well as the whole cluster.[3–5]

(*c*) **RAM:** A slave node with enhanced RAM can run more processes concurrently, which reduces the processing speed of the slave as well as master.[3–5]

14.4.1.3 *Other Hardware Components*

As mentioned above, switch is more appropriate than a hub for building a cluster because of their increased speed. The presence of KVM (keyboard video Mouse switch) allows easy access to individual node in the network. The use of diskless nodes reduces the cost of building a cluster. More number of slave nodes in the cluster may generate more heat. So, the number must not exceed 50 and that too for AMD machines it is strongly recommended.[3–5]

14.4.2 Step B: Installing Linux

After all the hardware was setup for a cluster, the next step is to install Linux operating system into the systems. There are many advanced versions of Linux available. Of them Red Hat version 5 or more is best suitable for building a cluster. Any other Linux can also be used based on the awareness of the user. It is strongly suggested to know well about the p.c's on which Linux is going to be installed. The following four major aspects must be well known in order to explore p.c's before Linux installation.[3–5]

(*i*) **Monitor:** Collect maximum information such as refresh rate, screen resolution and color settings about the monitors that are involved in the cluster. This information is detected by the installation process when stored in the system during Linux installation. Hand copy of this information may help to avoid or prevent any damages in the configuration.[3–5]

(*ii*) **Video card:** As like monitor information, this information is also detected by the installation process automatically. Video card information gives the amount of RAM, graphical memory, cache, etc existing in the system. In general, this information may be skipped, as it is not much important.[3–5]

(*iii*) **Hard drive:** Hard disk information must be well known because it is more important later during the partitioning of the memory of the system in the Linux installation process. Based on this information only the computations are performed and computational tasks are assigned.[3–5]

(*iv*) **Network card:** Network card information is very much needed while transmitting data through the network from node to node. In general, this information is detected during the installation process. It is strongly recommended to manually configure network.[3–5]

After knowing this information thoroughly, install Linux on to systems that are involved in building a cluster. The installation procedure is well explained in the reference [2].[3–5]

14.4.3 Step C: Configuring the Nodes

After the Linux operating system is successfully installed on all the systems, they must be configured with clustering software as well. The software for cluster will be available as free wares or open sources in the internet. They can be downloaded and installed on all the p.c's. This configuration process can be found in detail in [2]. The development kit used for this process is *Portland Group's Cluster Development kit.* All the configuration process is done mostly on the root directory indicated by a starting symbol '/'.[3–5]

14.4.3.1 *Testing the configuration*[3–5]

(*i*) Restart all the systems after installation and configuration process for changes to take effect.

(*ii*) Be sure that rsh will work without a password from master node to rsh and then to slave node.

14.4.3.2 *Add user*

After the setup was completed users are added from the master node and a user log file was created. After the users are created they cloned onto slave nodes (this process of cloning is done as explained in [2]). During this processes entire path is given starting from root for better performance.[3–5]

SUMMARY

A cluster is a group of homogenous systems connected by a LAN, which work on particular problem concurrently. The mixture of configurations is not allowed in the building of a cluster. Building of a cluster is mainly of three steps gathering of all the hardware requirements, installation of Linux and clustering software and finally testing the configuration. Hardware requirements are nothing but processor speed, disk speed, network speed and RAM of all the systems including master node that are involved in the cluster. Clusters are restricted to solve small problems only. When it is the case of solving any complex tasks, some of these clusters (homogenous or heterogeneous) are combined together to form a large infrastructure. This infrastructure was combined called as ***Grid*** and the computing that was performed using a grid is called ***Grid computing***.

KNOWLEDGE TESTING

1. What is a cluster? What are the basic steps involved in building a cluster? Explain in detail.
2. Describe the process of installing Linux operating system to implement a cluster using those installed systems.
3. Describe the process of configuring Linux installed system for implementing a cluster. How users are added to that system?
4. Take for example 4 Intel systems with 512 MB RAM, 1 MB cache and without any Hard disk. Let a system may have 80 GB hard disk which is set as master node. With this configuration and with the help of rough sketch explain how to build a cluster of 5 nodes can be built. All the nodes are connected by a hi-speed Ethernet.

REFERENCES

1. Mark Baker (University of Portsmouth), Rajkumar Buyya (Monash University), Dan Hyde (Bucknell University),Technical Activities Forum, *Cluster Computing: A High Performance Contender*, July 1999.
2. Joshy Joseph and C. Fellenstein, *Grid Computing*, Pearson Education, 2005.
3. *www.docstoc.com/docs/7188483/How-to-Build-Linux-Cluster.*
4. *http://www.mcsr.olemiss.edu/bookshelf/articles/how_to_build_a_cluster.html.*
5. *www.cse.mtu.edu/cseri.html.*

❑❑❑

15

Grid Technologies, Systems and Scheduling

15.1 INTRODUCTION

There are many problems exist in this world which are related to communication and practical systems. These communications are either between the fixed connections, servers, applications, databases or storage machines. Grid computing solves this type of problems. Grid computing applications are primarily used in scientific and academic communities. In grid world, we can solve the problems by connect a variety of systems into a virtual supercomputer capable of accessing unused resources within a network, such as processing cycles.[1–2]

For doing applications, grid uses five main attributes in computing. These attributes are conceptual oriented.[1–2]

- Virtualization.
- Dynamic resource provisioning.
- Pooling concept.
- Self- adapting.
- Unifying models.

Many applications can benefit from the Grid infrastructure, including collaborative engineering, data exploration, high-throughput computing. Grid applications are generally large- scale and multidisciplinary. These applications are typically developed using grid languages and utilities such as MPI or HPC++. Application (problem) can be broken into pieces and each part is solved by either super computer or other participating systems. For doing this grid tools are helps to users to easily write/run grid applications.[1–2]

Definition

"The Grid application is a combination of cooperating Grid resources (application elements) joined together to achieve particular functionality".

—Ian Faster

The following real examples show where grid applications can be used.

More than 150 virtual organizations from different fields like Biomedicine, Earth Sciences and High-Energy Physics uses the grid applications in their projects. Some of them are:[1–2]

- Health-e-Child project to build on Grid technology—This project run on clinical decision support systems on a secure and reliable distributed platform.
- Processing and data storage capability projects—offered by the EGEE Grid.
- The Enabling Grids for E-science (EGEE) project is made by the European Commission. The project operates the largest multi-science Grid infrastructure in the world.
- DKRZ project(the German Climate Computing Centre) which provides state-of-the-art supercomputing, data service and other associated services to the German scientific community to conduct top of the line Earth System and Climate Modeling.
- CERN project—the European Organization for Nuclear Research.

Now we will see about the some of the production grids that developed by core companies.

15.2 ORACLE GRID

The recent versions of Oracle (Oracle 10g) allows grid computing which as great impact on their applications. Oracle's new technology meets the requirements of grid computing especially in databases, servers, applications, storages. The central idea beyond using the grid in products is to make the computing more reliable, transparent as utility and pervasive. For better outcomes Oracle.[2]

- Oracle creates a dynamic computing environment for sharing resources and intermediate results.
- Scalability (ability to extend) concept applied for storing peta bytes of data.

With grid computing, the practical approach of Oracle involves virtualization, consolidation and automation. Because of using grid in products Oracle increases its quality by decreasing the cost. The following benefits will occur in business.[2]

- Scalability and performance at lower cost.
- Better self-managing.
- Securing.
- Self-managing.

15.3 SUN GRID

Sun grid was developed by Sun Microsystems. Sun Grid Engine (SGE) is a open source system software which as world's leading batch queuing system and distributed resource manager. It collaborates to sun grid utility computing system. The newly released sun grid engine 6.2 Beta 3 version supports the resource sharing among two or more sun grid engine clusters. Some of the benefits and features from SGE are:[4]

- Significant scalability—Scale up to 63,000 *core* CPU's.
- Advanced resource reservation—Resources can be reserved advance by users such as host's nodes, memory etc.
- Parallel job support and interaction between job supporters.
- Array task dependency—Run the software more effectively and faster execution/production times.
- Allows two or more SGE clusters for sharing resources.
- Graphical User Interface (GUI) for frontiers.

15.4 IBM GRID

IBM, pioneer organization for building grids and it is the first one which releases the business on demand concept. The same concept can be used by many organizations for in their grids. On demand business provides dynamic environment to the businesses, cost matters and focus on core business competence.[4–5]

15.5 GRID SCHEDULING

In a grid environment, resources are dynamic, autonomous, heterogeneous, and wide-area distributed. To manage these resources advanced scheduler tools are needed. The Grid Computing discipline chooses tools for networking services and connections of a potentially unlimited number of ubiquitous computing devices within a grid.[4–5]

Scheduling the tasks and resource allocation are two main jobs for grid. A task is a sequence of commands that describe the user's requirements. Schedulers are responsible for managing the jobs like allocating resources, partitioning jobs /tasks, data management and service- level management. Jobs are managed either in single system or multiple systems grouped together. The main idea beyond scheduling is to minimize the overall completion time. Scheduling can be done in two ways: static and dynamic schedules. These two schedulers are mainly applicable in parallel programming. In static scheduling, the program's behavior is known before execution but is not in the case of dynamic scheduling. In dynamic scheduling, program completion time is minimized and scheduling overhead can be reduced.[4–5]

The functionalities provided by the schedulers are:[4–5]

- Securing the batch jobs until they are executed.
- Bring the jobs from system.
- Run the jobs according to their arrival (by using FIFO, FILO algorithms).
- Submit output back to the required system/user.

> **Note:** If schedulers use the complex management policies/functionalities, then scheduling algorithms should achieve distributed, QoS, Security and resource reservation.

What is the difference between the job scheduler and job manager?

In grid, scheduling concept generally applied in between networked systems. Job schedulers are responsible for submitting, controlling and monitoring the jobs in multiple networked computers. Jobs are tasks which are run in a particular time interval after allocating resources if they need. If jobs need resources we should preserve/avoid deadlock situation. Some of the popular job schedulers are portable batch systems, Local scheduler Framework etc.

Simply saying a job manager is responsible for execution of jobs. Job manager is a master for job services, configurations, integration to job schedulers and testing the jobs etc. Job manager provides a single interface for execution of jobs. A set of these interfaces are called Globus Resource Allocation Manager (GRAM).[4–5]

The following figure shows the simple scheduling hierarchy.

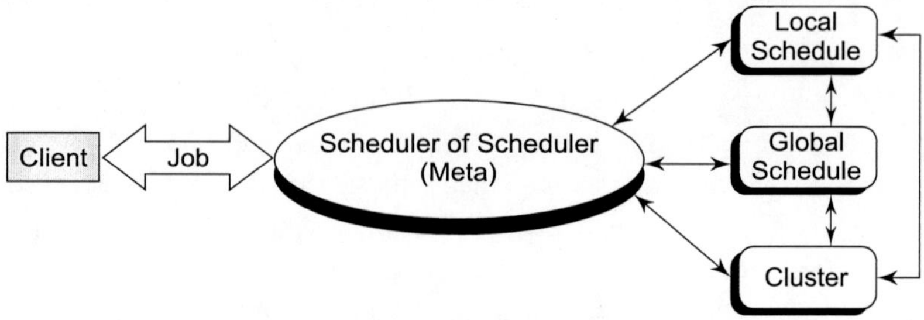

Fig. 15.1 Scheduling hierarchy.[3–5]

Drawback for normal scheduling is that it doesn't provide so many services between providers and consumers and it doesn't provide the resource provision and reservation of resources more effectively. To solve this type of problems *resource brokering* concept was introduced in the grid schedulers.[4–5]

15.5.1 Resource Brokering

A resource broker can provide futures like selecting particular scheduler, resource selection, task information etc. The main job of resource provider is it provides pairing services between the service requester and service provider. It holds the information of more than one resource and submits it to the scheduler. According to that information scheduler execute the tasks by using any one of the resource and it also provides feedback information back to the user. It also returns the job- execution times to the user. Brokering concept is generally used in complex and large composite applications.[4–5]

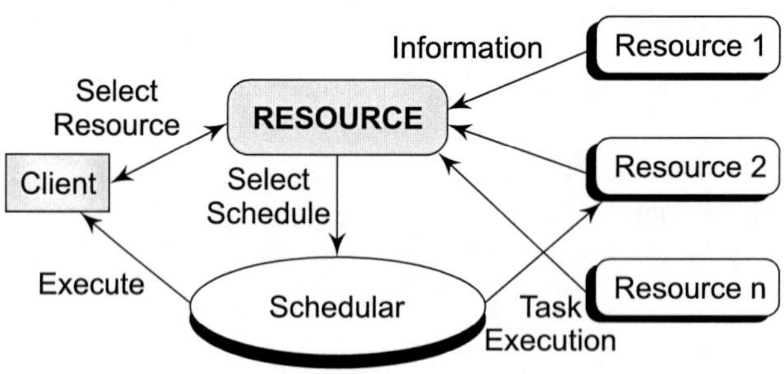

Fig. 15.2 Resource brokering in scheduling.[3–5]

User interacts to resource broker for solving resource discovery, scheduling and processing application jobs. Resource broker performs other tasks also like calculates the time for data transfer between nodes by using network management functions. However we are not going to discuss about network management, but some of the functionalities that provided by the network management that relates to resources in scheduling are:[4–5]

- Reserving networking paths (single/multiple).
- Required information for network resources.
- Controlling network events and finally maintain topology information.

15.5.2 GridWay

GridWay is best example to the grid scheduling concept. It is the open source meta scheduling technology. It provides a scheduling framework to the end-users and application developers. It allows, monitor, synchronize and control jobs. It work as a execution management tool for globus toolkit. In Globus Toolkit 4.0.5, GridWay is defaultly included. The following are the some tasks performed by the GridWay[4–5]

- Job execution management.
- Resource brokering.
- Heterogeneity, dynamic and loosely-coupled environment.
- Job scheduling and fault recovery mechanisms.

15.6 GRIDSIM TOOL

Grid sim is a tool for developing grid scheduling applications. It is a java- based toolkit which useful for modeling and simulation of computational resources for evaluation of resources. For developing the applications gridsim uses the effective resource algorithms and policies. We like to simulate millions of resources and thousands of users with varied requirements and study scalability of systems, algorithms, efficiency of resource allocation policies and satisfaction of users. We are also interested to explore how significantly the local economy and the global positioning (e.g., the time zone) of a particular resource play role in securing jobs under various pricing and demand/supply situations. The main drawback of the simulation is it consumes large amount of computing power especially in parallel and cluster computing systems.[3]

15.7 DATA GRID

The idea behind the data grid project is developing the middleware's. A distributed system can store the large amounts of distributed data. For storing peta bytes of data data grids are generally used. A data grid is a grid computing system which controls and manages the large amounts of distributed data. For storing tera and peta bytes of distributed data, data generally combined with computational grids. Some of the data grid projects are:[3]

- Southern California Earthquake Center (SCEC).
- Biomedical Informatics Research Network (BIRN).

The data grid creates virtual collaborative environments that support distributed but coordinated scientific and engineering research.[3]

15.8 WWG

WWG stands for World Wide Grid. WWG is a large- scale test for grid computing. It has heterogeneous and distributed resources across multiple organizations. It has fall into the category of application development. For more information visit www.buyya.com/ecogrid/wwg.[3–5]

15.9 CASE STUDY: MOBILE GRID COMPUTING

The term "mobile" has the meaning continuous or on the move. People who are using mobiles they are migrating in environment and applications are run almost in anywhere. Laptops, smart phone and Personal Digital Assistants (PDA) etc are best examples to mobile devices. When mobile term is used in grid we concentrate on wireless communication, addressing, routing issues, trust, security and privacy.[5]

"Mobile computing" is the term used for describing the application of small, portable and wireless computing. In mobile grid both mobile and grid computing concepts plays a good role and additional things like mobile users, seamless, transparent terms are added. In mobile grid mobile users are allowed to access the grid resources by themselves. Mobile users are act as interfaces to grid activities in an 'anytime' 'anywhere' mode. These users are some constraints and limitations for accessing the grid enabled resources. In simple words mobile grid is the platform that should address mobility issues by enabling fixed and mobile users for accessing mobile grid resources.[5]

There are three types of mobility's are there in mobile grid computing:[5]

User mobility—Multiple users are move around different terminals and ask session movement. Sessions are opened by user at some place and ask its movement at different place.

Terminal mobility—Ending point of the communication.

Service mobility—Maintains the services for a user while he is mobile.

15.10 CLOUD COMPUTING

The future computing to grid is cloud computing. Cloud computing is another way of technology in which resources are virtualized and provided as a service over the internet. Cloud computing is described as a sub set of grid computing concerned with the use of special shared computing resources. It incorporates:[1–3]

- *Platform as a Service* (PaaS)—It offers full or partial application development that users can access.
- *Infrastructure as a Service* (IaaS)—Consumer can get the service from a infrastructure computer through internet.
- *Software as a Service* (SaaS)—Provides a complete application, such as Enterprise Resource Management through the Internet.

We can access the business applications from cloud computing, while the data and applications are stored at server. In cloud computing we have to consider three things: *thin clients, grid computing and utility computing*. In grid computing disparate computers are form a large infrastructure, harnessing unused resources. Utility computing is paying for what you use on shared servers like you pay for a public utility. Cloud computing evolves from grid computing and provides on-demand resource provisioning.[1–3]

What are the similarities of between cloud computing and grid computing? What are the advantages of cloud computing?

- Both are scalable. Applications are running on variety of operating systems and they are connected through web services.
- In both cases network bandwidth is allocated and de- allocated on demand.
- In both cases customers can perform different tasks, accessing a single or multiple application instances. Both supports service level agreements.

15.10.1 Advantages[1–3]

- Easily handle load situations without any additional hardware infrastructure.
- Provides more economical infrastructure.
- Processing power can be decreased by storing data in the cloud.
- The system delivers greater scalability as it is possible to add “on-demand” computational resources.

- Large businesses are moving to cloud. One of the greatest advantages is that the user is no longer tied to a traditional computer to use an application.
- Fewer maintained issues. Users will not have to worry about storage capacity, compatibility or other matters.

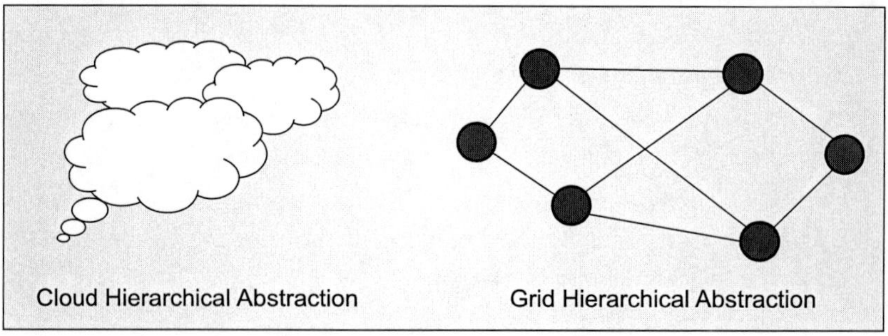

Fig. 15.3 Cloud and Grid hierarchical structures[9].

15.11 GARUDA

The motivation of GARUDA, originated from the need of sharing of high-end computational resources with the larger scientific and engineering community across India. Emerging High Performance Computing (HPC) applications in the country require integration of geographically distributed resources. Seamless, transparent access from anywhere in the country is also needed.[3–5]

The clusters designed by C-DAC, are called PARAM. The network interconnect they use is PARAMNet. Reconfigurable computing systems specially designed for bioinformatics and cryptanalysis have been completed. In total GARUDA connects 45 institutions all over India. 22 institutions are connected using 100 Mbps and 23 using 10 Mbp are bandwidth connections. To monitor the Grid, Paryavekshanam a grid-monitoring tool is used.[3–5]

15.11.1 Objectives

GARUDA aims at strengthening and advancing scientific and technological excellence in the area of Grid and Peer-to-Peer technologies. The strategic objectives of GARUDA are to:[3–5]

- Create a test bed for the research and engineering of technologies, architectures, standards and applications in Grid Computing.
- Bring together all potential research, development and user groups who can help develop a national initiative on Grid computing.

- Create the foundation for the next generation grids by addressing long term research issues in the strategic areas of knowledge and data management, programming models, architectures, grid management and monitoring, problem solving environments, grid tools and services [*source:* C-DAC India].

SUMMARY

When sharing resources the following questions may arise:

- Where are the resources?- *Resource Discovery* (Resources are may disparate geographically).
- What type of resources are available- *Resource Characterization.*
- What policy is applied when assigning the resources? What is the actual process of assigning the resources? Who gets how much?- *Resource Allocation.*
- For what purpose resource can be used and at what time- *Resource Management.*
- How many resources are used and what's there rating- *Counting and Service Level Agreement (SLA).*
- Finally considering security issues like *authentication, authorization and policies.*

From all these discussions one way to accomplish is to imagine a grid implementation that is trying to run on one machine X with the help of some resource located at site Y, subject to virtual community policy P, providing access to data at Z according to policy Q. So there is no rule that resources are nearer to machine.

KNOWLEDGE TESTING

1. Define the grid application. Where grid applications are useful?

2. Briefly explain the following:

 (*i*) Sun Grid Engine

 (*ii*) Oracle Grid

 (*iii*) IBM's Business on Demand

3. What are the functionalities provided by the grid schedulers and what's the difference between job manager and scheduling jobs.?

Contd...

4. Explain the role of resource brokering in grid scheduling? Is resource broker necessary for scheduling concepts? Explain why.
5. Take any area where grid computing as applied and explain.
6. Explain grid computing in mobile devices.
7. Write short notes on:
   - Cloud computing
   - Mobile grid
8. In cloud computing we are discussed about similarities. After understanding write at least three differences between cloud and grid computing.

REFERENCES

1. *http://www.dkrz.de.*
2. Miranda Nash Oracle, *10 g: Infrastructure for Grid Computing,* An Oracle White Paper, September 2003.
3. Penka Martincová, Michal Zábovský University of Zilina, *Comparison of Simulated GRID Scheduling Algorithms.*
4. Philipp Wieder, Dortmund UoT, Joachim Lepping, Dortmund UoT Ariel Oleksiak, PSNC Alexander Papaspyrou, Dortmund UoT, *Grid Scheduling Architecture Requirements and Recommendations.*
5. Antonios Litke, Dimitrios Skoutas, Theodora Varvarigou, *Mobile Grid Computing: Changes and Challenges of Resource Management in a mobile Grid Environment.*
6. *http://blogs.sun.com/templedf/entry/a_little_history_lesson.*
7. Ian Foster *et al.*, *A Security Infrastructure by Computational Grids.*
8. E. Huedo, R. S. Montero and I. M. Llorente: *A Framework for Adaptive Execution in Grids.* Software - Practice and Experience 34 (7): *GT 4.2.0 GridWay*, pp. 631–651, 2004.
9. Francesco Maria Aymerich and Gianni Fenu., *An Approach to a Cloud Computing Network.*
10. Joshy Joseph and C. Fellenstein, *Grid Computing*, Pearson Education, 2005.

❑❑❑

Glossary

- **Grid Computing** provides sharing of resources globally for solving a particular task.
- Grid is a type of parallel and distributed system that enables the sharing, selection, and aggregation of geographically distributed resources. These resources are autonomous.
- Grid is applied in the application areas like commercial, numerical and scientific applications. The reason is you can build more powerful systems, more cheaply, by more efficient utilization of available computing resources.
- A grid is a distributed system. Without distributed computing there is no meaning to grid computing. A distributed computing deals with hardware and software systems containing more than one processing element or storage element, concurrent processes, or multiple programs.
- Grid computing connects users and resources in a transparent, openness and scalable way.
- The overall motivation for "Grids" is to facilitate the routine interactions of these resources in order to support large-scale science and Engineering.
- Grid technology also provides the ability to store, share and analyze large volumes of data, ensuring that people have access to information at the right time.
- Grid technology improves resource utilization and reduces costs, while maintaining a flexible infrastructure that can cope with changing business demands, yet remain reliable, resilient and secure.
- There are mainly three issues in grid computing- heterogeneity, scalability and adaptability.

- Clusters are usually deployed to improve performance and/or availability over that provided by a single computer, while typically being much more cost-effective than single computers of comparable speed or availability.
- A computer cluster is a group of tightly coupled computers that work together closely so that in many respects they can be viewed as though they are a single computer.
- Networking, distributed computing, high performance computing, web services and cluster concepts are building blocks to grid computing.
- Distributed computing is a process of computation, where a program is divided into modules and is processed on different computers of a network in parallel.
- A grid is a hardware and software infrastructure that provides dependable, consistent, pervasive, and inexpensive access to computational resources.
- A grid is a collection of machines, sometimes referred to as "nodes," "resources," "members," "donors," "clients," "hosts," "engines," and many other such terms.
- Grids are super Internets for ***high-performance computing***: worldwide collections of high-end resources—such as supercomputers, storage, advanced instruments, and immersive environments.
- Distributed computing environment (DCE) is a software system developed by major companies like Hewlett-Packard (hp), IBM, etc in 1990's. DCE provides a framework and toolkit for developing client-server applications, which includes *remote procedure call* (RPC) mechanism.
- A *resource* is an entity that is to be shared. It can be computational such as a personal digital assistant, laptop, desktop, workstation, server, cluster, and supercomputer or a storage resource such as a hard drive in a desktop.
- The difference between web and grid is web provides us information where as grid process it.
- The resource in peer-to-peer networks is the storage capacity of each (mostly desktops) node. Each computer is responsible for setting up and maintaining its own security for those resources.
- OGSA, OGSI, Semantic Grid, web services, SOA, Autonomic computing and business on demand are the road map to grid computing and these are included in third generation.
- Demand business fills the gap between IT promises and product delivers. Demand business (e-business) connects its core business systems constituencies using intranets, extranets, and the Web.

- The Semantic Grid is clearly useful in providing support for investigations using social simulations. Semantic grid is the combination of semantic web services and grid services.

  Semantic grid= Semantic web service + grid services

  Semantic web service= Semantic web + web service technology.

- There are mainly two technologies for building semantic webs

  XML and

  Resource description Framework (RDF)

- Grid offers low cost and high throughput solution that allows companies to optimize and leverage existing IT infrastructure and investments.
- In Grid environment, resources do not have prior information about each other nor do they have pre-defined security relationships.
- *Virtual organizations* can span from small corporate departments that are in the same physical location to large groups of people from different organizations that are spread out across the globe. Virtual organizations can be large or small, static or dynamic.
- A virtual organization can made for a particular project and disabled once the project is complete.
- Internet protocol architecture (defined by OSI- Open Systems interconnection) has been closely assigned with the grid architecture model.

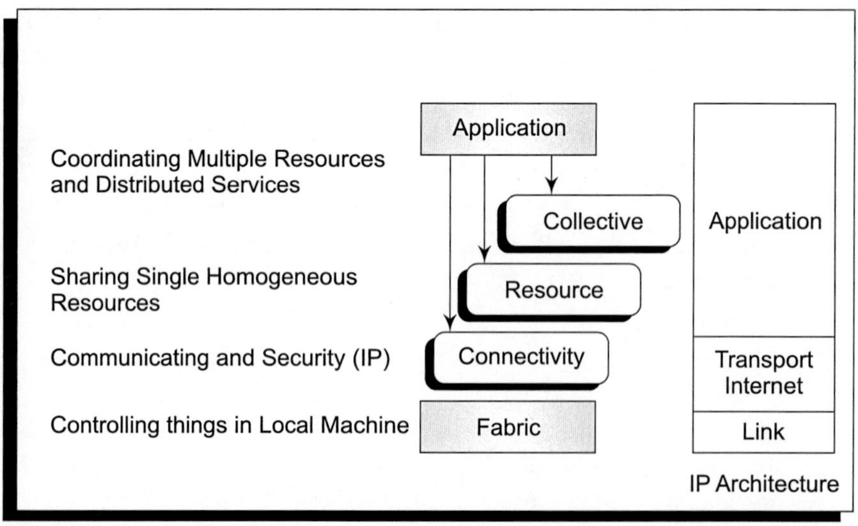

Comparing Grid computing architecture model with IP.

- Grid protocols are:

  GridFTP- used for transport and upper layer data acess

  Grid Resource Allocation Manager (GRAM)- controlling resources, remote allocation, scheduling and monitoring.

  Grid Resource Information Service (GRIS)—Access to structure and state information.

  Grid Security Infrastructure (GSI) –It define extensions for Secure Socket Layer/ Transport Layer Security (SSL/TLS) and X.509 have been defined to allow single sign-on (proxy certificate) and delegation.

  All these protocols are defined in resource layer which initiate and control local resources.

- Grid FTP is a secure, robust, fast, efficient, standards based, widely accepted data transfer protocol.
- Meta- directory services, resource brokering and resource availability are defined in collective layer.
- Security credentials and proxy certificates are created using X.509 Certificate.
- A Resource Specification Language (RSL) is a common notation for exchange of information between applications, resource brokers, and local resource managers. Resource requirements and job configurations are two types of information's in RSL.
- A *service* is a specific function, typically a business function, such as analyzing an individual's credit history or processing a purchase order.
- Service may be *multiple* or *aggregated*, or *composite*. A service is a function that is well-defined, self-contained, and does not depend on the context or state of other services.
- SOA bridges the gap between IT and business. Business processes can be done using the concept of SOA.
- WSDL, UDDI, and SOAP are the fundamental elements/pieces of the SOA infrastructure.
- NET and J2EE- Developers are mainly working on this area. They are trying to develop the applications that meet the SOA's issues and design goals.
- DCOM, DCE, CORBA and Java RMI all are distributed technologies.
- Web services provide a framework for remotely invoking an object and exchanging data.

- Web services are platform neutrality and Standards such as XML, SOAP, UDDI, and WSDL address the basics of interoperable services.
- XML will be standard language for describing information in the grid.
- SOAP may become a standard RPC mechanism for Grid services.
- SOAP, important component in web services, which is used to define a standard way of packaging a message for interoperability.
- The SOAP package is transferred over protocols, such as FTP or HTTP. SOAP is not a network or a transfer protocol.
- SOAP doesn't allow you to check for errors at the time of compiling the document. You can only test for errors at run time.
- The process of calling a procedure from a remote computer is called RPC. The request for the procedure can be made using SOAP in the form of SOAP message.
- Web Services Description Language (WSDL) is a format for describing a Web Services interface. It is a way to describe services and how they should be bound to specific network addresses.
- A service description maintains some documents that combine describe the interface to a service. It may also include the service road map and functionalities.
- The WSDL defines services as collections of network endpoints, or ports. The WSDL specification provides an XML format.
- A WSDL document is simply a set of definitions.
- GXA provides a functionality for maintain consistent data. It reduces the time spent on developing applications, so that application transparency duration using protocols are reduced.
- The main vision of GXA is it provides basic open standards based designs for interoperable messaging across multiple vendors.
- The main principle of GMA includes:
    - XML information set.
    - Open standards.
    - Service policy and
    - Security.
- Open Grid Services Architecture (OGSA) is a set of technical specifications and it defines a common framework to businesses for building grids.

- OGSA architecture defines behavior of grid services, service description mechanisms by using Web Service Description and protocol binding information by using web service enhancements.
- Another work of OGSA is it defines the standards for both commercial software and open source.
- It proposed an enabling infrastructure for systems and applications that require the integration and management of service within distributed, heterogeneous, dynamic "virtual organizations."
- In clearly OGSA defines the technology to grid services and Open Grid Service Infrastructure (OGSI) specifies the framework to grid services.
- OGSA is build on top of OGSI. Whatever standards that specified by the OGSI those must poses by the grid services.
- In grid services OGSA concentrate on high- level models and types. It also supports multiple protocol bindings for grid services.
- OGSA standard groups are security, work flow, data and resource management.
- The architecture of OGSA is an extension of the Web Services architecture and the descriptive language such as Web Service Description Language (WSDL).
- OGSA theme is collecting individual services and builds web service standards among them so that finally we have to achieve the relevant grid services.
- OGSI defines the basic level of functionality to grid services. It defines language for constructing grid services.
- Remember OGSI does not define how Grid Services are implemented within a particular hosting environment.
- How clients deal with Grid Services. For this question OGSI provides the specifications, basic interfaces and naming.
- Globus toolkit is the framework for developing and hosting OGSI grid services. Globus is implemented by java.
- Grid services are descriptive in nature. A grid service is a web service packaged that provides state information, objects in the state and a set of well defined interfaces and that follows specific conventional methods.
- It aimed to provide transparency, dynamic service creation, lifetime management, location discovery and manageability.
- Grid services are state full web services where as web services are state-less.

- Registry, discovery, factory and lifetime are interfaces for managing grid services.
- It is possible to make grid services as virtualized. OGSI helps for doing this.
- OGSA's main aim is to achieve the heterogeneous environment between the virtual organizations.
- OGSA is open- architecture. It develops the standards and specifications that address the distributed infrastructure, high- throughput computing and service mobility.
- GGF proposed OGSA as a standard platform for Grid Computing, and represents the definition of grid technology and functionality as Web Services.
- Internet standards such as XML, W3C standards such as Simple Object Access Protocol (SOAP), Web Services Description Language (WSDL), and Web Services Inspection Language (WSIL) are helped for defining conventions for a service provider and a service consumer to exchange messages in a protocol and programming language independent way.
- The platform of OGSA is made up of three components-Open Grid Services Infrastructure (OGSI), the OGSA Platform Interfaces, and the OGSA Platform Models.
- OGSI definitions can be grouped into four categories: WSDL extension and conventions, service data, core grid service properties, and portTypes for basic services.
- For managing grid services both OGSA and OGSI are needed.
- Confidentiality, integrity, Authentication, single-sign on and delegation are basic security fundamentals used in grid computing.
- The grid security taxonomy mainly characterized into three groups.
    - Architecture
    - Infrastructure
    - Management
- GSI enabling secure authentication and communication over an open network provides a number of useful services for Grids, including mutual authentication and single sign-on.
- GSI based on public key encryption, X.509 certificates, and the Secure Sockets Layer (SSL) communication protocol.

- WS- Security is a standard released by OASIS. There are mainly three levels of security namely Secure Socket Level (SSL), Message Level Security (MLS) and Transport level security (TLS).
- The WS-Security core specification also defines the application of XML encryption and XML digital signatures to provide end-to-end messaging integrity and confidentiality without the support of the underlying communication protocol.
- The Globus Toolkit is an open source software toolkit to build computational grids and grid-based applications. Globus is one of the core-level middlewares.
- The GT4 architecture is divided into three main parts

  Core part

  Globus base services

  User- defined services
- The data in the globus can be virtualized. Grid software beyond that provided by these suites are being defined and implemented by many organizations and universities.
- Job management services provide a way of submitting and monitoring jobs remotely that is, submitting jobs in the Grid. It follows the interfaces defined in OGSI by using WSDL, which is based on XML.
- A collection of computers that work concurrently on a particular problem and connected by a network (LAN) is known as a *cluster.*
- Generally, a cluster is designed to work combined on a particular problem, so that the cost of computation reduces and performance increases.
- A computer cluster is a small group of computers that work together and seems to be working on a single computer.
- Commercial clusters are Tandem Himalaya (a circa 1994 high-availability product) and the IBM S/390 Parallel Sysplex.
- One of the implementations of High Performance computing is '*Beouwulf*' cluster, which is build on Linux Operating System and a free software to implement parallelism.
- The main concept of *Beowulf cluster* is to produce a cost-effective alternative to a supercomputer by using commercial off-the-shelf computers.
- Building of a cluster is mainly of three steps gathering of all the hardware requirements, installation of Linux and clustering software and finally testing the configuration.

- Hardware requirements are nothing but processor speed, disk speed, network speed and RAM of all the systems including master node that are involved in the cluster.
- They are many pre-requested software that are to be installed very carefully by setting there paths according to the gtk4.0.1 requirements. Some of the pre-requested software are:
  - Apache Ant.
  - postgre sql.
  - jakarta tomcat.
  - junit.
  - xineted.
- According to Ian Faster "*The Grid application is a combination of cooperating Grid resources (application elements) joined together to achieve particular functionality*".
- Scheduling the tasks and resource allocation are two main jobs for grid.
- A task is a sequence of commands that describe the user's requirements. Schedulers are responsible for managing the jobs like allocating resources, partitioning jobs /tasks, data management and service- level management.
- A resource broker can provide futures like selecting particular scheduler, resource selection, task information etc. The main job of resource provider is it provides pairing services between the service requester and service provider.
- GridWay is best example to the grid scheduling concept. It is the open source meta scheduling technology. It provides a scheduling framework to the end- users and application developers.
- The future computing to grid is cloud computing. Cloud computing is another way of technology in which resources are virtualized and provided as a service over the internet.
- In cloud computing we have to consider three things: *thin clients, grid computing and utility computing.*
- The idea behind the data grid project is developing the middleware's.
- A data grid is a grid computing system which controls and manages the large amounts of distributed data.
- There are some similarities between world wide web (WWW) and grid

  Uniform Naming.

  Seamless, scalable information service.

  Powerful new meta-data language: XML, SOAP etc.

- Grid computing concentrate on solving the following problems like

  Resource sharing

  Large storage, sensors, networks.

  Heterogeneity, policies and Sharing .

  Coordinated problem solving

  Integration of distributed resources

  Quality of service (QoS) requirements

  Dynamic, multi-institutional virtual orgs

Serial	***Parallel***	***Grid***
• We can fetch the data and store it. • Compute the data.	• We can fetch the data and store it. • Not only compute but also communicate.	Same futures like in parallel and additional are: • Resource discovery • Security • Interaction with remote application • Dynamic, virtualisation • Scheduling • Geographically independent etc..

Fig. Comparison of serial and parallel computing with grid computing.

❑❑❑